IONESCO

A COLLECTION OF CRITICAL ESSAYS

Edited by

Rosette C. Lamont

Prentice-Hall, Inc.  Englewood Cliffs, N.J.

A SPECTRUM BOOK

Library of Congress Cataloging in Publication Data

LAMONT, ROSETTE C   comp.
   Ionesco: a collection of critical essays.

   (Twentieth century views) (A Spectrum book)
   Contents: Lamont, R. C. Introduction.—Doubrovsky,
J. S. Ionesco and the Comic of absurdity.—Schechner, R.
The bald soprano and the Lesson: an inquiry into play
structure. [etc.]
   1. Ionesco, Eugene. I. Title.
PQ2617.06Z74   842'.9'14   73–5500
ISBN 0–13–504977–6
ISBN 0–13–504969–5 (pbk.)

To Ludmilla and Fred,
my two wonderful friends

We are grateful to the following publishers for their permission to reprint
from the works listed below:

To Grove Press, Inc., and Calder and Boyars Ltd., for quotations from these
works by Ionesco: *Amédée* (© 1958 by John Calder, Publishers, Ltd); *Rhinoceros*
(© 1960 by John Calder); *Jack, or the Submission* (© 1958 by Grove Press, Inc.);
Victims of Duty (© 1958 by John Calder); *The Lesson* (© 1958 by Grove Press,
Inc.); *The Bald Soprano* (© 1956, 1965 by Grove Press, Inc.); *Notes and Counternotes* (© 1964 by Grove Press, Inc.).

To Editions Gallimard, for quotations from Ionesco's *L'Impromptu de l'Alma,*
in *Théâtre II* (© Editions Gallimard).

To Calder and Boyars Ltd., for quotations from *Three Plays,* trans. Donald
Watson (Jupiter Books, London, John Calder, 1963).

To Holt, Rinehart and Winston, Inc. and Faber and Faber Ltd., for quotations
from *Conversations with Eugene Ionesco,* by Claude Bonnefoy. Trans. Jan Daw-
son. (© 1970 by Faber and Faber Limited.)

10 9 8 7 6 5 4 3 2 1

PRENTICE-HALL INTERNATIONAL, INC. (*London*)
PRENTICE-HALL OF AUSTRALIA PTY. LTD. (*Sydney*)
PRENTICE-HALL OF CANADA LTD. (*Toronto*)
PRENTICE-HALL OF INDIA PRIVATE LIMITED (*New Delhi*)
PRENTICE-HALL OF JAPAN, INC. (*Tokyo*)

Contents

Introduction   1
by Rosette C. Lamont

Ionesco and the Comic of Absurdity   11
by J. S. Doubrovsky

The Bald Soprano and *The Lesson*: An Inquiry into Play
    Structure   21
by Richard Schechner

Amédée: A Caricatural Ionesco   38
by Jean-Hervé Donnard

Ionesco ex Machina   55
by Jacques Guicharnaud

Science and Fiction in Ionesco's "Experimental" Theatre:
    (An Interpretation of *The Chairs*)   64
by David Mendelson

Eugene Ionesco: The Existential Oedipus   99
by Hugh Dickinson

Ionesco's *L'Impromtu de l'Alma*: A Satire of Parisian Theater
    Criticism   120
by Peter Ronge

Utopia and After   135
by Richard N. Coe

Eugene Ionesco and the Metaphysical Farce   154
by Rosette C. Lamont

iv   *Contents*

Chronology of Important Dates   184
Selected Bibliography   186
Notes on the Editor and Contributors   188

Introduction

by
Rosette C. Lamont

In June 1959 in the course of a talk that inaugurated the *Helsinki Debates on the Avant-Garde Theatre,* Ionesco made the following declaration:

> It has been said that what distinguishes man from the other animals is that he is the animal that laughs; he is above all the animal that creates. He introduces into the world things which were not there before: temples and rabbit hutches, wheelbarrows, locomotives, symphonies, poems, cathedrals and cigarettes. The usefulness of all these things is often only a pretext. What is the use of existing? To exist. What is the use of a flower? To be a flower. Of what use is a temple or a cathedral? To house the faithful? I doubt it, since the temples are no longer used and we still admire them. They serve to reveal to us the laws of architecture, and perhaps of universal construction, which are apparently reflected in our mind since the mind discovers these laws within itself.

For the playwright, a work of art is an autonomous universe, governed by its own laws. It is not an imitation of what we call our world, nor is it totally unlike that world; one could say that it is a self-contained construct, parallel to ours.

How do we as readers, or viewers of plays, approach and understand this strange world? It could be said that we are like a person who enters an unfamiliar house. We wander from room to room, floor to floor, sometimes in the dark, till, gradually, we get to know where the hallway leads, what is behind each door, how the architect has apportioned space, and what materials he has used. If this house is well put together we may linger, and if it speaks to us, fills us with its peculiar charm, we may be inclined to dwell there forever, or at least to return to it frequently. If we are teachers, or critics, or both, we will describe this home, lovingly, wishing to draw our friends' attention to cunning detail of the moulding, to a secret passage between rooms, or simply to the soundness of the whole construction. On the surface Ionescoland is deceptively like our own. The mod-

1

est clerks, mailmen, police officers, *concierges,* maids, married couples, maidens to marry, and apprehensive bachelors are the very people we see and overhear on the streets of Paris every day. We are lulled
into believing there will be no surprises. One of the creators of Surrealism, Philippe Soupault, writes in a special Ionesco issue of *Les
Cahiers des Saisons* (Hiver 1959) of Ionesco's "natural tone." The
same Soupault, however, recognizes a younger brother, or an heir,
when he suggests: "Eugene Ionesco, perhaps without meaning to,
unleashes something scandalous the moment actors agree to speak
his lines as he has written them." (p. 230) Is it because of the playwright's inner search for sincerity, his desire to reach a truth beyond
that of so-called reality? Is it because, as Pierre-Aimé Touchard says
in the same issue of the review, Ionesco has re-invented and resur-
rected myths? At any rate, we realize quite soon that the overstuffed
pieces of furniture so much like the ones we inherited from aunt
Marie, the clichés which pass for conversation, have deceived us into
believing we knew exactly where we were. We are actually on the
other side of the looking glass. There, one is condemned to run as
fast as one can just to stay in place. Under our feet the earth sinks,
the air sucks us up. The low fire we started in the fireplace to warm
our bones becomes a conflagration, engulfs our planet. A little affection turns into an ocean of eros and drowns us. The four elements
fuse into "deserts of ice, deserts of fire battling with each other and
all coming slowly towards us . . ." *The Stroller in Air*). We have
awakened in the world of our private nightmares, issuing from a very
ancient deposit to which all mankind may lay claim. This universe
of myth, the crystallization of a poet's meditation, is as intimate as
the secret recesses of our bodies, and as wide as the unconfined
reaches of our dreams.

It took a while for Eugene Ionesco to become Ionesco. He was
thirty-eight years old when his first play, *The Bald Soprano,* was
presented to a very small public at the *Noctambules* theatre. It was
not written as a play, but as a kind of exercise coming out of the
future playwright's painful attempts to master the English language.
Using the *Assimil* conversation method, Ionesco found himself in
the company of an English couple, Mr. and Mrs. Smith. The Smiths
seemed to find it necessary to inform one another that the ceiling
was overhead, the floor underfoot, the week made up of seven days,
and that they were having a fine English meal served by their maid
Mary. It was at this point in the textbook reading that Ionesco was
possessed by a strange excitement, utterly out of proportion either
with the discussion held by this dull couple, or the task of learning

English. Dizzy, as though he had received a solid knock on the head, the would-be student had to lie down, and not unlike the narrator of Proust's *A la recherche du temps perdu*, turn within in search of reasons for his rapture. Intelligence soon registered that what had happened was a take-over by the characters of *L'Anglais tel qu'on le parle*; the latter were writing their own lines. Thus what had begun as a didactic form of plagiarism obeyed, all of a sudden, mysterious laws surging from some dark night of the soul. Ionesco's *Discours de la Méthode* which he had considered calling *English Made Easy* or *The English Hour* kept on growing into a distorted vision: worthy bourgeois couples, struck with amnesia, failed to recognize one another even upon discovering they shared the same room and bed; inhabitants of a city—"men, women, children, cats and ideologists"—were all called Bobby Watson. To add to this confusion, "a fifth and unexpected character turned up to cause more trouble between the peaceable couples: The Captain of the Fire Brigade." The announcement of this emergence must have failed to surprise Ionesco's Italian audience at the French Institute where he was explaining, in 1958, the genesis of his play. In Italy the Captain of the Fire Brigade has a famous predecessor. Madame Pace, a dressmaker in *Six Characters in Search of an Author* whose shop is also a brothel, appears out of nowhere at the moment the Daughter relives before us the incestuous encounter with the Stepfather. Pirandello's character "comes to birth," evoked by the sheer magic of dramatic re-enactment. In *The Bald Soprano,* as in Pirandello's play, the strange happenings serve to sever the drama and the author from the habitual, an element in which most of us are constantly immersed as in some tepid bath. To be "bludgeoned" (*Notes and Counter Notes,* p. 26) out of our natural mental sloth, we must be ready to endure the dangers of anarchic humor whose cathartic violence mingles with that brought about by the feelings of pity and terror. From then on, Ionesco was committed to the wild exaggerations of parody, for in the creation of what he had assumed was "a comedy on comedy," he had actually written "the tragedy of language."

Ionesco's plays are neither tragedies nor comedies but tragicomedies or comitragedies. Since 186 B.C., when Plautus spoke of *tragicocomoedia* in his *Amphitryon,* the clearly separated genres began to come together. Till our own era, however, this meant that comic scenes came to relieve tragic events. Today, an interfusion has occurred lending comic coloring to tragic happenings and somber coloring to comic ones. Like Gogol's *Dead Souls,* the anti-plays of Beckett, Ionesco, Adamov, Dubillard, Arrabal, and Weingarten elicit "laughter through tears." In his essay, "Experience of the Theatre," published in *Notes and Counter Notes,* Ionesco states:

> It seems to me that the comic is tragic, and that the tragedy of man is pure derision. The contemporary critical mind takes nothing too seriously or too lightly. In *Victims of Duty* I tried to sink comedy in tragedy: in *The Chairs* tragedy in comedy, or, if you like, to confront comedy and tragedy in order to link them in a new dramatic synthesis. But it is not a true synthesis for these two elements do not coalesce, they coexist: one constantly repels the other, they show each other up, criticize and deny one another and, thanks to their opposition, thus succeed dynamically in maintaining a balance and creating tension. (p. 27)

It is becoming increasingly evident that this tragicomic mode expresses our ironic age. Comedy, which traditionally involved detachment and even a sense of superiority on the part of the viewer, who was not forced to imagine that such absurd reverses of fortune could happen to him, seems less and less likely to speak to a generation that has witnessed shifts in political ideologies, violent upheavals, the disappearance of societies, the genocidal annihilation of millions. We can no longer afford to be detached from the rest of humanity, though we tend to be detached from ourselves. This brings us closer to tragedy which, traditionally, presents to the viewer the fate of individual human beings, and thus an image of his own destiny. At the same time we are distanced from it by the fact that its usual hero, the personage in high position, is one that our modern era is wary of, seeing in him or her more often than not the destroyer, the embodiment of tyranny. Tragicomedy, on the other hand, presents basically ordinary characters, types we can identify with. Thus when Ionesco writes—"When the fallen Richard II is a prisoner in his cell, abandoned and alone, it is not Richard II I see there, but all the fallen kings of this world; and not only fallen kings, but also our beliefs and values, our unsanctified, corrupt and worn-out truths, the crumbling of civilizations, the march of destiny. When Richard II dies, it is really the death of all I hold most dear that I am watching; it is I who die with Richard II" (*Notes and Counter Notes,* p. 31)—he gives a perfect definition of the meaning of tragedy. His own dying king, Bérenger I, is a mixture of grotesque dignity and clownish fears; he is the common man facing dissolution. We laugh not *at* Bérenger but at ourselves; we share his anxieties, his desperate clinging to life; we cry because he must die at the end of the play, and because we must die at the end of the play which is our life.

Ionesco's *Exit the King* is a triumphant example of the tragi-comic mode. It is a play about the apprenticeship of death which provides an affirmation of the act of living. This farce manages to blend humor and anguish, echoing at the same time the fear and trembling of Pascal and Kierkegaard, and the patient wisdom in regard to physical suffering of the Montaigne of *De l'Expérience.* It is a philosophical cartoon, bitter, yet immensely tender.

Nor does the playwright limit himself to portraying a dying man; he depicts a dying world, and the ultimate, apocalyptic disappearance of our planet. Scientific progress and the development of civilization are brilliantly derided in this play. The King, we are told by the Guard who serves as chorus, has lived for hundreds of years, not unlike Rabelais' giants. During that time he has invented steel, balloons, airplanes, has built Rome, New York, Paris, and Moscow. He has made revolutions and counter-revolutions, Reformation and Counter-reformation. He has created literature by writing *The Iliad* and *The Odyssey,* and it is he, not Bacon, who composed the tragedies and comedies of Elizabethan England under the pseudonym of Shakespeare. Yet, after his death, he will be only a page in a book of ten thousand pages, in a volume placed in a library among a million libraries. Then the books will yellow, the pages turn to dust. The planet will grow cold and die. All so-called immortality is temporary, and thus relative. "What must come to an end is already ended," cries out Bérenger. The unavoidable truth is man's mortality, and by making this the theme of one of his greatest tragicomedies, Ionesco has also written one of the most profound dramatic poems on death and dying in our century.

There are a number of different Ionescos. The author of *The Bald Soprano, The Lesson, Jack or Submission* sets in motion the mechanism of the theatre to portray aimless passions. Later in *Amédée,* even in *The Chairs,* metaphysical considerations are expressed by the motion of objects, the proliferation of matter. *Victims of Duty,* Ionesco's favorite drama, is confessional, *Hunger and Thirst,* allegorical. The most philosophic of Ionesco's plays is *Exit the King. Rhinoceros, The Killer,* and *Macbett* are mostly political.

Ionesco says over and over again that he is not a political writer. In "The London Controversy" which opposed Ionesco and Kenneth Tynan, one can follow the outlines of two programs. Tynan expresses fear at the thought that Ionesco's bleak new world may infect the age. An admirer of Brecht's Marxist theories, Tynan believes that art and ideology interact and "spring from a common source."

In an answer which was never published by *The Observer* but which appears in *Notes and Counter Notes,* Ionesco makes his position clear: Tynan defends a narrow realism, socialist realism. True society is extrasocial. Socialist paradises have not been able to abolish, or even diminish the pain of living, the pain of death. What we have in common is our human condition. A revolution is a change in mentality; a language must be created to convey this change. Gradually what Tynan "calls anti-reality (becomes) clear, . . . the incommunicable (is) communicated." Man is not a social function; he is a solitude. Only by probing that solitary state, and bringing to the stage some of the images crystallizing at the bottom of the soul, do we rejoin other human beings.

Though Ionesco may not admit to it, he is passionately interested in politics. His view is not narrow; he neither preaches nor teaches, but he is always ready to denounce the cruelties of so-called ideologies, the inhumanity of man to man, in the name of future generations. His *Journals (Fragments of a Journal, Present Past Past Present),* the numerous articles he has written for *Le Figaro,* testify to his gifts as a pamphleteer, and to his commitment to fighting oppression, or the more subtle pressures of cliché opinions. It will become obvious as one looks back upon his body of work that Ionesco has written some of the most potent political satires of the second half of the twentieth century.

"My hero, if you can call him that," says Ionesco in conversation, "is not so much an anti-hero as a hero in spite of himself. When I was a young man in Rumania—that was after I left France to spend some time with my father—I remember how everyone around me converted to fascism, till it seemed to me that I was the only one left in the world. My own father had chameleonic gifts, and could always persuade himself that the present government was in the right. After all, History knew where it was going. It seemed to me at the time that although I was the most insignificant of creatures a terrible responsibility had befallen me, and that, somehow, I would have to do something, or rather *everything.* Isn't this the plight and privilege of the modern hero?"

Ionesco's Bérenger, the protagonist of *The Killer* and of *Rhinoceros* is indeed that hero-in-spite-of-himself who has become the central figure of much of our contemporary literature. He is the common man—"Bérenger, an average, middle-aged citizen." Unlike Molière's *raisonneur,* he speaks for unreason; for however modest or even humble he is, he thinks and feels as poets do. Patience, passive resistance, the silent rebellion of the spirit are his virtues.

Rhinoceros shows an entire community afflicted with *rhinoceritis,* the malady of conformity. Average men and women, but also philosophers, intellectuals, all catch the bug. Only Bérenger retains his humanity, and towards the end, when he is all alone, he begins to feel most uncomfortable with his white, human skin covered with light body hair since the brutes around him seem to rejoice in their thick, green hides.

The protagonist of *The Killer* (The French title is *Tueur sans gages* which is a reversal of the expression *tueur à gages,* hired assasin, thus stressing the gratuitous quality of this murder) tries to make his way to the police station through the goose-stepping throngs of Mother Peep's followers. Mother Peep, the new leader, who bears a disturbing resemblance to the *concierge* of Act I, shouts: "We'll replace the myths by slogans." Bérenger must reach the police, for he has found in the briefcase of his office friend, Edouard, the plans of the murderer who is destroying the citizens of the "radiant city." A week, sickly man, Edouard denies any knowledge of the documents found among his papers; the killer's schedule second by second, the colonel's picture the murderer uses as bait, the complete list of his victims—all these have just slipped in among other plans. When Bérenger says with some indignation: "After all you don't mean to say that these things got here all by themselves!" Edouard answers, not unlike Eichman at his trial: "I can't explain, I don't understand." Edouard believes that these documents, which were handed to him with a view towards publication, were "only projects, imaginary projects." So was Mein Kampf! At the end of the play, in an empty lot, Bérenger meets the killer, face to face. In a soliloquy which seems to be half of a dialogue—but the assassin's only answer is a shrug of the shoulders, a snicker, the flicker of a knife—Bérenger attempts to reason with the killer. Does he hate all human beings? Does he have any conception of happiness? Soon, it becomes clear that communication with such a creature is impossible. To take life is an absurd action. To argue with absurdity is to deliver oneself to its blind forces. Bérenger finds that he is driven to argue not against the murderer but with him, for him; the more he talks, the more reasons he finds for killing, or rather being killed. Though he is armed, Bérenger knows that he, a humanist, will not be able to bring himself to shoot even an enemy who means to destroy him. He says: "And what good are bullets against the resistance of an infinitely stubborn will?" He lays down his pistols, accepting his demise with a strange dignity and despair. In his *Journals* Ionesco writes:

> The greatest crime of all is homicide. Cain kills Abel. That's the crime *par excellence*. And we keep on killing. I have to kill my obvious enemy, the one who is trying to put me to death, in order that he shall not kill me. In killing him I find relief, for I am obscurely aware that I have killed death; I am not responsible for his death, I can feel no anxiety on that account, if have killed my adversary with the approval of the community; that's what wars are for, to enable one to kill with a clear conscience. By killing I exorcize my own death; the act of killing is part of a magic rite. (*Fragments of a Journal*, p. 92)

Does Bérenger realize that he is the sacrificial victim of a magic rite? At least, we can say that Ionesco knows that our society is based on the ruthless eradication of individuals, sometimes of a whole class. Yet, "History is shrewd" as Lenin said. This is the *leitmotiv* of many of Ionesco's *Journal* entries. It reappears in his *Macbeth*.

Ionesco's cartoon version of *Macbeth* is a witty exposition of that well-known fact that absolute power corrupts absolutely. In this great mechanism put together by Ionesco "to make you laugh for fear you'll weep instead," rulers and their generals are strapped to the tiny wheels of the infernal machine of power. Sovereigns, barons, princes of the church, those in power and those who seek that power pursue each other, dethrone one another, slaughter enemies, former friends and allies, entire nations. A king falls; another takes his place and his wife. Le Roi est mort, vive le Roi! Each succeeding sovereign is more blood-thirsty than his predecessor, grown monstrous through the pursuit of power, and the desire to retain what he has gained at the price of his former virtue, his loyalty, his innocence. Ionesco, by his own admission, is giving us a re-reading of *Macbeth* filtered through the grotesquely ironic text of Jarry's *Ubu*.

Jarry, the inventor of Pataphysics—the science of imaginary solutions—is in more ways than one Ionesco's spiritual ancestor. Ubu the King is the first destroyer of language. His expressionistic opening word, a variation on a famous curse word, marks the beginning of that malady the philosopher Brice Parain diagnoses as "word ache." The new idiom of the avant-garde theatre is the result of the inflation suffered by language after the First World War. Inflation, as we know, is characterized by the fact that although prices remain the same currency decreases in value. Language suffered a similar crisis. War, with its inflated rhetoric, its propaganda, its diplomatic double talk allowing for broken promises, sapped the very essence of communication. In the lull between two world wars, Communism and Fascism flowered upon the debris of words and ideas. They made a meal of the clichés available to them while clamoring that words should be action. The Dadaists during the war of 1914, the Surrealists in the twenties were the first to realize the state of bankruptcy that had befallen language. They sought to create works which would be adventures in linguistic terrorism. Words would have to be destroyed by words. To perform this task the poet had to place side by side words which would ignite one another and be consumed. These exiled humanists, whose hatred for language is a disguised form of longing and love, admit that man, the only animal who speaks, *is* his language; that man secretes words to make of them his protective shell. Left with clichés, empty words for empty minds, the contemporary dramatists use them with a vengeance, not unlike the way in which Pop artists make use of Coca-Cola bottles, or Campbell soup cans. Thus the new writers weave from the web of commonplace expressions a language whose new synthetic texture reveals the monstrous realities of our atomic age.

Did Ionesco invent a new language or was he invented by it? The question need not be answered though it must be posited. "I write to know what I am thinking," he likes to proclaim. But the manner in which one writes alters one's thought patterns. "Man is language" affirms the poet Francis Ponge, while the young American poet, Robert Sward writes: "A dog is said Dog! Or by name." Once a writer has given an object a name, the word becomes the thing. Poets knew this before it was stated by the philosopher Wittgenstein, for the poet must constantly give birth to language anew, and thus reinvent his basic tools. Words are charged with previous associations. To free himself of dead images, to fight his way through the tangle of signs, the writer must strip words of the layers of filth which obscure their meaning, lifting the filmy surface as skillfully as a surgeon removes cataracts. In his essay on the poet Ponge, Jean Paul Sartre says that one must learn to "décrasser les mots" (scrub words clean). Once this is done a private vocabulary is formed, what we call style, or literary form. The reader who is invited to enter a private universe is like the child invited to enter a game the rules of which he must learn. These rules create boundary lines, visible only to the initiate, and serve to isolate the magic world created by the artist-magician. The writer may appear to speak the language of everyday life, but actually he never does; the artist's vocabulary is always a language within language.

In *Notes and Counter Notes* Ionesco states: "Each new author seeks to fight in the name of truth. Boileau wished to express truth. In his Preface to *Cromwell,* Victor Hugo considered that romantic art rather than classical contained more truth and was more complex. The aim of realism and naturalism was also to extend the realms of reality or reveal new and still unknown aspects of it. Symbolism and later surrealism were further attempts to reveal and express hidden realities. The question then is simply for an author to discover truths and to state them. And the manner of stating them is naturally unfamiliar, for this statement itself is the truth for him. He can only speak it for himself. It is by speaking it for himself that he speaks it for others. Not the other way around." (p. 43) In the same talk about the avant-garde, Ionesco calls the latter a "pre-style." You cannot see the avant-garde, he explains, until it has taken place, has turned in fact into the rear guard.

Though the essays in this collection testify to the fact that the avant-garde is not yet a classical monument, and though Eugene Ionesco, even as a member of the *Académie Française,* is still too much a Satrap of the *Collège de Pataphysique* to be immobilized into eternity, we can, at this point, look back upon a body of work and begin to see the outlines of a face. The portrait is unfinished, but an expression has been caught. The face appears to be that of a melancholy but smiling clown. The eyes are bemused. A finger is held up to the lips as though the man in the picture were sharing a secret with himself. The round head reminds one of Socrates, and the folds of the flesh, apparent even under the clown mask, reveal that the taste of hemlock is not unfamiliar. The man is poised amid the moving architecture of his newly erected environment. The lower part of his body is embedded in what he calls "the warm slime of the living," partaking of the heaviness of matter, but the torso is stretched up, ready for flight. Under his feet, over his head, yawn Pascal's abysmal, silent spaces. To his right and left stand open-mouthed monstrous creatures who have retained in their state of metamorphosis something of the human traits they once possessed. The man in the unfinished portrait is alone, but knowing the depths of his solitude, he has formed a world, consubstantial with himself, which we can now explore.

Ionesco and the Comic of Absurdity

by J. S. Doubrovsky

For the last nine years during which Eugene Ionesco has filled
the theater with his presence, his reputation, by a stage effect not unworthy of the corpse in *Amédée*, has kept increasing and stretching
to the four corners of the earth. In spite of some critics' reservations,
he has conquered a vast public. One might almost say that this
extreme avant-gardist has become, in a way, a classic. Such a theater,
upsetting all conventions and habits and destructive of the theater
itself, seems to have been expected. At any rate, it has been immedi-
ately recognized and acclaimed. This is due to the fact that Ionesco's
plays, which some commentators have tried to dismiss as mere ex-
travaganzas born of the author's dreams and anxieties, are a response to the demands of a given personal situation in history. His
feelings are those of a man of his time, plunged in the agony of his
century. As he says in *The Alma Impromptu*: "The creator himself
is the only valid witness to his own time, he discovers it in himself,
he alone, mysteriously and freely, expresses it." We must therefore
understand the very impulses, desires and nightmares which he projects on the stage as constituting his *testimony* on the present condition of man, in no way inferior to any moral or political preach-
ing. In case we wonder what evidence he intends to give, Madeleine
is most explicit in *Victims of Duty*: "There are always things to say.
Since the modern world is in a state of decomposition, you can be a
witness to decomposition." If Ionesco's works appear at first so
strange and disconcerting and seem so fond of the weird and the
monstrous, it is not because they are immured within the universe of
dream or delirium, but precisely because they open out into our
world.

"Ionesco and the Comic of Absurdity" by J. S. Doubrovsky. From *Yale French
Studies*, no. 23 (Summer 1959), 3–10. Copyright © 1959 by *Yale French Studies*.
Reprinted by permission of the author and the publisher.

The aim of a theater of decomposition will be the decomposition of the theater. If the central theme of literature during the last twenty years is the absurdity of a world where man is left alone to fill in the void of God, give a name and a meaning to things and freely, but unjustifiably, create his own values, literary expression, it must be admitted, up to Beckett and Ionesco, had trailed far behind philosophical intent. In the same manner as Pascal strove to ruin reason in the eyes of the libertine by virtue of a rational dialectics, Sartre and Camus, in the exploring of absurdity which they undertook in *Nausea* or *The Myth of Sisyphus,* use an admirably logical language to express the illogical, the internal necessity of their sentences to convey the total contingency of the world, and resort to literature in order to negate literature. A genuine experience of the absurd, however, will invent its own language and create forms that are not those of rational discourse. "I dream of an irrationalist theater," says the Poet in *Victims of Duty.* "A non-Aristotelian theater?—Exactly." What must be carried onto the stage is the radical revolution which, in the twentieth century, substituted many-valued logics for the logic of the excluded middle and Einsteinian for Newtonian space. Therefore an irrationalist theater is not merely a theater that attacks the idols of rationalism, indefinite-progress-towards-happiness-through-science (although Ionesco makes no bones about tilting at them many times, from *Victims of Duty* to *The Unrewarded Killer*), it is, above all, a theater which is meant to be a genuine expression of the irrational. The traditional theater was coherent because the human beings it presented were coherent. In this respect, even writers of the absurd, like Sartre or Camus, remain, in their plays as well as in their style, very conservative. Sartre's plays especially are exemplars of the "well-made" play and *Les Mains Sales* is a masterpiece of what Ionesco would call the "police" type of drama. The reason for this is that man as the source of "Sinngebung," as a universal dispenser of meaning and the measure of all things, is intact. Although he is like a sickness of being, that sick man retains both his cohesion and his coherence. An authentic rendering of absurdity will demand a double disintegration, that of personality and that of language.

The already famous passage in which Ionesco has one of his characters declare: "We shall give up the principle of the identity and unity of character, to the benefit of motion and dynamic psychology . . ." is a highly significant text. But its interpretation remains a delicate affair and we must not be misled by the author's choice of terms. The words he uses are those of classical psychoanalysis ("dynamic psychology," "contradictory forces") and we might be tempted to construe the decomposition of personality we find in Ionesco's theater through analogy with dream manifestations. Some critics have even yielded to the temptation. But if it were only a matter of psychoanalysis, rationality would fare well. We must not forget that the play from which the quote is taken is meant to be a sharp satire on the claims of psychoanalysis, whose formulas the writer enjoys parodying. In *Victims of Duty* we see a policeman-psychoanalyst (with all the ratiocinative connotations of the word for Ionesco) ruthlessly pursuing "Mallot with a t at the end" through the dreams and memories of another character called Choubert and asserting: "I don't believe in absurdity, everything is coherent, everything becomes understandable . . . thanks to the endeavors of human thought and science." This manifesto could have been signed by Freud himself and the whole play aims at ridiculing it. "Mallot with a t at the end" is nowhere to be discovered, for the good reason that he cannot be recovered: "You *cannot* retrieve Mallot," cries out the exasperated Policeman, "you have a hole in your memory. We shall *fill up* that hole in your memory." The final scene of the play, with its extraordinary crescendo of frantic chewing and eating on the part of Choubert, brings out one of Ionesco's central themes and illustrates the symbolism of the "hole," analysed by Sartre at the end of *Being and Nothingness*. What all that manducation is trying to achieve is to fill an absolute gap and give thought a substantial existence.

But Choubert gorges in vain and his thought really is an unfillable void. In that sense, one might say that Ionesco's is an ontological theater. He seems to be one of the first playwrights to have taken seriously the philosophical assertion that thought is not a region of being, but, on the contrary, a nothingness in the plenum of the world. In spite of all his theoretical analyses tending to disprove the existence of an ego, Sartre still created characters with a "personality." Hugo in *Dirty Hands,* for instance, can be described by a series of predicates: bourgeois, weak, idealist, a misfit, etc. It would be very easy to write a non-Sartrian analysis of Sartre's works, in terms of traditional psychology, which is in keeping, of course, with the classical structure of his plays. But if we take seriously the assertion that consciousness is a nothing, personality and character disappear for good. Within the total impersonality of consciousness, it is now possible, as Rimbaud says, that "I be another." In this respect, the comments of the Belgian scholar A. de Waelhens on "the One" in Heidegger's philosophy[1] could apply word for word to Ionesco's characters: "The real 'subject' in daily life is that impersonal *Man,* since at all times and in all occasions it dictates to me what I must do or be. *I* become lost in *it.*" There is, so to speak, a void of being and a fall into the "one does" or "one says" which constitute man's original sin. Such a play as *The Bald Soprano* can only be understood as the unfolding of human existence on the level of "the One" described by Heidegger. The characters, absent from themselves, become as interchangeable as the lines they speak: hence their perpetual duplication, the unending series of Jacques, father, son, mother, sister, etc., all with the same name, the identity of Roberte I and II in *Jacques or the Submission,* of Amédée and Madeleine I and II in *How to get rid of it,* etc. If, by that repeated device most characteristic of Ionesco's theater, we are faced with an endless game of hide-and-seek to the point of dizziness, if the selves can thus be substituted for each other and the lines come most weirdly out of the wrong mouth, it is because the identity of the selves is like that of a vacuum. In *The Chairs,* the Old Man and the Old Woman, cut off and estranged from the world (the scene is laid on an island), seek to attain salvation through communication with mankind. What follows is well known: over the array of empty chairs on which the guests are supposed to be sitting extends an unfillable void, a total absence. No one is to be seen or heard. The Orator who was to deliver the Message cannot find his words and humanity is thus a wilderness where it is not even possible to preach.

Within that metaphysical perspective, the traditional "comique de caractère" is replaced by what might be called a "comique de non-caractère." You think you have one human being in front of you and you suddenly find another. This is the kind of comic effect due to abrupt change of balance and cheated expectation which Kant stressed. Hence a sort of vicious circle of human existence and a special brand of comedy which one might term a comedy of *circularity.* But destinies, like personalities, are interchangeable. There could not be any story or plot, in the usual sense, since these pre-

[1] This unfortunate expression is the usual English translation for the German "man" and the French "on" in the sense of *"one* does," *"one* thinks," etc.

suppose a linear progression. We are faced with yet another endless vicious circle, which explains why the denouements of *The Bald Soprano* and *The Lesson* exactly repeat the beginning, with other characters who happen to be the same; by virtue of the same device, the entrance of Bartholomeus II in *The Alma Impromptu* is the very replica of that of Bartholomeus I. That eternal return is not an eternal assertion of the self, as it was for Nietzsche, but its perpetual negation. Moreover, to man's absence corresponds the all-pervading presence of things. In the same way as Sartre's Roquentin experienced Nausea in front of a pebble or a root, the spectator experiences the essential emptiness of man before the monstrous kingdom of objects. The comedy of *proliferation,* on the level of things, is complimentary to the comedy of circularity, on the human level. The chairs in *The Chairs,* the cups in *Victims of Duty,* the pieces of furniture in *The New Tenant* or the eggs in *The Future is in the Eggs* are multiplied until they crowd and choke the stage, the corpse and the mushrooms in *Amédée* keep growing until there is no more room for the characters. Although Ionesco is occasionally tempted to abuse that device, this is no merely mechanical and facile trick. That uncontrollable growth and geometrical progression of objects, for the most part of human fabrication, that finally drive man out, convey both the futility of man's attempt to give himself through boundless material production the fullness of being which he lacks, and the inevitable ultimate triumph of object over subject. Things are like the nightmare of consciousness. Our laughter is tinged with anxiety. Against the spreading tide of things and the dissolution of the human, there remains one barrier, language. This last defense Ionesco will now proceed to storm.

This onslaught is the most striking and destructive element of his comic. "It is in talking that one finds ideas, words, and then ourselves in our own words, and also the town, and the garden, maybe one finds everything again and *is an orphan no more,*" declares the Old Woman in *The Chairs.* Like Claudel, she believes that language will wed and weld man and the world and that it affords the only access to the truth of things. But her hopes will be dashed and the playwright will expose the duplicity and failure of words on all levels. For we try to conceal our inner void and the absurdity of the world under the veil of the universal logos. The rationality to which we desperately cling only exists in and by our words, it is merely their creation. Unbearable talkers, Ionesco's characters all have a passionate, diseased urge to "understand."

"There is something I don't understand," Mr. Smith says in *The Bald Soprano,* "it's just meaningless." "This is understandable through an inner mathematical reasoning. You've got it or you haven't," the Professeur in *The Lesson* peremptorily declares. From the policeman-psychoanalyst, whom we already met, to the all too human Bérenger in *The Unrewarded Killer,* everybody wants to understand everything, and even man. If Molière's "reasoners" are firmly established within language and drift happily along the logical currents, they are, at least, cautious enough never to push their medium to extremes. Sade's reasoners, on the contrary, naive or fearless, are not afraid to carry their ratiocinations to the point where logic becomes sheer madness. As for Ionesco's reasoners, they demonstrate that language, in its essence, never was anything but systematic delirium. From that viewpoint, his theater can be considered as a complete treatise on the pathology of linguistics. The mechanical combination of terms reflects the automatic association of ideas. Capable of saying everything, words say nothing. Contraries are equivalent and can be substituted for each other at any time: "When all is said and done, we still don't know, when the bell rings, if there is someone at the door or not!—No one ever.—Always someone.—I'll set you right. There is something in what you both say. When the bell rings, sometimes there is somebody at the door, and sometimes there is nobody.—That seems logical to me.—To me also." Ordinary truths are as empty as the "One" in which they originate: "*One* says so.—One also says the contrary.—The truth is in between.—That's correct." *The Bald Soprano,* like all the plays of Ionesco, offers a complete range of that "everyday talk" on which Heidegger is such an acerb commentator and in which human stupidity is deposited in maxims and sayings clearly recognizable as they flit by, since they adorn our daily conversation. Common sense wisdom, fallen from the distinguished lips of the bourgeois or culled from the caretakers' gossip, the vociferations of the police, the clichés of the administrators, Mère Pipe's marxist-inspired demagogy as well as the liberal slogans of the Drunkard in *The Unrewarded Killer,* the jargon of critics and the tomfoolery of philosophers, and even the humanist beliefs which are dearest to our hearts, like those of Bérenger ("There must be some common ground, some common language . . ."), all that reveals the utter inanity of human logorrhea. We discover not without dismay that, for thought, words are not simply a frame of reference or a support, but the whole of reality. A prisoner of his speech, man thinks himself protected by his own psittacism. It is enough to show us for one moment our language *from the outside* to tear down that fragile barrier. From then on, the poet's imagination plays havoc with words. A French critic had the patience to count up to thirty-six stock tricks in Ionesco's comedies. As far as language is concerned, the latter displays prodigious verbal invention: his accumulation of puns, spoonerisms, equivocations, misunderstandings and a thousand and one other nonsensical drolleries, down to outright disintegration of articulate language into onomatopoeias, brayings and belchings, does not merely betray a childish or diseased inclination, on the part of the author, for verbal fireworks; it is a perpetually renewed act of accusation against language, a language that lends itself to all possible coaxings and inveiglements, torsions and distortions, that can utter contrary statements in one breath and believes itself to be an emanation of the universal Logos! Instead of men using language to think, we have language thinking for men. That mask must be torn from their faces. Thus is the "anti-character" comedy completed by "anti-wit" witticisms and speech-destructive speeches.

Now Ionesco has reached the total decomposition of the stage and achieved the irrationalist theater of which he dreamt. The frame of the stage-world, the fetters of ordinary language are broken. It is like a rebellion of the theater against itself. Yet it must be remarked that this all-out challenge allows a spectacle to subsist which calls for the presence of spectators. Such an "anti-theater" differs *toto caelo* from the "a-theater" of a Pichette, where action becomes lost in words and the show vanishes into flights of lyricism. There remains in Ionesco's works (and that characteristic is even more emphasized in his most recent play, *The Unrewarded Killer*) a certain theatrical consistency and structural coherence, which alone would necessitate a long analysis. To simplify matters, let us say that what keeps his plays from being mere rantings and ravings is the very weight and denseness of their reality, one might almost say their realism. For, as far as we are concerned, we refuse to consider those literary works as "dream-like" (*oniriques*) or "surrealistic." That would mean forgetting the meticulous care with which the playwright stresses, without omitting a single one of them, all the details of his deliberately familiar settings, "a middle-class English home," "a study, used also as a dining-room," "an old dusty armchair in the centre of the stage and a night-table," etc. Even the most fantastic and whimsical plays, like *Jacques,* are set in a decidedly familiar, everyday environment. What must be wrenched off its moorings, after the fashion of Rimbaud's Bateau Ivre, what must overturn and capsize is *reality* itself, for, according to the very words of the Architect in *The Unrewarded Killer,* "reality, *contrary to dream,* can turn into a nightmare." If Ionesco's theater is viewed as compounded of "the stuff dreams are made on," it will lose all its force and be neutralized. On the contrary, once the barrier of language is disposed of, reality will suddenly assume a monstrous appearance. This is an experience reminiscent of the one Sartre describes in *Nausea,* only more radical. Far from our rising then to a "surreality" (let us not forget that surrealism is optimistic and purposes to renovate and resuscitate man through the imagination), it would be more accurate to say that we lapse into an "infrareality," we retrace the path of evolution. Articulated speech falls apart and becomes once more a succession of syllables, cries and breathings. Man goes back to the original beast, witness the end of *Jacques:* "One can still see the Jacques and the Roberts *swarm* on the stage. One can hear their *animal* groans . . . Everybody is gone, except for Roberte, who is lying, or rather *crouching,* on the floor . . . One can only see her nine fingers stirring like *reptiles.*" Everything returns to the primeval magma and initial absurdity from which it issued. Face to face with the Killer, Béranger in *The Unrewarded Killer* looks for that ultimate confrontation with Death, which La Fontaine's Woodcutter had hastened to flee: but Béranger is unable to bring forth a single reason for the Killer to spare him. He is fundamentally guilty of seeking reasons where there are none. He falls a victim to his own tragic passion for "understanding," and his rational yearnings make his encounter with absurdity all the more painful. There is in Ionesco an all-pervading feeling of guilt. It would be a misinterpretation to construe it, as some critics did, as the author's private guilt feeling, in a Freudian sense, for what here becomes manifest is the essential, ontological culpability of man, the author's and ours. Thus we reach a "théâtre total," and it is total not because bits of movies, ballet and song are added to it, but because it involves the spectator in the spectacle totally. Since the subject at hand is human reality and since the actors are nobody in particular, they are precisely *ourselves* and what they are enacting is *our* drama. When I laugh at Molière's Miser or Misanthrope I can set my mind at rest, on leaving the theater, with the thought that I am neither a miser nor a misanthropist. In traditional comedy, there always is a safe distance between the actors and me. But when I laugh at "everyone" and "anyone," I laugh at myself. There is no more separation between the spectator and the spectacle, the latter becomes a mirror, just like consciousness; and what it reflects is our bad conscience. "Everything must arouse in the spectator a painful feeling of shame and uneasiness." (Stage directions at the end of *Jacques*.)

This non-Aristotelian theater presents us with a problem which Aristotle had not foreseen: that of pity and fear for which *laughter* is a catharsis.

It is in this perspective that we must ultimately view the comic in Ionesco. One might wonder, indeed, by what miracle that theater of "shame" and "uneasiness" can elicit laughter. The revelation of absurdity is usually accompanied by anguish, the anguish of man's dignity for Camus, that of man's responsibility for Sartre. But if one goes further in the experience of absurdity, man becomes suddenly so unimportant that tragedy turns into a farce, and an absurd laughter bursts forth. That kind of laughter had already been heard at the end of *The Wall* by Sartre and at the most humiliating point of the French defeat in *Roads to Liberty*. But this laughter is still inauthentic, it plays the part of a "safety valve," which André Breton assigned to grim humor; it is a type of human behavior which consists, once our projects have lost any possible transcendance into the future, in shifting the responsibility for an absurd situation onto the world and thus getting rid of it. In Sartre's eyes, as he wrote in *Nausea*, "nothing that exists can be comic." But let man cease to be a "humanist" and to view himself in a tragic light or even to take himself seriously, let him stand back at the theater and look at himself from the outside at last, let him see himself as the puppet he really is, and then, as Nicolas, in *Victims of Duty*, exclaims: "No more drama nor tragedy: the tragic becomes comic, the comic is tragic, and life becomes so gay . . . life becomes so gay . . ." This determination to be gay in face of the utter confusion and final disappearance of all values offers no salvation, it does not conquer absurdity, it stresses it, it does not try to dodge it, it revels in it. It is an act of accusation against man much more than against the world. It is man throwing doubt on the possibility of being a man. In our awkward moments, Bergson saw what he called a mechanical something grafted upon life: in our best moments, we discover ourselves to be but a living something grafted upon mere mechanism. The "useless passion" which existentialists thought man to be now becomes eminently laughable. The laughter that suddenly rings out is Ionesco's.

The Bald Soprano and *The Lesson:*
An Inquiry into Play Structure

by Richard Schechner

In April, 1951, a few months after the world premiere of *The Bald Soprano* in Paris, and two years after the play was written, Ionesco began to talk about the structure of his play.

> *The Bald Soprano,* like *The Lesson,* among other things, attempts to make the mechanics of drama function in a vacuum. An experiment in abstract or non-representative drama. [. . .] The aim is to release dramatic tension without the help of any proper plot or any special subject. But it still leads, in the end, to the revelation of something monstrous: this is essential, moreover, for in the last resort drama is a revelation of monstrosity or of some monstrous formless state of being or of monstrous forms that we carry in ourselves. [. . .] The progression of purposeless passion, a rising crescendo that is all the more natural, dramatic, and exciting because it is not hampered by content, and by that I mean any *apparent* content or subject which conceals the *genuine* subject from us: the particular meaning of a dramatic plot hides its essential significance.[1]

Ionesco packs a lot of fundamental theory into these 175 words. He claims for his first two plays an architectural, structural pristinity; he says that drama is the revelation of that monstrous (and I am reminded here of Greek myth, and the myth-rites of many other peoples as well) rising suddenly and perplexingly from the depths, as a vast whale from the sea. He says that drama is best which is least plotted because the plot is a veil concealing the action of the play.

[1] Eugène Ionesco. *Notes and Counternotes.* Translated by Donald Watson. New York: Grove Press, 1964, pp. 180–81.

In 1970 these assertions may seem passé, but they are not. We must locate Ionesco's dramaturgy properly. He is a writer; he is talking about plays and not performances. He raises for us the questions of play structure, and questions put powerfully twenty years ago have not been resolved. Rather, performers have intervened and solved the questions for themselves (and, maybe, for the theater) by dismissing the writer and substituting the performer and the director. In considering Ionesco's claims we are, perhaps, delving into an archaic problem. But, I think, before we are through, we shall come to a fuller understanding of some current baffling situations. After all, we do not want to eliminate words from the theater, but find for them proper places. The writer is not the money-changer to be chased from the temple, nor even the hypocrite. He has simply been off somewhere, doing something else. And Ionesco was among the first to suggest through his theory and his practice how the writer might re-enter the work of the theater.

Ionesco wants to reveal the structure by sucking out the content. He is an architect and a musician. He is interested in what supports drama, where the connections are, and in what direction the stresses run. The process of writing led him from parody to originality, a very difficult circle to close.

> In my first play, *The Bald Soprano,* which started off as an attempt to parody the theatre, and hence a certain kind of human behavior, it was by plunging into banality, by draining the sense from the hollowest clichés of everyday language that I tried to render the strangeness and the farcical, the prosaic and the poetic, the realistic and the fantastic, the strange and the ordinary, perhaps these are the contradictory principles (there is no theatre without conflict) that may serve as a basis for a new dramatic structure. In this way perhaps the unnatural can by its very violence appear natural, and the too natural will avoid the naturalistic.[2]

Stripping away, as a technique, eliminates the accustomed order of things, the causative world, and reveals rhythms. These may be thoracic—like breathing and heartbeat—or "natural"—like sunrise and sunset; or even metaphysical and "logical" as when Mrs. Smith concludes that "experience teaches us that when one hears the doorbell ring it is because there is never anyone there." Here the structure of logical thought is laid out—namely, that one reasons from par-

[2] *Ibid.,* p. 28.

ticular instances in accord with certain rules of induction and deduction. This structure is put up against the structure of theater—namely, that one can arrange whatever business one wishes.

Rhythms are automatic and often unconscious. They are patterns that are not necessarily causative. Night follows day but night does not cause day. To strip away the causative necessities that make a plot is to leave theater naked and to liberate the energies of rhythms. It is making theater approach music, that first art of rhythm-making and playing. These rhythms are alive in *Soprano,* but not the people, who are empty, mechanical, and dying. The drama's language is alive; it has its own logic, it reproduces itself (the play's climax), it creates people (Bobby Watsons), and situations (the courtship of the Martins). *Soprano* turns classic comedy on its head, and in doing so earns itself a place within the comic tradition. For that tradition is nothing other than finding new solutions to the oldest problem: how to beat death. Comedy does this by uncovering again and again life in the least likely places. In *Soprano* language is life. The obstacles to life are the Smiths and the Martins. As in the science-fiction film *The Invasion of the Body Snatchers,* a new life-force enters people, hollows them out, and takes over their shells. Inside the dead and dying people a new life-force stirs. It is not an evolution or a moral development. It is wholly new and alien.

Soprano opens with seventeen clangs of the clock—and Mrs. Smith says, "There it's nine o'clock." Her talking is automatic, as if whatever is speaking is not yet used to English. "We've drunk the soup and eaten the fish and chips," etc. Something is talking through Mrs. Smith, making its report, struggling with English grammar and vocabulary. (No wonder Ionesco punched through to the bottom of the opportunity of *Soprano* while studying English in the *Assimil* primer.) Mrs. Smith talks English, but her language is no longer her own, nor is it that of the alien being inside her. That being, language itself, is *learning English* just as Hal does in Kubrick's *2001.* It is the instrument closest at hand. What is the difference between "language" and "English"? English is one of the limitless forms language may take as its expression. Mrs. Smith is not aware that she is the host for an alien being. Why should she be—are you aware of the millions of bacteria in your gut? As she dies to her old life she becomes the means of the new life.

She reports how she feels. She looks at herself and her family as if they were at a far distance from her. She is not involved emotionally. In fact, each time she says "we" she could more correctly say "they." Of course, from one perspective this is a protest against the "dehumanization" of man; a typical theme of the forties and fifties. But I think we are ready for a new interpretation. Mrs. Smith is not using language. It is using her. She is "they" because language is "I." The language needs people because it is not able to live on its own, purely; people are its means of being, its host. But we ought not to prematurely or prejudicially abhor such a language. And surely we must not underestimate its power or deny to it *a priori* compassionate feelings. Some parasites are intelligent and cunning; and some the agents of high cultures. We have no reason to be contemptuous of these life-forms; such contempt is a function of ethnocentrism. "While writing this play," Ionesco says, "I felt genuinely uneasy, sick and dizzy. [. . .] When I had finished I was nevertheless very proud of it. I imagined I had written something like the tragedy of language."

The triumph of language is more like it. But Ionesco's malaise is understandable. He is writing of possession in its pure and absolute sense; writing from within the experience of being possessed. When Ionesco finished his play it appeared a tragedy because the author was unable to fly away from his humanity—he is no traitor to his species. But he is a traitor to an aspect of his culture—that part which values individualism above everything else. *Soprano* is triumphant, comic, bouyant, and proud if you do not value individualism. The author is dizzy because his whole career indicates a deep problem concerning individualism, about which he has the most ambivalent feelings.

Looking behind the drama at some of its social implications, some twenty years after its premiere, we recognize that language is the most salient stirring of a wholly vivified environment—a world of teeming life where not only words but gestures, clocks, doorbells, servants—things which we expect to be dehumanized, manageable, "in their places"—spring alive with shocking energy. The Smith and the Martins are dying; the Fire Chief is the messenger of a new culture (this needs looking at later); and Marie is a liberated woman— the maid who won't do what she's told, the Fire Chief's first lover, Sherlock Holmes.

Customarily we think of culture as the secretion of human living and experience. To use a visual metaphor, human beings are the core and culture the meat of the apple. The relationship between the biological and the sociological species is as between core and meat. But *Soprano* reverses that. At the core is the cultural, and around that, serving it, are the people. What we experience in this drama is a world in which culture (language, things) is alive and the people are secretions and by-products. The Martins don't even know they are married until they discover so through deductive logic; and even then they are wrong (so Marie tells us). The Bobby Watsons proliferate as they are talked of because they are the children of language, not of human parents. The clock strikes as many times as it wants to. Sometimes when the doorbell rings there is someone there, and sometimes not. Even the stage directions have a rhetoric which identifies them with the rest of the drama, not with the author.

Words do not identify the Bobby Watsons. They live only as they can be talked about. They are the creations and the toys of a language just starting to explore its own possibilities. As Vannier says, "language has been promoted to the dignity of a theatrical object." [3] Words are no longer the vehicles of thoughts or feelings; they are themselves actions—the initiators of dramatic events. Conceivably, if we could *see* the Watsons we could tell old from young, male from female, living from dead.[4] But the Watsons do not exist as people offstage (anymore than the invisible people of *The Chairs* are "real"); the Watsons are what they are—part of a conversation. Language makes the Watsons, and language can multiply, confuse, kill, birth, or do what it wills with them. The Smiths cannot interfere with this wordplay because ultimately the Smiths are like the Watsons. As Mrs. Martin reminds Mr. Martin, "This morning when you looked at yourself in the mirror you didn't see yourself." And he nicely answers, "That's because I wasn't there yet."

In *Soprano* there is little conflict between the drama's protagonist —language—and the human beings. Even the mad dance finale is a dance of triumph, a celebration of language's liberation from people. Perhaps, as Doubrovsky believes, this is an indication of despair, a revelation of monstrosity.

[3] Jean Vannier. "A Theatre of Language," *Tulane Drama Review* 7, No. 3 (Spring, 1963), p. 82.
[4] One of the Bobby Watsons can't even be visually "true." "She has regular features and yet one cannot say she is pretty. She is too big and stout. Her features are not regular but still one can say she is very pretty. She is a little too small and thin." The clock is very amused by language's play and it rings five times.

Instead of using language to think, we have language thinking for
men. That mask must be torn from their faces. Thus is the "anti-
character" comedy completed by "anti-wit" witticisms and speech-
destructive speeches. [. . .] Once the barrier of language is disposed
of, reality will assume a monstrous appearance. This is an experience
reminiscent of the one Sartre describes in *Nausea*, only more radical.[5]

Doubrovsky's reference to *Nausea* is significant. He ties *Soprano* to
a mood which reached one of its climaxes just before World War II,
and the other in the decade following the war. This mood was somber, even full of despair. It is not the mood of the seventies—which
on the one hand is apocalyptic and on the other millennial. Why
should language communicate for men? Why oughtn't it have its
own integrity and rights? Surely, as Doubrovsky says, Ionesco may
have wanted to show the nothingness that lies coiled in the heart
of being; or he may have wanted to deplore the subjugation of man
by his former servants. Ionesco himself says, "for me, what had happened was a kind of collapse of reality. The words had turned into
sounding shells devoid of meaning." [6] But we must set aside the
author's intentions if we are to look freshly, more than twenty years
after it was written, at a work that seems today to have relevance
and liveliness. From this new perspective I discern in *Soprano*
triumph and celebration—not of individualized human beings, but
of the possible next phase of cultural development.

The Fire Chief and Marie are not dead like the Smiths and the
Martins. They live purposeful lives; are lovers; go to fires and
movies; act as servants and confessors and detectives. The Fire Chief
is the man who looks for fires; Marie recites the poem, "Fire." R. D.
Laing says, of fire: "There are many images used to describe the
related ways in which identity is threatened. [. . .] The image of
fire recurs repeatedly. Fire may be the uncertain flickering of the
individual's own inner aliveness. It may be a destructive alien power
which will devastate him." [7] Not in the usual narrative way, but in
a musical and associative way the Fire Chief and Marie reinforce
the major themes of *The Bald Soprano*. When Marie's fire is put
out by Mr. Smith's hammer, the Fire Chief prepares to leave. "I

---

[5] J. S. Doubrovsky, "Ionesco and the Comic of Absurdity," *Yale French Studies*
23 (Summer, 1959), pp. 8–9. Also reprinted above, p. 11.

[6] *Notes and Counternotes*, p. 179.

[7] R. D. Laing. *The Divided Self*. Chicago: Quadrangle, 1960, p. 47.

must tell you that in exactly three-quarters of an hour and sixteen minutes, I'm having a fire at the other end of the city." The exit of the Fire Chief is the signal for the start of the final explosive dance. Marie's "death" is a prelude to rebirth—at the "other end of the city."

The two scenes which precede the dance finale (Marie's poem, the Fire Chief's exit) are more easily understood structurally than narratively. It is futile to search for meaning in the lines themselves. "During rehearsals," Ionesco recalls, "we discovered that the play had movement: in the absence of action [plot] there were actions, a rhythm, a development without plot, an abstract progression." [8] It is unfortunate that modern art took the term "abstract" as a description of a kind of nonfigurative structuring. Abstract suggests nonconcrete and general. Nothing could be more misleading. Abstract art is as concrete as the most vivid landscape and as specific as an image from one of Shakespeare's sonnets. The "abstract progression" Ionesco alludes to in *Soprano* is the movement from the finish of individuality to the assertion of a new life-force; and the dropping of all "characterization" in the drama. In most productions of *Soprano* this has led to a mechanical way of performing— as if the Smiths, Martins, Marie, and the Fire Chief were puppets. It is possible that Ionesco intended this kind of performing. Indeed, at the very long run of the first revival of *Soprano* at the Théâtre de la Huchette in Paris, it was this kind of acting that I saw. That production had Ionesco's approval, and, I believe, his assistance during rehearsals. But if a fresh interpretation of the play is possible, then maybe a fresh way of playing is called for.

We have examples of performing without playing "characters." Grotowski's work, some of the pieces directed by Joseph Chaikin, and elements of *Dionysus in 69, Makbeth,* and *Commune* which I directed, approach the performer's task differently. The text of a play and the actions it suggests are not aspects of a person (called a "character"). They are evocative stimuli working directly on the feelings of the performer. The performer performs "vis-à-vis" the text of the drama. He sets himself in front of the text and systematically removes those blocks that would prevent him from reacting openly and wholly to the text. He is not bound by the surface logic of the text, but is open to the farthest associations and most personal

[8] Eugène Ionesco. *Cahiers des Saisons* 15 (1959), p. 283.

evocations.[9] Thus, in this way of working, the Smiths, Martins, Marie, and the Fire Chief are not people, or puppets. They are "parts"—that is, sets of verbal notations, just as a musical part is a set of musical notations. These parts in themselves have no feelings. Each part is, however, a stimulator of feelings within the performer. To play these parts is not to recreate or create for the first time living people, but rather to allow these notations to stimulate whatever feelings are there within the performer. The living life is the performers; the text outlines the structure of the *mise en scene*. These two bases of the performance need not harmonize with each other. They may be in counterpoint, or utterly contradict each other. The performer's task, and that of his director, is to remove all the obstacles preventing or impeding the free flow of feelings within the discipline of the verbal and (later during rehearsals) gestural notations. Ionesco's early work would seem particularly well suited to this approach because of his drama's architectural and musical qualities.

Whether intentionally or not, Ionesco in *Soprano* goes beyond bourgeois drama and makes a play without individuated characters. He has also side-stepped the solution put forth by the German Expressionists and their "mass" characters. In Ionesco's drama we are able to have the creativity of the performers and the vitality of a liberated language. To perform *The Bald Soprano* this way would be to radically reinterpret it, and make of it what I think it wants to be, a driving life-force comedy. "But words, it will be said, have metaphysical powers; it is not forbidden to conceive of speech as well as of gestures on the universal level, and it is on that level moreover that speech acquires its major efficacity, like a dissociative force exerted upon physical appearances, and upon all states in which the mind feels stabilized and tends toward repose." [10] Once again, Artaud speaks prophetically.

The Lesson is in many ways the opposite of *Soprano*. But like so

[9] For a more detailed discussion of these techniques see Jerzy Grotowski, *Towards a Poor Theatre* (New York: Simon & Schuster, 1969) and Richard Schechner, *Public Domain* (New York: Avon, 1969) and "Actuals: A Look into Performance Theory," in Alan Cheuse and Richard Koffler, eds., *The Rarer Action* (New Brunswick: Rutgers University Press, 1970).

[10] Antonin Artaud. *The Theatre and Its Double,* trans. Mary C. Richards. New York: Grove Press, 1958, p. 70.

many oppositions, underlying them is an identity: for *Lesson* too is about life-force and triumph dancing. The difference is that *Lesson* uses familiar human beings.

Here, too, language is the hero/villain. Not that language possesses the Professor; no, it is his ally, his shield, his weapon, and his alibi. Truly in *Lesson* language has "metaphysical powers" and it operates like a "dissociative force exerted upon physical appearances." The knife that rapes and kills, like the philology lecture itself, is a verbal knife: a concrete being whose substance is grammatical.

Power is the X-factor of *Lesson*. When the Pupil has it, the Professor is a timid old man; when he gets it, she is helplessly gripped by numbing pain; when Marie disarms the Professor, he becomes a whining baby—but while he has the power and is strong in his rage, Marie can do nothing with him. There is just so much power, and the game/ritual of *Lesson* is the flow of this power from one to another. The power is in the language. At its deepest level, *Lesson* is a magic play, replete with special formulae and occult incantations. To know how to speak is to have power. But speaking is not ordinary English or French or any *national* language; rather, in the circularity so liked by Ionesco, the verbal language of the Professor's lecture is the worded manifestation of the language of sexual power. But this does not make of verbal language merely a mask in the debased sense of masking. No, like the Elema *hevehe* ritual, the power is the mask: without the mask there is nothing, with it everything.

The orderly transfer of power is important. It is the rhythm of the play, its dancelike repetitiveness, its circles within circles. There is no "exaltation" until all the power is concentrated in the Professor's magic knife. At that moment both the Pupil and Marie are *empty*.

Remember photos of dancers in which a torch or flashlight is carried so that after a long exposure the developed picture shows the pattern of movement? These are not motion pictures, but pictures of motion. *The Lesson* is a picture of motion and the torch is the power which flows among the three characters.

The setting does not prepare us for the play's action. There is no hint in "the office of the old professor, which also serves as a dining room" that here a rape/murder will be committed, one of an unend-

ing series. The concealment of the *insolite*[11] within the banal is a
favorite Ionesco device, and part of a set of contrapuntal details in
Lesson. Others are the Professor's age *vs.* his act; the Pupil's apparent innocence *vs.* her behavior; Marie's subservient social position *vs.* her control over the Professor; the seemingly passive role of
language *vs.* its deadly power. Both the romanticism and the farce
of *Lesson* come from these oppositions.

As soon as the Pupil enters, and the Professor sees her, the power
flow begins. A quickly suppressed "lewd gleam" dances in his eyes.
Marie, who lets the Pupil in, surely knows from experience what is
going to happen. She is a sullen accomplice, a goad who guarantees
the murderous outcome of events. (If *Lesson* were read as a political
parable, Marie would be the "people" who seemingly deplore but
actually assist each tyrant in his tyranny. The Nazi armband Marie
gives to the Professor while they carry the Pupil's body out supports the political reading.) The very presence of the Pupil—young,
apparently innocent, pretty—and Marie's warnings, cathect the first
flow of energy.

LATENT ENERGY	STIMULUS	OBSTACLE	OVERT ENERGY
	Pupil enters	*Marie's warning*	*Professor's "gleam"*

Power is expressed among the characters, and flows from one to
the other. It is ideally theatrical. Finally, power is the ability to use
language, "to pronounce the word knife."

Despite the Pupil's inability to answer the most simple questions,
the Professor is at first very pleased with her. He sees nothing standing in the way of her getting the "total doctorate." The flirtation
is obvious, and of that especially titillating kind between a very
young girl and an old man. The language between Professor and
Pupil is transparent, and behind it we experience the sexual play.
In *Soprano* language burst through the Smiths and Martins to express its own life; here a subtext is revealed behind the text. Several
times early in the play the whole rhythm of the "progressive exalta-
tions" that make the play's action is enacted. *Lesson* is structured

---

[11] *Insolite* is a difficult French word to translate; it is one of Ionesco's favorites.
It means the astonishing, the *unmaskingness* of experience—as when the side of
a building falls down to reveal your wife (or husband) in the arms of her (his)
lover.

musically—it develops not through the revelation of plot but through the intensification and repetition of moods and patterns. These increase in intensity and widen in amplitude, are played in varying keys of anger, amusement, love, and fear.

When the Professor asks the Pupil about the seasons, when she and he sit down together, when they begin arithmetic, when he is warned by Marie, when they start philology—each of these games are properly *dances* modeled on the "scalp dance" that ends in rape/murder. These dances are sometimes introductory, sometimes titillating, sometimes climactic. It is from a musical perspective that we ought to appreciate them and to see their sexual function; it is from this same perspective that we ought to know the uses that the Professor makes of Marie's meddling and warnings which only further raise his temperature. The small reservoir of power which is teased into play at the start builds rhythmically and in waves until it possesses the Professor and overwhelms the Pupil. This wavelike, musical development can be detected in the text, but fully appreciated only during performance.

I can outline this structure by discussing my staging (Province-town, 1961) of the scene in which the Professor asks the Pupil to sit.

> *Professor.* Then, may I ask you to sit down . . . there. . . . Will you permit me, miss, that is, if you have no objections, to sit down opposite you?
>
> *Pupil.* Oh, of course, Professor, please do.
>
> *Professor.* Thank you very much, miss. [*They sit down facing each other at the table, their profiles to the audience.*] There we are. Now have you brought your books and notebooks?
>
> *Pupil* [*taking notebooks and books out of her briefcase*]. Yes, Professor. Certainly, I have brought all that we'll need.
>
> *Professor.* Perfect, miss. This is perfect. Now, if this doesn't bore you . . . shall we begin?
>
> *Pupil.* Yes, indeed, Professor. I am at your disposal.
>
> *Professor.* At my disposal? [*A gleam comes into his eyes and is quickly extinguished; he begins to make a gesture that he suppresses at once.*] Oh, miss, it is I who am at your disposal. I am only your humble servant.
>
> *Pupil.* Oh, professor . . .

The text is super-polite. It is like two animals first meeting during mating season. Taking this as my subtextual action, I had the Professor gesture the Pupil to her seat. But she, being a well-brought-up girl, does not sit down before the Professor. He, in turn, cannot sit until after the "lady." She, then, is playing a child who does not sit while adults are standing, and he a gentlemen who does not sit until the ladies are seated. Both these roles are games—for she is no child, and he no gentleman. But these are precisely the roles that can excite each of them most deeply. As he begins to sit she rises, and as she begins to sit he rises. The physical rhythms are not unlike sexual intercourse, and the feeling-center of their bodies for this scene is in the pelvis and very base of the spine. The performers played this game with each other, enjoying its combination of teasing and overt but not acknowledged sexuality, until the Professor cuts it off with "There we are." He has been excited because a child has toyed with him; she has been excited because a man treated her as a grown-up. They now know for sure that a sexual exchange is possible between them. The Professor quickly changes the subject to "books and notebooks" and the Pupil answers with a double-entendre, "I have brought all that we'll need." The Professor picks up her cue and, speaking as much to himself as to her, replies, "Perfect, miss. This is perfect." At each of his speeches, I had the Professor make the most subtle move toward the Pupil. He wants very much to reach out and just take her; but he doesn't dare. She knows she is safe, and so she teases him by the way she sits, with her knees apart, absolutely open. The Professor wants to keep himself from going too far, the Pupil wants to go as far as she can; he is testing his restraining mechanisms and she her adventurous ones. The power flow is very evident here as both Professor and Pupil give and take. When she suggests that she is at his "disposal," that is all he can bear. He has a mini-orgasm, reaches for her, suppresses his gesture, and apologizes. The bundle of energy that has been building during the scene is discharged. The Pupil senses that something has happened, and her "Oh, Professor" is a lilt of pleasure. She is pleased because she has been "recognized" sexually; he is pleased because he has come, ever so subtly and slightly.

There are seven beats to this brief scene.

1	2	3
OPENING GAME	INTERLUDE	SEXUAL STIMULATION
Who will sit first?	*From "There we are" to "This is perfect"*	*From "Now, if this doesn't bore you" to "I am at your disposal"*

4	5	6
OVERT LEWDNESS	PLEASURE	SUPPRESSION
"At my disposal?"	*Pupil's laugh,*	*Professor stopping*
And the gleam in	*Professor's*	*himself from going*
the Professor's eye,	*orgasm*	*further*
his gesture		

7

GRATIFICATION

Pupil's "Oh,
professor"

This is an ebb-flow game/dance. It definitely takes two to play; its overall rhythm is that of coitus. This same structure is repeated several times during *Lesson*. It is the rhythmic *leitmotif* of the play. Ionesco says that the play works through a "progression by intensifying states of soul, feeling, situation, [and] anguish" that leads to an "exaltation." This "progression" is the seven-beat pattern outlined above.

This pattern is repeated during the addition scene and during the subtraction-by-taking-away-ears scene. This latter is complicated because the Professor is frustrated, and the last beat is not gratification but frustration. When the Pupil does not respond "correctly" and the Professor is frustrated, his first response is to try another approach—new avenues to gratification. But these fail, he gets angry, and his anger arouses fear in her. The small pleasure sources released in the early scenes are frustrated after the addition scene. There is no release. Instead there is the build-up of energy and the transformation of fear in the pupil first into her toothache and then into the numbing pains in her legs, genitals, and breasts. Each frustration further stimulates the Professor, whose kindness is transformed into anger. This transformation is not necessarily psychologically valid; it is musically valid, like the shift in a symphony from the tonic to the dominant. The progression from geography to arithmetic to philology parallels the other transformations.

The philology lecture follows the same general plan as that of the earlier scenes. It would be hard to schematize the lecture into seven clear movements/beats because the lecture is long and complicated. The game/dance of the lecture—like that of the play as a whole—is that of a lesson. The Professor will "teach" the Pupil

something. Each speech of his, each protestation of hers, augments
his energy store. He can no longer put down his impulse to touch
her, and by now his gestures are not gentle—he "seizes her wrist and
twists it." Like the Smiths and the Martins, the Professor is possessed. But he is not the host to some alien power. Rather his own
vital and sexual energies are manifesting themselves; and his language is the magic formula/incantation to further evoke and stimulate these energies. Brushing aside Marie's interventions, he pro-
claims that he must make his Pupil "understand." He picks the
inevitable example that "will serve for all the languages"—the *word*
knife. It is not a knife, but the *word*—the magic noumenon. The
verbal rape/murder follows precisely the seven-beat scheme.

1	2	3
OPENING GAME	INTERLUDE	SEXUAL STIMULATION
Pronouncing the word "knife"	*"Look at it"*	*Pupil "caressingly touches the parts of her body as she names them"*

4	5	6
OVERT LEWDNESS	PLEASURE/PAIN	EXPRESSION
Professor's "scalp dance"—his pleas-ure as she repeats the word "knife"	*Pupil's pain in her whole body. Profes-sor's exalta-tion*	*The change in the Professor's voice just before he strikes her*

7
GRATIFICATION
Professor's "Aaaah! [. . .] That does me good!"

Here beat five is both pleasure and pain; beat six is no longer
suppression but its opposite, expression. These inversions do not
disturb the flow of the action which has been prefigured several
times in the play; and which itself recapitulates the whole play.

Much of the force of *Lesson* comes from this repetition of scene
structure. Without being able to specify exactly what is being repeated, an audience is aware that something fundamental is happening again and again.

There is *uncovering* as well as repetition—the sexual actions, barely visible at the start, are overt and direct in the rape/murder. Therefore a musical mode, repetition, is combined with a theatrical one, uncovering. Considering the play as a whole, we find the same seven movements.

1	2	3
OPENING GAME	INTERLUDE	SEXUAL STIMULATION
The Lesson, Marie lets the Pupil in	*First meeting between Pupil and Professor; addition; mutual easy pleasure*	*Throughout, but increasing during ear game and intensified by Marie's warnings*

4	5	6
OVERT LEWDNESS	PLEASURE/FEAR/PAIN	EXPRESSION
The transformation of the Professor from an old man into a young man; ultimately the exposure of his "knife"	*Pleasure at first when Pupil cooperates; fear as she resists; his increasing frustration with her; after the murder, his submission to Marie*	*Rape/murder; Marie's disarming the Professor*

7
GRATIFICATION
Rape/murder; becoming a child again with Marie as mother

Of course, the play isn't "neat." That would render it mechanical —my schematization is not an exact rendering but an approximate, and I hope useful, model. Taken as a whole *Lesson* is particularly rich and complicated because the relationship between the Professor and Marie parallels in some ways and contradicts in others the relationship between the Professor and the Pupil. Marie is servant, accomplice, mother, doctor, priest, and prophet. She helps the Professor, after warning him. She disarms him when he tries to do to her what he did to the Pupil. She consoles him when he is overwhelmed with remorse. She tells him how to get rid of the corpse and helps him do it. Not least, she answers the door and lets new pupil in.

Marie is there before the Professor and the Pupil; she is there when both of them have gone. She is the first and last person an audience sees on stage; she is the referee and the rule maker. Fundamentally she is uninterested in all that goes on. The Pupil is a victim of curiosity and vitality; the Professor is the object of his own compulsions and of a language of magic powers. But Marie is free because she doesn't care. Her role is the most contemptible ethically, but the freest metaphysically. The others are trapped by the repetitions; she sets the wheels moving, and keeps them going.

It would be unfair to call *Lesson* a study of psychological compulsion. Individual psychology is not the object of the play, nor its subject. If anything, *Lesson* might be regarded as a study of *sociological* compulsion, a parable of destruction by habit and magic. Everyone is "guilty"—the servant who makes all the arrangements before and after and who does not back her warnings with effective sanctions; the all-too-willing victim; the murderer who will not believe what he has experienced innumerable times before—that "arithmetic leads to philology and philology leads to crime." It may sound ridiculous, but it is history.

Much of the so-called Theater of the Absurd is now far enough behind us to be of marginal interest. It has blended with earlier movements—dada, surrealism, varieties of existentialism—and exerts its influence as part of a large mass of literature protesting the dehumanization of the spirit and the encroachment of mechanization, and it regards modern civilization as a threat to liberty and an object of ridicule. Some of Ionesco's theater fits this movement— from *Rhinoceros* through *Thirst and Hunger,* his "middle period." But his first period—from *Soprano* to *Victims of Duty* (1949–1953) and including, especially, *Soprano, Lesson, Jack, Chairs,* and *Victims* —transcends the movement of which these plays are a part. These works, though having their quotient of despair, are, in my view, celebrations of life-force. The individual is no longer powerful; bourgeois living is empty. But I glimpse in these comedies a celebration of alien life-forms, an acknowledgment (no matter how ironic and grudging) of collective experience and living.

These plays have an original and highly musical style. It is this style whose structure I have tried to reveal. Ionesco himself calls *Soprano* and *Lesson* "experiment[s] in abstract or nonrepresentative drama [. . .] the progression of purposeless passion." Purposeless because it is not the slave of plot, but the direct apprehension of the flow of energy from within the dramatic structure itself.

Ionesco feels that these plays reveal "monstrous forms that we carry in ourselves." I agree but think of the monstrous as evil only from the perspective of individualism. Otherwise, "monstrous" means only something unusual and rarely glimpsed; and perhaps a harbinger of new times. In *Soprano* the characters are dying and language is the true protagonist. In *Lesson* the characters are masks of social compulsions. The Professor, the Pupil, and Marie are the objects of a willful grammar—not merely a language starting to know itself and its hosts, as in *Soprano,* but of an already highly developed *system,* a grammar whose chief law is that "arithmetic leads to philology and philology leads to crime." The Professor refuses to believe this, and so he repeats rape/murder again and again. We are leaving an age of individualism and entering a collective age. We are leaving "rationalism" and entering a time of sacral magic. Whether we deplore or welcome these changes will to a large degree condition our response to *Soprano* and *Lesson.* What is triumphant to one mind will be horrific to another.

In both plays Ionesco masterfully builds closed systems that are integral and complete. These systems relate to other systems only by analogy: what happens in *Soprano* and *Lesson* is parallel and homologous to what happens in society. The plays are not "about" anything; they refer only to themselves. That is why I call their structure musical. But they are not nonsense plays; and there is nothing wrong with pointing out analogies between them and society. I think *Soprano* and *Lesson* are good plays for practitioners of the new theater to work with because these plays' structures are compatible with the procedures of the new theater.

Soprano and *Lesson* will probably stand up very well in time. They do not depend on tricks, but on the cohesion of their parts. They probe deeply, and originally. They are playable and offer performers a creative challenge. Most of all, they suspend in balance a difficult tension—that between the social and the structural. Enough of the mood of the postwar and cold war days is in these plays to give them substance and historicity. But they have been put together by a mind fine and sensitive enough to transcend their historicity. For a long time they will evoke interpretations on stage.

Amédée: A Caricatural Ionesco

by Jean-Hervé Donnard

During the romantic period, skeletons stayed quietly in closets. It is M. Ionesco's fault that nowadays they have lost this discretion and invade apartments. If you kill someone, you will no longer have recourse to concealing the body in your home; this is the lesson to be drawn from the misfortune of Amédée and Madeleine.

The writer has told us this fantastic story twice, first in a short story entitled "Oriflamme," next in a play.[1] A murder has been committed a number of years ago; nobody knows anything about it, since the culprits share their home with the mortal remains of their victim, while confining themselves to a totally cloistered existence. The secret is well kept until the day the corpse is affected by geometrical progression, that "incurable disease of the dead." The scandal is about to break; the concierge and the neighbors begin to gossip, the police prick up their ears. Amédée and Madeleine lead a frightful life, little by little driven out of their house by the deceased person, who is growing by leaps and bounds. Since they must get rid of him at any cost, Amédée, taking advantage of midnight darkness, pulls the huge corpse out of the apartment, without overturning the china, then drags it toward the Seine. At that point an extraordinary phenomenon occurs, so extraordinary that it is better, for the moment, to put off describing and explaining it.

This mad plot is played with an exemplary seriousness. The reader asks the same question as an illustrious marshal: what is it all about? The answer presents itself more clearly in the story than

"Amédée: A Caricatural Ionesco" by Jean-Hervé Donnard (editor's title). From *Ionesco dramaturge ou l'artisan et le démon* by Jean-Hervé Donnard (Paris: Lettres Modernes, 1966). Translated by Judith Kutcher. Copyright © 1966 by Lettres Modernes. Reprinted by permission of the publisher.

[1] "Oriflamme," published by the Nouvelle Revue Française in February, 1954, has been incorporated in *The Colonel's Photograph. Amédée or How to Get Rid of It,* a comedy in three acts, was created on April 14, 1954.

in the play; contemplating the corpse, whose white beard reaches down to his knees, the narrator reflects: "Who would have recognized him as the fine young man who one evening ten years ago had come to call on us, had suddenly fallen in love with my wife and —taking advantage of my five minutes' absence—had become her lover that very evening?" *I,* then, has committed a crime of passion which he distinctly recalls. It is a different story with Amédée, who gets "everything so mixed up," confuses "dreams and real life," and wonders in seemingly good faith: "Did I really kill him?" He even doubts the victim's identity: ". . . it seems to me that the young man had already left . . . when the crime was committed . . ." This cadaver which ages and grows so quickly is perhaps that of a baby, entrusted to them one day by a neighbor who never came back for it. Its wailing made Amédée nervous, provoking "a fit of justifiable rage . . . a clumsy blow . . . a bit brutal . . . killing babies is as easy as killing flies." Moreover, perhaps there never was a murder: "A baby's very delicate. It holds to life by a thread." But this quibbling does not shake Madeleine's conviction; she asserts: "My memory's more reliable than yours. It was the young man." If the narrator in "Oriflamme" accepts his guilt without dodging, Amédée in the play is compelled by his wife to assume his responsibilities. This modification, in all probability, was imposed by dramaturgical necessities, the conflict imparting a faster rhythm to the comedy.

Whatever the reason might be, the man in both cases became an assassin because of being insufficiently loved. In the story and in the play, he utters these significant words: ". . . if we loved each other, if we really loved each other, none of this would be important. [. . .] Why don't we try to love each other, *please,* Madeleine? Love puts everything right, you know, it changes life" ("Oriflamme," p. 17; *Amédée,* pp. 52–53). But, her eye dry and her mouth set, Madeleine spurns her husband's advances. A scene in the comedy, which has no equivalent in the story, throws a naked light on the buried sources of this marital misunderstanding. While awaiting the hour to dispose of the corpse, Amédée lets himself drift into a melancholy reverie. The past returns: in the presence of a Madeleine wearing white gown and veil, the young bridegroom's joy overflows: "I'm bursting with song . . . la, li, la, li, la, la, la!" Yet the new bride snubs him harshly: "Stop singing in that cracked voice . . . It's earsplitting! [. . .] You're deafening me! Hu-urting me!"

Sexual incompatibility is unequivocally suggested: "I won't, I won't . . ." screams the bride. "I'm frightened! Aaah! . . . You horrible b-e-ast! [. . .] they're digging red-hot pins into my flesh. Aaah!" The wedding night ends in rape. Brutality or inexperience of the husband? Inherent or temporary frigidity of the wife? Ionesco deliberately refrains from analysing the reasons for this failure. He does not infringe upon the domain of the psychologist, the doctor, or the moralist. What interests him, as a playwright, are not so much occult causes as visible consequences. Poetic images reveal the young couple's discord. To the exaltation of the one is opposed the sombre despair of the other:

> *Amédée.* House of glass, of light . . .
> *Madeleine.* House of brass, house of night!

Amédée cannot believe in his misfortune: "Of glass, of light," he repeats obstinately, whereas Madeleine answers like an echo: "Of brass, of brass, of night, of brass, of night . . ." In the end, Amédée, conquered, joins in unison: "The brass and the night, alas . . ."

Mr. Pronko proposes a bold and seductive hypothesis: the assassinated lover, he writes, is perhaps "none other than the young Amédée." [2] In any case, the corpse seems to symbolize dead love; it grows in pace with rancors, aversions developed through the years which will culminate in a definitive separation. Banal and human drama, banal because it is human. Yet it makes the heart of even an indifferent public pound, because it is presented in an entirely novel dramatic form wherein extreme realism allies itself with extreme fantasy.

Appearing to repudiate his former artistic principles, Ionesco reverts to certain methods of conventional theatre, making them, however, entirely his own. In his preceding plays, he had cast out that undesirable: the Persona. The Smiths and the Martins, the Jacques and the Roberts, the Professor and his Pupil are animated by erotic and aggressive impulses, but they do not have any *character*, any more than they can be said to possess an identity, a social position, a past. The Old Man and the Old Woman, equally anonymous, possess as their only individual personality traits, private obsessions. The Policeman and Nicholas are marionettes whose function it is to make particular demonstrations. As for Choubert, he is

[2] *Avant-Garde: The Experimental Theater in France* (Berkeley and Los Angeles: University of California Press, 1962), p. 94.

content to be the author's spokesman, expressing the latter's ideas on theater as well as his anxieties and phantasmata. In *Amédée,* for the first time, one finds "characters" in the traditional sense of the word. Here, Ionesco speaks (who would have believed it?) in the voice of François Mauriac. As did the novelist, the playwright claims to allow the beings he creates the exercise of their free will: "They do whatever they want, *they* control *me,* for it would be a mistake for *me* to try and control *them.* [. . .] But creation [. . .] is life and liberty, it can even stand against accepted ideals and turn against the author" (*Notes et Contrenotes,* p. 197; in reference to *Amédée*). In the same vein, Mauriac affirms, in *The Novelist and his Characters,* that he often finds himself blushing at what the heroes of his novels say and do. He experiences, however, a secret joy in so doing, for if one of them "docilely submits to what we expect of him, that proves, most often, that he has no life of his own, and that we grasp nothing but a hollow shell." Yet, he loves his "most pitiful characters" as a "mother who instinctively prefers her most homely child." Not unlike the author of *Knot of Vipers,* Ionesco feels himself overcome "by a kind of pity" while following his creatures; when his comedy darkens, however, turning to drama, he is overcome by "revulsion" and, to protect himself against what he considers to be a weakness, transforms the character into caricature.

Amédée, then, is Ionesco, but a caricatural Ionesco. Far from being a prolific playwright, Amédée is an unfortunate man of letters, beset by intellectual impotence. In "Oriflamme," the narrator does not specify his profession; he acknowledges that he is "lazy, indolent," living shamelessly at the expense of his wife, who writes poems and sells them to increase her meager resources. Obviously a shift has occurred since, in the play, it is no longer Madeleine but Amédée who is "the literary one." The latter's production, however, is so limited that it scarcely allows him to improve his income. He writes plays, or rather he is trying to write a play, one which could well be entitled *The Chairs.* Alas, he is still on scene 1 and, in the course of fifteen years has come up with only two lines: "The old woman says to the old man, 'Do you think it will do?' [. . .] The old man replies: 'It won't do by itself.' " On the other hand this would-be playwright is inexhaustible when he must find excuses for his sterility. His health is at fault: "I feel so tired, so tired . . . worn out, heavy. I've got indigestion and my tummy's all bloated. I feel sleepy all the time." He also laments his physical environment, which prevents him from devoting himself to literary creation with a free and easy mind. When Madeleine asks him to do the shopping, he cries out with irritation: "In such circumstances it's not easy to write. And you're surprised I can't get on with it. [. . .] I can't work, I can't work! I don't have the normal conditions necessary to intellectual creation." Ultimately, the strange misfortune which has befallen him immobilizes his muse; seeing the dead man's legs continue their progressive growth through the dining-room, Amédée announces, brokenheartedly: "What about my plays? I shan't be able to write any longer now . . . We're finished. . . ." Although these complaints are somewhat justifiable, bad faith plays a part in prompting them. Sartre would most certainly classify Amédée as one of the "salauds" and consider Madeleine right in refuting his sophisms. When her husband places the responsibility for his lack of inspiration on material destitution, by saying: "You'd need to be a hero, a superman, to write in my situation, in such wretched poverty," Madeleine sneers: "Have you ever seen a superman living in poverty? You must be the first!" Amédée complains that the corpse is preventing him from writing; Madeleine flings the truth in his face: "It's an ideal excuse for you to stop work altogether!" Hell is the Other; before this inflexible judge, Amédée is forced to see himself as he is: "Yes, Madeleine, you're right. Anyone else could manage better than I do. I'm like a helpless child, I'm defenseless. I'm a misfit . . ." It is moving to hear a failure humbly admit his defeat, without cynicism and without sourness. Amédée has succeeded at nothing, neither in literature nor in love.

In his relationship with his wife, one notices a mixture of weakness and kindness, of bitterness and tenderness. His attitude does not cease to be ambiguous and his solicitude often barely, masks a moral shortcoming. Full of good will at the moment of the catastrophe, he tries to comfort Madeleine, who is close to hysteria, but he is too mediocre to utter anything but banalities: "Everyone has problems, Madeleine. [. . .] Some people are worse off than we are!" In the beginning, he insisted that his wife put an end to her too frequent and too lengthy vigils in the dead man's room: "You see, it's because I'm really sorry for you that . . . I'd rather you didn't stay in there and watch him. It doesn't do you any good, and it doesn't help . . ." In calling him a hypocrite and a liar, Madeleine is both right and wrong. Her husband is sorry for her, sincerely sorry, without any doubt, but he is equally sorry for himself. When he urges her to shorten her visits with the corpse, he is motivated by mixed feelings, of which he cannot be fully aware; if he is anxious not to compromise any further the already shaky well-being of his wife, he also suffers pangs of jealousy in relation to this strangely fascinating corpse; finally, solitude weighs heavily upon him, and in this definitely morbid atmosphere he requires a living presence at his side.

Cowardice as much as compassion leads him to subterfuge. Discovering that the mushrooms continue proliferating, Madeleine is harsh with him: "Why didn't you tell me straightaway? You're always hiding things from me!" Amédée finds the perfect excuse: "I didn't want to upset you . . . You've plenty to worry you as it is." Yet perhaps it is himself he did not wish to upset. He might have submitted to this additional unpleasantness, silently, because of his dread of his wife's laments and reproaches. In addition, silence is a way of denying a fact's existence; not to name the mushroom is to will it away. Amédée flees before reality. Forced to acknowledge these unwonted cryptogams, he tries to at least calm his spouse by suggesting that this phenomenon is natural, perhaps beneficial: "They *are* very tiny. [. . .] Perhaps it's only the damp . . . It often happens, you know, in flats. And you never know, they may be good for something: perhaps they keep spiders away . . ." As for the corpse, why get alarmed if it grows: "It's quite normal. He's branching out."

Amédée proves to be incapable of making a decision and of acting on his own. He is constantly in need of the Other, and calls for help: "It's so unfair . . . And in a case like this . . . no one to turn to for help and advice! . . . " His arms folded, he waits for Heaven to come to his rescue. He makes furtive visits to the dead man's room: "Suddenly, I began to hope . . . I wondered if . . . I thought he might have disappeared . . ." Though he is ready to admit that" the day of miracles is past . . . unfortunately . . . ," nevertheless he continues to hope for the impossible, insisting upon it: "It'll be all right, it really will, it'll be all right . . . I'm sure it will . . . it's simply got to be all right . . ." Still, the heavens remain silent, devoid of signs. In the meanwhile, the disaster is acquiring monstrous proportions, and Madeleine's recriminations turn violent; clearly, something must be done at once: "When? When? When?" shouts Madeleine, at the height of exasperation. A war-weary Amédée answers: "Tomorrow . . . Let me have a bit of rest first." Madeleine's experience with this kind of promise has been too bitter for her not to resort to threats: "Now, listen to me! If you don't get rid of him, I'm going to get a divorce." Compelled to act, Amédée falls prey to extreme hesitancy, something beyond his ordinary abulia. Overcome by sudden pity, he contemplates the corpse he is getting ready to evict from the apartment: "He's still goodlooking, though . . . It's funny how, in spite of everything, I'd got used to him." For once, Madeleine agrees with her husband: "So had I . . ." She adds, however: "But that's no reason for keeping him here." This corpse is the symbol of a great hope, doubtlessly dead, yet hope just the same. "He's been the silent witness of our whole past," recalls Amédée, "which has not been so pleasant, I admit . . ." This very past is about to be put to an end; by carrying off the corpse, Amédée is going to separate forever from the wife whom he has never stopped loving.

It is this feeling which redeems this puppet. A tiny flame glows in his heart, which the squalls have not managed to extinguish. He has awaited, for over fifteen years, a kind word from his wife, looked for an affectionate gesture on her part, reaping only snubs. Alluding to the care the corpse has received, he muses: "Has he forgiven us yet? . . . We put him in the best room, *our* bedroom when we were first married . . ." With these words, Amédée tries to take his wife's hand; she withdraws it. This time, however, for a single moment, he is filled with an immense hope as the bewildered Madeleine begs him: "Please, please darling, do something. . . ." Overcome with feeling, drunk with a budding happiness, he exclaims: "What did you say?" Alas, annoyed again, Madeleine answers: "I simply said 'Do something' . . ." And when Amédée bemoans his companion's harshness, we can only commiserate: "You don't give me a moment's peace . . . Do you think I'm not suffering too? I'm not the same as I used to be, either . . ." The liar, the hypocrite, speaks at this moment with sincerity, the straw man takes on human proportions.

Having reached this degree of emotional intensity, fearing that he will fall into sentimental and psychological drama, Ionesco bursts into a shout of laughter, and in one swoop takes away the life that he had given to his creature. When he decides to bring the corpse out of the apartment, Amédée is "if not calm, at least detached from the proceedings, acting like a robot." He is emptied of all thought, of all feeling, in a word, of all human nature. In the street, he meets an inebriated American soldier, and, without provocation, launches into a declaration of literary beliefs, professing principles contrary to Ionesco's: "I'm all for taking sides, Monsieur, I believe in progress. It's a problem play attacking nihilism and announcing a new form of humanism, more enlightened than the old." He will finish by uttering sentences devoid of all meaning. Even before disappearing into the air, this character has stopped existing. To adopt Jung's terminology, let us say that if Amédée reveals an overly soft *anima,* Madeleine's *animus,* on the other hand, appears too strong. This marriage is not harmonious; the woman does not complement the man, she "compensates" for him, which results in an irreparable discord. Madeleine proves to be even more disagreeable in the play than in the story; it is true that the emphasis on this defect is due to dramaturgical motives as much as to psychological ones. Since theatre comes alive through the interplay of antagonistic elements, Ionesco is led to stress the divergent characteristics of his protagonists; Amédée is thus shown as particularly sluggish, while Madeleine is decidedly willful.

In "Oriflamme," the narrator prides himself on having at least one quality: lucidity. "I have a realistic turn of mind; I may be lacking in will power but on the other hand I reason clearly." Yet he examines his total character without complacency:

> Oh, I am lazy, indolent, untidy, I'm fagged out doing nothing! I can never remember where I put my belongings. I waste all my time, I wear out my nerves, I destroy myself looking for them, rummaging in drawers, crawling under beds, shutting myself up in dark rooms, burying myself in wardrobes . . . I am forever undertaking a lot of things I never finish, I give up my plans, I drop everything . . . I've no will power, because I've no real aim! . . .

It would have been awkward to transpose this confession into a monologue in the play, an arbitrary procedure to which the dramatist is loathe to resort. As Madeleine, however, lists her husband's failings, the confession turns into an indictment, self-criticism into critical appraisal:

> *Madeleine.* You can't deny you're lazy, idle, untidy . . .
> *Amédée.* Dead tired, more than anything, dead tired.
> *Madeleine.* You never know where you put your own things. You waste three quarters of your time looking for them, rummaging about in

drawers. And then I find them for you under the bed, all over the place. You're always taking on jobs you never finish. You make plans, give them up and then let everything slide.

Amédée intervenes only once in order to ask consideration for attenuating circumstances in view of his deep exhaustion, a sign of ill health.

Far from seeming a mere dramatic device, Madeleine's bitterness is psychologically motivated by a two-fold deception, emotional and social. This woman is not resigned to being deprived of love's pleasures. Once, only once, she did perhaps furtively enjoy them, and this memory has been haunting her. Far from feeling ashamed, she flaunts it as she says to Amédée: ". . . You always said you thought he was my lover . . . And I never denied it . . ." This challenges her partner, who nevertheless does not pick up the dare. He struggles to plead not guilty, attributing the young man's death to a "stroke" brought on by intense erotic desire. Madeleine scornfully rejects this explanation: "To start with, it takes more than *that* to kill a young man of twenty. *He* doesn't suffer from hardening of the arteries, like one old crock I know . . ." This reply is accompanied by explicit stage directions: "When she says 'old crock' Madeleine stresses the two words glancing significantly at Amédée; the latter pretends not to understand." Deprived of the permissible pleasures of the marriage bed, this woman has not even found the satisfactions of self-esteem as a poor substitute. She calls her husband a "lazy so-and-so," and does not tire of reproaching him: "I'd rather you wrote that play of yours . . . You don't seem to have made much progress . . . You'll never finish it!" Incapable of winning glory, neither does Amédée possess the wealth which would allow his wife to lead a decent, if not a comfortable, life. "I've got to sweep up, haven't I? After all, someone's got to look after the house. We've no maid, and there's no one to help me. *And* I've got to earn a living for both of us." Madeleine despises her companion's weakness: "Do something, can't you!" she repeats sharply. She suffers from his inferiority, all the more so because she worries about her neighbors' opinions: "What will people say!" She belongs to that group of people who, reduced to humble or unfortunate circumstances, take refuge in dreams. She criticizes bitterly her husband's "looking on the bright side," his tendency to adorn harsh reality with the glamor of literature: "There's no point deluding ourselves, we've got to face facts." But this so-called realist distorts the facts when she persists in shifting the entire responsibility for the catastrophe onto her companion alone. "I've been telling you it's all your fault . . . And it's all because you've no initiative . . . [I] tell you we'd never been in this state, if you hadn't been so careless and always let things slide." Again, one must recognize a grain of truth in these excessive reproaches. But Madeleine makes little of logic when she insists that had the "demise" been reported, the fifteen years for amnesty would have elapsed; Amédée can well object that "the fifteen years would never have had time to elapse . . ." Madeleine interprets this commonsense remark as a personal insult. Her passion carries her to such a point that she accuses her husband of all the sins on earth; she goes as far as suspecting him of alcoholism. Amédée risks a protest: "You know I never touch anything but tomato juice . . ." Madeleine retorts: "Well, then, if you've always been such a sober-sides, if you've nothing seriously wrong with you, if all your faculties are still intact, wake yourself up a bit, get to work, write your masterpiece . . ." No matter what he does or says, Amédée is always wrong. But the nerves of this spirited, overly self-righteous woman finally snap. Seeing the corpse invade the dining room, she bursts into tears. In the end, she "gradually loses her calm and her self control"; at the moment when her husband, whom she has finally galvanized into action, prepares to do away with the dead man, she stammers, distractedly: "I'm frightened . . . We shouldn't have made up our minds so quickly . . . We couldn't do anything else . . . We should have waited . . . No, we shouldn't have waited . . . It's all your fault . . . No, it's not your fault, I was right all the same, we simply had to . . ." Madeleine is more antipathetic than Amédée, even though her ill-humor and insincerity are not without excuse. This shrew is capable of having a good impulse: "Listen, today I'll let you break your rule. Have a glass of wine, go on, you look so miserable!" This gesture of pity redeems her a little. Madeleine represents that type of woman who is not fundamentally mean, but who turns bad-tempered through disillusionment. However, like Amédée, and for the same reasons, this vibrant and perhaps moving character "disintegrates" in the third act, where one sees only a dishevelled housewife in search of her husband who has gotten involved in a shady adventure.

Ionesco, that smasher of idols, has therefore come to follow in the path of the great creators of human characters, who from Racine to Mauriac have established a solid tradition. In spite of this concession, he remains faithful to his own dramatic art, a bold innovator, although every now and then he permits himself to use traditional techniques. Thus, the first act contains a genuine "exposition"; the return to psychological comedy must, it is true, employ this classic procedure. Yet one is surprised that the author of *Amédée* should contradict the theoretician of *Victims of Duty*. For *Amédée*, at least in the beginning, is a "detective" play. This "repudiation" is all the more curious in that the original story did not present any enigma, the opening lines of "Oriflamme" giving a perfectly clear picture of the situation. " 'Why,' Madeleine asked me, 'did you not register his death in time? Or else get rid of the corpse sooner, when it would have been easier!' " By contrast, the opening exchanges in the comedy lead its spectators to consider a certain number of problems. As the curtain goes up we see Amédée picking a mushroom and muttering: "Oh, that Madeleine, that Madeleine! Once she gets into that bedroom, she's there for ever! She must have seen enough by now! We've both seen enough of him! Oh dear, oh dead, oh dear!" Who *is* this fascinating, bothersome guest? The plot thickens when Amédée says, after taking his turn at glancing in the room: "I was only looking to see if he'd grown! . . . You'd almost think he had, a little." Is it then a plant, an animal? Moreover, the extraordinary proliferation of mushrooms and the presence of the unknown seem to have some relation to each other: "It'll be quite impossible if he makes them grow in [the dining room]." Life goes on; one of them tries to write while the other sweeps. However these occupations do not succeed in dissipating their anxiety. Again Amédée has gone to look at the "thing"; he comes back upset and announces what he has seen: an aging, growing, corpse. But the spectators must wait until Act II to learn the (probable) identity of the deceased, revealed much earlier in the short story.

What creates the interest of this first act is not wholly the "suspense," achieved through well-proven formulas; it is rather the effects of original staging and unusual sketches, characteristic elements of the avant-garde theater, expertly controlled so that the tension increases continuously until the breaking point. During the first part of the act, one does not see the corpse. Each time he returns from the room, Amédée's report is more pessimistic: "He's grown again. Soon, the divan won't be big enough for him. His feet are over the end already. [. . .] What big nails he's got. [. . .] His toenails have grown right through his shoes." Then the corpse himself makes his presence known by "slight" cracking noises which rapidly become "tremendous" ones, until finally "a violent bang is heard against the wall"; "dumb with terror," Amédée and Madeleine, and along with them the spectators, see "two enormous feet slide slowly in through the open door and advance about eighteen inches on to the stage." Like a tragedy by Racine, Ionesco's comedy opens at the moment of an imminent crisis; but where in classical theater the dialogue expresses the pathetic in an abstract way, the modern playwright has recourse to concrete expression through production techniques. The "machine" replaces spiritual analysis.

Similarly, a series of well-directed sketches reveals the couple's inner dispositions. Nine o'clock strikes; "I must go to work . . ." sighs Madeleine, "I shall be late!" She is a switchboard operator. Ionesco shows in a striking way the deadening aspects in this kind of job, where man's stupidity is given free rein. Here is a fragment of the ridiculous conversations Madeleine carries on with anonymous callers:

> No, Sir, there are no gas chambers left, not since the last war . . . You'd better wait for the next one . . . [. . .] Hallo . . . I'm sorry, the firemen are away on Thursdays, it's their day off, they take the children out for a walk . . . But I didn't say today was Thursday . . . [. . .] Hallo, yes, can I help you? . . . No, Madame, no, we're a Republic now . . . Since 1870, Madame . . .

As Ionesco justly writes, "We need humor and fantasy. [. . .] Humor brings us a free and lucid realization of the tragic or derisory condition of man; [. . .] To become fully conscious of the atrocious and to laugh at it is to master the atrocious" (*Notes,* pp. 142–44). The sketch illustrates painful realities: Madeleine's slavery, her interlocutors' unconscious foolishness, ignorance, or cruelty. However the tone remains comic, for with an apparent detachment, Ionesco alters the course of reality to make it even more distorted. Thus the switchboard is set up in the couple's own dwelling. The two characters lead a cloistered life, never leaving their house and refusing to open their shutters to the world. To concretize this withdrawal, Ionesco had the ingenious idea of transporting Madeleine's place of work to her apartment. It is so true that many individuals consider social and professional life lacking in interest; while taking part in it by force, they constantly think of their private lives.

Ionesco's observation is therefore correct; the idea which he develops is simple, if not banal; but the concrete form which it assumes gives it a striking originality. The dramatist thoroughly exploits his finding, with an implacable "logic" from which spring droll and unexpected effects. As noon approaches, Madeleine says to her husband, between two telephone calls: "You might go and do the shopping, or we shan't have anything for lunch. Take the basket." Amédée raises the Venetian blinds, lowers the basket at the end of a rope and gives his order to an invisible grocer: "Put in a pound of plums, please! . . . A cream cheese . . . Two rusks, two pots of yoghourt . . . fifty grammes of table salt . . ." Such will be the frugal lunch for these two recluses. Although this sketch is sufficient unto itself, it would be awkward, if not impossible, to cut it out of the act, for it helps to create an "atmosphere." The same is true for the famous postman scene, which follows this one. A play composed of sketches, *Amédée* is not an episodic play.

If in the extremely dense first act the inner and outer, psychological and visual events succeed one another at an accelerated pace, by contrast the second act, which is noticeably longer, seems less charged and provokes a milder interest. The surprises are, if one can express it this way, concentrated in Act I; in the next act, although the mushrooms reach a monstrous size and the corpse encumbers the stage, the same emotional shock is not produced. From a theatrical point of view, there is only one new element, the "strange music" coming from the dead man's room, which the couple contemplatively listen to. Night has fallen, the stage has become dark, when it "is suddenly lit by a not unpleasant green light." Amédée murmurs to Madeleine: "It's his eyes shining . . . like two beacons . . ." This harmonious but strange music, this soft light, are without doubt the couple's memories, their regrets, and their vague hopes. While the first part of the play shakes the public's nerves, the second stirs it to melancholy. Rhetoric, alas, comes back into its own. The characters have too great a tendency to explain events and themselves. Amédée and Madeleine, looking back on their past, reveal the remote origins of their misunderstanding. These regressions to the past are sometimes accompanied by repetitions, and the formerly rapid action ends by marking time. Amédée, for example, after much equivocation, admits his responsibility for the young man's murder; he may do so halfheartedly, but nevertheless admits it. The debate is barely over, when the accused retracts his confession: "Listen, there's no real proof I did kill him. I'm not at all sure I did." Madeleine remarks, with good reason: "Off you go again!"

As for Act III, the critics concur in deploring its inconsistency.[3] It is the weak part of the work, and one regrets it all the more because it contains the denouement. Let us mention a few eloquent numbers in respect to this:

Act I: 27 pages.
Act II: 37 pages.
Act III: 14 pages.

It is fitting to add that only three characters appear in the first two acts: Amédée and Madeleine, the main characters, and a single episodic character, the postman; this moderation aids the dramatic force. On the other hand, in Act III, which is very short, there are no less than eight secondary characters; the result of this is a divided interest. Ionesco realized the disadvantage, since a somewhat revised second version of this part no longer constitutes an independent act, but forms the final scene of Act II.

Amédée has managed to get the huge corpse out of the house. With great difficulty he drags it through the street, the object of astonished, sympathetic, or reproving stares from American soldiers, a prostitute, and the owner of a bar. Attracted by the noise, people post themselves at their windows, while policemen chase after the suspect. All of a sudden a wondrous event occurs. The corpse is transformed into a parachute and, lifted by an irresistible elevating force, carries a helpless Amédée off into the air. Soon he disappears in the Milky Way. Madeleine sheds a tear: "It's such a pity! He was quite a genius, you know, really!" To which the publican adds: "All that talent wasted! It's a bad day for literature!" And the prostitute concludes: "No one is indispensable!"

It is not a question of a simple puppet show, conceived of in order to obliterate the painful impression created by the drama. As Martin Esslin writes,

> We see the two basic moods of Ionesco's experience of the world side by side: heaviness and proliferation of matter in the first two acts,

[3] Martin Esslin, *The Theatre of the Absurd* (New York: Doubleday/Anchor Books, 1961), p. 110; Pronko, *op. cit.*, p. 94.

lightness and evanescence in the third. As Amédée gets rid of the corpse of his dead love, that stifling presence turns into lightness and lifts him into the air.[4]

This explanation seems judicious. Amédée's flight is, moreover, prefigured by Choubert's, although there are evident differences. Amédée, fully conscious of the phenomenon, begs to be excused for this hasty and involuntary departure. On the other hand Choubert, absorbed in his dream, hears neither the reproaches nor the promises heaped upon him in the hope of convincing him to descend. Amédée disappears like a meteor, and it is unlikely that he will return; on the contrary, Choubert falls heavily to the ground. Finally, where Amédée is actually lifted up by a "machine" under the eyes of the public, Choubert relates and mimes his flight, while his feet never leave the stage.

Surely, Ionesco seeks to be original; but in the present case might he not have been influenced by a work of Vauthier, *Captain Bada,* anterior to *Amédée* by more than two years? It matters little whether or not a *source* can be said to exist. If one discovers a series of puzzling correspondences between Ionesco and Vauthier, the two works remain original, for different temperaments and opposing artistic conceptions are manifest in both. Vauthier's truculence and his verbosity are antithetical to Ionesco's exactness, which does not exclude poetry. The protagonists in *Bada* speak a great deal, a great deal too much; the author of *Amédée,* on the other hand, accords a special place to the spectacle and avoids garrulousness; he is less lyrical and more dramatic than his colleague. That said, if we set up a parallel between the two plays, it is less to judge their respective merits than to try to throw light on one by means of the other.

The plots present so many traits in common that one could give them the sub-title "History of a Poorly-Matched Couple." Bada and Alice's wedding night was just as disappointing as Amédée's and Madeleine's. "No caresses! Don't touch me!" scolds Alice. Madeleine defends herself with the same vigor, and in the same terms: "Don't come near me. Don't touch me." Alice loses her head: "Somebody help me! An evil person wants to harm me!" Madeleine exhibits an equal terror: ". . . help! help! I'm suffocating, help! [. . .] [You're] Hu-urting me!" The two women consider sexual union a dirty and painful act. "You sting, sting, sting," screams Madeleine, "You hu-urt me! [. . .] Don't rend my darkness! S-a-dist! S-a-dist!" Alice expresses an aversion no less profound: "I won't be an animal for your pleasure. I won't die under you. I won't drown in sin. I won't be tortured." Vaudeville is mixed with drama. In both plays, the bridegroom dressed in the classic black suit runs after the bride, whose veil and long gown do not hinder flight. Yet the scene by Vauthier is real, occurring in the present, whereas Ionesco treats it as a flashback, the evocation of a remote memory. The action in *Bada* is spread out in time: in Act I we see the engagement, in Act II the marriage, in Act III the definitive separation twenty-seven years later. On the contrary, the highly condensed duration of *How to get rid of it* does not exceed the twenty-four hours of classical tragedy; the past appears only in a fleeting double exposure.

In spite of this formal difference, the resemblances are still striking. The two couples tear each other to pieces behind closed doors, in apartments where shutters are never opened. They suffer from their poverty, which borders on destitution. "Our income was modest," Bada complains, "but now it is dwindling to nothing!" "My skimpy income . . ." moans Madeleine, and now *that's* gone . . ." Bada, like Amédée, is an uninspired writer who collapses, exhausted, over his manuscript, once he has written a single word. Alice, like Madeleine, grumbles while performing the lowliest domestic chores. However, whereas Amédée admits his faults, Bada shows himself arrogant and odious. Domestic tyrant, he calls his wife "hussy! filthy beast!" He holds her responsible for his frustrations, demands that she put his shoes on for him and that she spoon-feed him. One is an ashamed failure, the other an insolent failure; one has retained his kindness, the other becomes more and more embittered and selfish.

In spite of these character differences, the two men experience the same fate, and will take leave of the earth under more or less analogous circumstances. Having reached the end of his life, Bada listens with rapture to beautiful and mysterious music coming from an unidentified place. How can one not think of the music from the dead man which charms Amédée and Madeleine just before their separation? Bada tries to locate the source of this improvised concert; perched on a tall chest, he sounds the ceiling, suddenly loses his balance, and fatally wounds himself in his fall. A little while before this accident, a clerk in a gilded cap had appeared in the doorway and—what a peculiar coincidence—had said his name was Amédée, "assistant chief clerk of the new Society of Undertakers, section I." Assuming a mistake was made, Bada dismisses him rather abruptly. When Bada's misfortune occurs, the clerk returns and invites the dying hero to sit "in the cockpit of a flying machine." Contrary to Madeleine, Alice is enraptured by this flight: "O my husband! do not rue going off into the starry night; you will rise as though borne aloft upon a coleopteron's wings."

One comes to wonder if Amédée's departure does not have the same significance. While going up into the clouds, the character drops his shoes, cigarettes, and vest upon the ground where the onlookers shamelessly divide them amongst themselves; is this a satire of inheritance? Amédée, incontestably, frees himself from the past; but does he still have a future? Is he dead, is he alive? He has disappeared, that is sure, but the crowd indulges in speculative commentary: "He won't come back . . . He *may* come back . . . Oh, no! He won't come back . . ." In fact, nobody, doubtless including the author himself, knows anything about it. And who could say which planet Bada and Amédée will settle upon? Do they not run the risk of circling indefinitely in space, like sputniks? The show is over, the drama goes on.

Ionesco Ex Machina

by Jacques Guicharnaud

A man recounts his dreams—caves and fire—linking them to his temperament: "Bilious and melancholic." Moreover, in what he calls his "prime," it seemed to him that, as he slept, he kept growing lighter and then rose into the air, thus fleeing from a gang of murderers. His flight, however, inevitably and finally, came to a stop because of the presence of a wall—unless, of course, the flight itself had been an illusion. Actually, he was close to the ground, and his enemies had only to reach out to grab him. "All my dreams have been similar to that one ever since I can recall," he adds. One night, however, after an especially delightful and festive evening, he finally dreamed that his body was weightless and that he could go on —up and up—all the way to "a palace where heat and light merged." But he was cruelly brought back to reality: he fell out of bed and awoke, his "bare belly on the floor." All this is, of course, the summary of a tale told by Cyrano de Bergerac in the first pages of his *Etats et empires du soleil*.[1] Gaston Bachelard mentions that passage in his own *L'Air et les songes*,[2] criticizing Cyrano for having spoiled a poetic emotion that could have been conveyed by merely recounting such dreams, instead of justifying the narrator's actual flights through the conscious use of machines that propelled him toward the Moon or the Sun.

I do not at all mean to go into a lengthy comparison between Cyrano's imagination and Ionesco's. Yet one obvious fact should be noted: such writers, with more or less similar temperaments, will produce rather dreamlike literature, with more or less similar im-

[1] Cyrano de Bergerac, *Histoire comique des états et empires de la lune et du soleil* (Paris: Jean-Jacques Pauvert, 1962), pp. 138–39.

[2] Gaston Bachelard, *L'Air et les songes* (Paris: José Corti, 1943), pp. 46–47.

agery. Cyrano's cave suggests—although perhaps not quite—the stifling, sinking atmosphere of Ionesco's apartments. There is no need
to compare the elements of fire in each case, nor the flight, the wall,
the danger, the failure, and the nostalgic longing for a magical place
where "heat and light merge." Besides, for both writers the enchantment of dream is accompanied by a feeling of anguish (Cyrano's
"anxieties") or ends in anguish. Still, while they may both start off in
somewhat the same way, their approaches are quite the opposite.
Cyrano, a Gassendist haunted by Cartesianism, gives up the tran-
scription of the spontaneous image in favor of an intellectual exercise: philosophical or para-scientific speculation. Ionesco, on the
other hand, "anti-intellectual" in this regard, preserves the spon-
taneity of the initial image for the sake of creating literary fiction as
close as possible to the experience of dream—at least in its jolt to
the emotions—in order to actualize existential metaphors rather
than introduce subversive ideas on the nature of the soul, matter,
or the cosmos in general.

For example, Ionesco knows the dangers involved in the machines
used by Cyrano as a means of transition from poetry to scientific and
philosophical meditation—and also knows them well in connection
with his own works. In his *Entretiens* with Claude Bonnefoy he of
course stands up for the use of machines in theatre ("I have been
attacked for my use of machines [in *A Stroll in the Air*]. Why not
make use of theatre machinery? In the seventeenth and eighteenth
centuries there were machine plays, complete with flying coaches,
divinities descending from heaven, etc."), but then, in characteristic
fashion, modifying the cliché by his inimitable hesitation between
the pros and the cons, he states: "When you resort to technical
means, you create not dreams but rather something fantastic or humorous. What interests people, in that case, is the feat itself. In *A
Stroll in the Air,* when Jean-Louis Barrault began to fly about, people laughed because they knew it was really a gimmick." [3] In fact,
Ionesco—with all the innocence of a sincere creator whom inter-
viewers and critics persist in making into a thinker—summed up
for himself one of the problems of baroque illusionism: faced with
the technically perfect representation of magic on the stage, to
what degree is the spectator truly taken in? What truly attracts his
attention? What is the source of his feelings and his delight?

[3] Claude Bonnefoy, *Entretiens avec Eugène Ionesco* (Paris: Pierre Belfond, 1966),
p. 116.

Obviously, flying machines proliferate in the baroque theatre (in the broad sense of the term: from the Medici Festivals, to Pierre Corneille's *Andromède,* to the Molière-Corneille-Quinault *Psyché,* not to mention the opera and the Théâtre Italien in Paris—both para-literary outcomes of the baroque), and it was perhaps they that were responsible for stimulating Cyrano's imagination. Now it is interesting to note that this baroque art not only had stagehands in the wings and up in the lofts, but also, within the actual world of the plays, had to *justify* the act of flying. Chariots, clouds, and occasionally winged spirits held up the god or the chosen mortal who was disappearing into the flies. A human being, or some creature in the shape of a human being, does not, in principle, levitate all by himself. *Something* must lift him up; if he leaves the ground, the *deus* (or *homo*) is necessarily *ex machina*—all of which actually comes down to the fact that, even in the baroque illusionist universe, a minimum of the laws of reason must prevail. In other words, enchantment is derived from the fact that that "something," in everyday life, does not rise (a chariot) nor does it hold anything up (a cloud), or it exists only in the imagination (a winged spirit). In any case, that type of magical world does have a familiar structure—that of cause and effect—which is precisely the structure that Cyrano adds to his dream as a basis for his "actual" adventures. Thus the ambiguity of the baroque, in the case of machine plays, consists in a mixture of astonishment at the sight of incredible wonders (a flying chariot, a solid cloud) and a certain satisfaction of the demands of reason.

Of course, the period of French classicism, while continuing to play the game according to the dictates of tradition (e.g., the 1671 *Psyché,* and opera at the end of the century), seriously challenged it. In *Les Amants magnifiques* (1670), for example, the play's only flight (a Venus *ex machina*) was verbally "dismantled" by Molière, who had one of his characters describe the remarkable operation of the mechanicians backstage, thus exposing the pseudo-wonder as a moral fraud. But from the start of the baroque period, the stage flight had to be based on a kind of "verisimilitude" within the magic world itself. Cyrano, in both of his novels, improved upon that need so characteristic of the age of Descartes and Gassendi. Although he began with a dream about flight, he shifted the focus of interest from the act of flying, which was clearly unreal, to the actual possibility of how it may be achieved. Perhaps the delirium of reason is, as it were, preferable to the insanity of dream. It is interesting to note, however, that the madly scientific glass cabin of Cyrano's trip to the sun is not all that different from the celluloid capsule[4] or the translucent plastic trunk[5] that Ionesco dreamt about when he was young—minus the presence of his double within the trunk. But, after all, Cyrano couldn't have everything in his pre-Freudian era.

Thus flight, sometimes even in dreams, would seem to need some kind of support or means of transportation. The boxes mentioned above can, of course, be interpreted as symbols of the mother's womb, which sends us out into the light or the horrors of this world, or—since the image is one of ascension—as symbols of the ecstasy or loathing experienced during the sexual act. But on the level of reason, they correspond to the mind's demand for an explanation, since logically a body cannot break with the natural laws of gravity and inertia if there is no cause for the phenomenon or, to repeat, no means of transportation. In the spirit of Pierre Bayle, I find that this is not the place to consider the divine mystery of mystic levitation, which is of another Order. So that outside the realm of faith, even in a world of fantasy, every effect must have a cause, although there is no need to explain the cause of that cause, as Cyrano does.

In Ionesco's dramatic works there are various attempts to resolve the problems of representing flights, its causality or noncausality, and the resulting conflict between subjectivity and a feeling of objectivity. There is also a relevant oscillation between the "realistic" image, as it were (despite the strange nature of the play's universe), of an ascension during which the character's feet never leave the ground and the actual act of flying: *Victims of Duty* was followed by *Amédée or How to Get Rid of It;* after *A Stroll in the Air* came *Hunger and Thirst.*

With regard to flying itself, *Amédée* would seem to be a machine play in which Ionesco respects the baroque tradition's necessary support, however fanciful, for the protagonist is wafted up by a kind of "enormous parachute," "a banner," which is merely a transformation of the corpse that continues to grow during the first two acts. Jean-Hervé Donnard was right to point out that Amédée's flight is not unrelated to that of Jean Vauthier's Capitaine Bada, which preceded it on the Parisian stage.[6] In fact, neither Ionesco's tale (*Ori-*

---

[4] *Ibid.,* p. 38.

[5] Eugène Ionesco, *Journal en miettes* (Paris: Mercure de France, 1967), p. 88.

[6] Jean-Hervé Donnard, *Ionesco dramaturge ou L'Artisan et le démon* (Paris: Minard, Lettres Modernes, 1966), pp. 101–4.

flamme, 1954) nor his play (1954) reached the public until after the performance of *Capitaine Bada.* But more important than a possible influence—despite the great differences stressed by Donnard—is the fact that Bada's apotheosis comes from the *outside:* quite unexpectedly, an official, wearing a golden visored cap, comes through the window of the hero's apartment by way of a nacelle hanging from a kind of flying machine. Vauthier's character—a frightful and sublime failure—is granted assumption to another world—as sudden and unforeseen as divine grace. In Ionesco's play Amédée apparently doesn't fly up all by himself either. *His* assumption has a double meaning: Amédée both rises and assumes full responsibility for himself. Indeed, the corpse which has been transformed into a balloon, or a rising parachute, is not at all an outside intervention: it is an integral part of Amédée's existence and being. One has merely to look at the photograph in a recent book by Richard N. Coe to see that the gigantic head of the corpse is the very portrait of Lucien Raimbourg, the actor who created and then revived the role of Amédée.[7] I do not intend to go into a detailed discussion of the various interpretations of the growing corpse; I mean quite simply to locate it: whether it represents generalized existential anguish, remorse due to some specific crime, or cancer, the airship-corpse issues from Amédée himself, not from some other world or place.

And so the machine at the end of *Amédée,* while justifying the protagonist's flight in the baroque manner, brings us back to the character himself, rather than suggest some mysterious beyond, since, unlike Bada's nacelle, it is part of him and, ultimately, he himself. The festivities at the end of the play thus correspond to the wondrous liberation through flight that results from an agonized creature managing to take his own agony in hand—all of which is very far indeed from the fantasy of opera. After the spectacle of Amédée's anguish and bad faith when faced with the growth of an embarrassing part of his being, the final integration—however ambiguous—is celebrated in an atmosphere of cosmic and collective rejoicing: comets, shooting stars, fireworks. On a suddenly crowded stage a privileged individual gloriously separates himself from the rest of the world through the dialectic of his personal adventure: obsessed and divided, he has managed to integrate himself by, in fact, trying to "get rid" of himself. An unhoped-for miracle ("I

[7] Richard N. Coe, *Ionesco: A Study of His Plays* (London: Methuen, 1971), plates following p. 152.

didn't do it on purpose, Madeleine, not of my own free will!''), it is
by gathering his sins about him that he disappears into the star-
studded paradise of wholeness—an individual saved from his wife
and the teeming world of all those others who doubtless experience
the same wrenching agony unawares. Madeleine's cry to the disappearing Amédée: "You haven't even finished your play!" is an
autobiographical allusion, a confession. And obviously. For would
Ionesco (or any artist of similar temperament) continue to write if
he managed, once and for all, to come to terms with the corpse whose
continuous rotting (or growth) feeds his writing?

Fireworks and a sort of "street-fair" display are not unrelated to
the transformation of the stage set which occurs at the end of
Ionesco's *The Picture,* a one-act play of the same period as Amédée.
But in *The Picture,* during which there is no flying but rather a
transformation of ugliness into beauty through a violent act of intense sexuality,[8] the protagonist fails on a personal level: the curtain
falls on the anguish of The Large Gentleman, who remains The
Large Gentleman, for no one shoots at him to achieve the final
metamorphosis. Amédée and his apotheosis (which makes him feel
"quite sprightly" despite all his apologies and his insisting that he
had no part in it) are a poetic illusion, a wish projected by his imagination. The complete Ionesco hero, or anti-hero, is doomed to failure. Cases of ascensions or journeys through light result, for example, in the murder of Bérenger in *The Killer,* the bitter fall and
martyrdom of Choubert in *Victims of Duty,* the demystification of
the radiant plateau followed by Jean's concentration-camp type of
imprisonment in *Hunger and Thirst.* And if the plague is no longer
rife at the end of *Death Games,* it is only so that it could be replaced
by the atrocity of fire—Ionesco's other obsession, and one diamet-
rically opposed to that of sinking into slime, but just as destructive. Considering only machine plays, it is thus *A Stroll in the Air*
that would seem one of the most comprehensive and subtle illustrations of the polarities of Ionesco's sensibility, actualized by an objective representation of the act of flying.

The most interesting of such elements in this play is the shifting
back and forth between the use of visible machines and pure levitation. In fact, *A Stroll in the Air* is a little festival of mechanical
gimmicks, some of which may, yet again, be compared with the
baroque marvels: a case in point is the small, pink, flower-festooned

---

[8] See Donnard, *op. cit.,* pp. 113–19.

column that suddenly rises straight out of the ground and is a phenomenon akin to those trees and classical ruins which the ingenuity of Italian set designers made appear and disappear right in front of the spectators at performances of court ballets and entertainments. Moreover, there is moving scenery and a floating arch (a vision that relates Ionesco's Bérenger to the Shelley of the Preface to *Prometheus Unbound*),[9] as well as a little train that might have choo-chooed right out of a store window at Christmas time. Aside from episodes such as Joséphine's nightmares, *A Stroll in the Air* appeals to that childlike ability to be dazzled by naïve and charmingly burlesque gadgets, including—in this play—caricatures of the English, portrayed as barely humanized talking dolls, weaving their way through Bérenger's "stroll" with his family. Now, although the whole universe of the play is animated by obvious machinery not unlike those little automated scenes created for the delight of children, the protagonist's own venture subtly uses but counters the machine. Bérenger begins by levitating on his own, and his terrifying final adventure will be the outcome of his again flying about without any outside help. But between those two episodes, there occurs what one might call "the temptation of the *machina*": a circus trapeze and rings, and—above all—a bicycle, which is omitted in the short story that corresponds to the play, although it is mentioned as a didactic analogy. The play's step-by-step lesson in the art of flying on a bicycle not only produces the charming effect of street-fair acrobatics, but serves to negate the bicycle—that is, the visible machine. Indeed, as Bérenger gradually rises above the play's characters and the spectators, his vehicle loses its parts one after the other, until nothing is left but Bérenger himself, "moving around in circles, still pedaling like a cyclist." Note that here the character flies with his feet: Bérenger's bicycle is related to Mercury's winged sandals, not to the wings of the angels so dear to Jean Cocteau and, before him, to Rilke. Besides, Ionesco pokes fun at flying with wings: one of the play's minor characters, the Second English Old Lady, informs us that her husband used to have two winged steeds—but they didn't fly; they were "purely decorative."

In other words, while almost everything within the universe of the play is obviously mechanical, the protagonist himself achieves the extraordinary feat of flying *under his own power*. An incredible accomplishment, an exalting liberation with the help of no one but

[9] See Bachelard, *op. cit.*, p. 51.

himself, Bérenger's flight is devoid of any artifice, of any mechanistic pseudo-justification. And it all ends with shattering revelations and a grievous fall. Thus *A Stroll in the Air* would appear to be, in that respect, the most "complete" of Ionesco's machine plays. On the one hand, the main character travels along the curve characteristic of all Ionesco's heroes: from minor miseries, to joyous exaltation, to a final and more disastrous misery. The play begins with Bérenger's fatigue and pessimism, which culminates in the destruction of his house by a bomb that happened to fall from a plane; then comes the stroll, during which he, feeling lighter and lighter, suddenly takes off and flies; and at the end he describes the apocalyptic vision of a devastated universe—a revelation that dwarfs the nervous discomfort and minor bombing at the start of the play. This curve, of course, is—if not identical—at least comparable to several other of Ionesco's plays: the Bérenger of *The Killer* lives in a sinister apartment, then visits a modern and luminous suburb, only to discover a dreadful blight and, in the end, meet his death; the Jean of *Hunger and Thirst* rises from a sinister underground dwelling to a plateau high in the sky, but the sky becomes tainted, does not satisfy his desires, so down he goes again to the terrors of La Bonne Auberge; and, by way of a strange detective psychodrama, Choubert, of *Victims of Duty*, starts with some discomfort, moves on to the nostalgia of a liberating ascension, and finally falls into complete victimization. On the other hand, from a perspective of theatricality rather than dramatic action, Ionesco, having chosen to represent an actual flight in *A Stroll*, made his play into a critical statement on the scenic illusion produced by wonder-working machines: he plainly eliminates the equivalent of baroque support (i.e., the bicycle) in order to offer the barest and most precise image possible of the feeling of levitation.

To conclude with the remarks addressed to Claude Bonnefoy quoted above: yes, the spectator directs his attention, at least in part, to the hidden "gimmick." And the more cleverly the gimmick is hidden (this was admirably done in the Barrault production), the more deeply the spectator is intrigued and tries to guess—as one does at a particularly successful performance of legerdemain. But, in fact, that form of interest or delight is far from negligible: Ionesco's world is one of perpetual astonishment which, in the rare cases that it is pleasing, consists in an exalted dazzlement at the sight of sunny meadows, towns, and gardens, and is experienced as a lightness of one's being, very close to soaring. Indeed, the feeling of entranced admiration provoked by the scenic ingenuity, the "feats" of the mechanicians, the set desiginers, and the actors, constitutes the theatrical transposition of that basic emotion. Besides, the spectator's consciousness is obviously never all of a piece: if, in the case of Amédée as in that of Bérenger, the spectator is conscious of "being at the theatre" (perhaps even, to some degree, at the circus), he will shift to an attitude of half belief (if only in the form of a wish or a reverie) in the real possibility of achieving that which is suggested by the very skillfully disguised lie of the spectacle.

Science and Fiction
in Ionesco's "Experimental" Theatre
(An Interpretation of *The Chairs*)

by David Mendelson

To write literature is to perform a function. Literary form at present is inadequate. The imagination can never be held in check. However, if the poet's imaginative function is to be reinvested with a certain value, some lapse of time is necessary during which the poet must assimilate the technological world which at the present time escapes him. For the time being, the field of literary exploration seems to be limited and any discovery must needs be of circumscribed importance. Among Telstar, Rattigan and even Saint-John Perse, it is Telstar that comes out best. . . .

What ought to be the essence of the theatre in our scientific world?

It should materially be an exploration, a concrete experiment; it should provide the opportunity of using our imagination to better advantage; it should be the unforeseen. . . .[1]

Eugène Ionesco

At first sight, science looks as though it has no other part to play in Ionesco's imaginary universe than to constitute a threat hanging over it like a vast atomic mushroom cloud menacing wholesale destruction both of matter and of the spatio-temporal bounds confining it: man, his thought and his language. "Theatre of the

"Science and Fiction in Ionesco's 'Experimental' Theatre" by David Mendelson. Trans. Michaël Janes. Used by permission of the author. This essay appears for the first time in this volume.

[1] Eugène Ionesco, in Claude Bonnefoy, *Entretiens avec Eugène Ionesco* (Paris: Editions Pierre Belfond, 1966), pp. 195, 197. Future references to *Entretiens* are cited in the essay.

atomic age," [2] it has often been called. Jacques Guicharnaud, for example, has some foreboding of an "end-of-the-world atmosphere" (Guicharnaud, p. 185) in *The Chairs* and he detects "a symbol of the world after the H-bomb (Guicharnaud, p. 185) in the image of the two wretched heroes of the play, the Old Man and the Old Woman, permanently driven out of their *espace vital* by the eruption of matter and by the ever-increasing number of those "chairs" moving about on stage like so many deadly particles. Guicharnaud, however, does not develop his analysis in this direction; for, he explains, there exists "but one precise suggestion in *Les Chaises*" of any such cataclysm:

> *The Old Lady*. Paris never existed, my dear.
> *The Old Man*. It must have existed since it collapsed. It was the city of light since the light has been out, out, for 4,000 years (Guicharnaud, p. 185).

In our view, a good deal of additional information in the play might allow us to determine this obsession with destruction which afflicts modern man as a result of scientific and technological development. To bring out this point, we need to emphasize that the drama, both physical and psychological, as lived by the two characters is enacted within the wider framework of a drama of space. From this standpoint, it is no longer merely the threat of a nuclear cataclysm that we should bring to mind to characterize the "atmosphere" of the work, but also that other element of danger which might be held in store for humanity by a more recent scientific triumph, namely the conquest of space. It was Robert Frost who, some years ago, expressed with uncommon vehemence the obsession of the best minds of our time, the poets in particular—those explorers of the universe of "fiction"—with the idea that man, launching out into the conquest of "outer space," would come to neglect the quest for his spiritual and imaginative "inner space." These two spaces, said Frost, echoing Werner Heisenberg and so many other philosophers of science, are "complementary"; in the theory of relativity the observer is an integral part of the observed system; scientific analysis, objectively developed on the basis of a certain technique in observation and expressed in symbolic, arbitrary and abstract language, should theoretically be able to be concretized

---

[2] Cf. Jacques Guicharnaud, with June Beckelman, *Modern French Theatre— Giraudoux to Beckett* (New Haven: Yale University Press, 1961), p. 185.

and subjectivized in the shape of a certain kind of "vision" of the world. We ascertain, however, that for the time being we are incapable of "imagining" this new universe brought to light by scientific knowledge; "thought conceived in images" [3] wrested from the spatial "plane" of Euclidean geometry,[4] which is no longer able to come to grips with the passing of time henceforth relativized and decomposed by non-Cartesian logic, withdraws into itself only to shrivel to a mere spot on the inner horizon of the spatio-temporal dimension of the "vécu." [5] The expansion of "outer space" is matched by a corresponding contraction of "inner space"; in the terminology of physics itself, this process might lead to a scission of being, a disintegration of mankind, a sort of inner atomic explosion of the mind. Hence the urgent need to find a solution of continuity between the two "spaces." Thus Ionesco explains in the words of Bérenger in *The Killer*: "In short, inner and outer world are bad expressions; there are no boundaries between the so-called two worlds. There is a fundamental impulse, obviously, which comes from us, and when it can't be exteriorized, when it can't be objectively realized, when there is no complete accord between my inner me and my outer me, the result is catastrophe, universal contradiction, the final break."

It is evidently the "experience" of some such "break" disintegrating both the "inner space" of the characters and the "outer space" of the objects which is described in *The Chairs*. In this respect the play might even be put forward as an authentic work of "science-fiction"; the conquest by man of space, considered from a scientific point of view, would quite simply turn into a conquest by space of man from the viewpoint of "fiction." There are numerous references in the text which allow us to outline this interpretation at the superficial level of the parable. Let us suppose, first of all, to come back to the passage quoted by Jacques Guicharnaud, that Paris, "the city of light," a symbol of civilisation, "has collapsed," "has gone out," not as the result of an atomic conflagration, but because it has faded in the memory of the two old people who are

[3] "Pensée imageantre": cf. Jean-Paul Sartre, *Imagination; a psychological critique*. Translated with an introduction by Forrest Williams (Ann Arbor: The University of Michigan Press), 1962.

[4] As Marshall MacLuhan points out, the "Gutenberg Galaxy" has exploded.

[5] We use here the opposition defined by Claude Lévi-Strauss between the intuitive perception of the "vécu" and the knowledge of the "réel" which comes to us via scientific logic.

like cosmonauts hovering about somewhere in inter-stellar space, "under the great black bridge of time" [6] at a distance of "four hundred thousand (light!) years" (*Three Plays*, p. 11) from the planet earth—"Ionesco's heroes are forever going on trips—fantastic journeys to impossible places." [7] Does not their "circular tower" (Martin Esslin's definition of the setting for *The Chairs*[8]) in fact resemble an interplanetary space capsule? No doubt they tell us that their "house" contains other rooms and that it is even surrounded by an island; but these are probably mere stray remarks: the "circular tower" in fact is completely surrounded by water, there is "water under the windows, water as far as the eye can see." (*Three Plays*, p. 8). The water, moreover, is not without connection with some gaseous element; although it is *"glaucous,"* (*Three Plays*, p. 58) it seems at any rate to diffuse the same light as the *"green light"* of the *"gas-lamp"* (*Three Plays*, p. 7). Hence the notion that one and the same element constitutes the atmosphere in the "inner space" of the "tower" and in the "outer space" of the "watery solitude" (*Three Plays*, p. 57) . . . or ether, we might add. The fascination exercised by oceanic depths:

> *Old Man.* I wanted to look, I *do* so enjoy looking at the water.

is inverted quite naturally, thus to produce a fear of heights:

> *Old Woman.* How can you dear? . . . It makes *me* quite giddy . . . I shall never get used to it all (*Three Plays*, p. 8).

The spatial and material factors of the setting (high and low, inner and outer, air and water) therefore seem to be relativized in a universe not wholly subject to the laws of terrestrial physics. For the tower, at any rate, does not move in the same orbit as the terrestrial globe: it is subjected to a completely different gravitational pull. The sun has faded into the distance:

> *Old Woman.* It's night-time my pet [. . .] (*Three Plays*, p. 8).

> *Old Man.* Six o'clock in the evening and it's dark already. Remember?

---

[6] Eugène Ionesco, *Three Plays*. Translated by Donald Watson (London: Jupiter Books, John Calder, 1963), p. 12. Future references to *Three Plays* are cited in the essay.

[7] Richard Schechner, "The Playwright Out of Time," in *Genet-Ionesco: The Theatre of the Double*. Edited by Kelly Morris (New York: Bantam Books, 1969), p. 183.

[8] Martin Esslin, *The Theatre of the Absurd* (New York: Doubleday/Anchor Books, 1961), p. 99.

It was different in the old days; it was still light at nine o'clock, at ten o'clock, at midnight (*Three Plays,* p. 9).

There was once, therefore, a time when the light of the sun shone in the middle of the night. Had the tower drawn closer to it before escaping from its field of attraction? Since then, the "semi-darkness" (*Three Plays,* p. 7) has been dissipated by a half-light: "When the weather's fine, there's a moon" (*Three Plays,* p. 22). For the moon itself goes on revolving around the "tower," which may after all be merely a depiction in microcosmic form of the macrocosm of the terrestrial globe drawn from the sun's orbit in the night of time . . . to come:

> Old Man. . . . the further we go the deeper the rut. It's all on account of the earth, which never stops turning, turning, turning . . .
> Old Woman. Turning, turning, my love . . . (*Three Plays,* p. 9).

It is not necessary to be "a great scholar" (*Three Plays,* p. 9) to define the sort of feeling induced in us by the playwright: we are indeed transported into the universe of science-fiction. We are thus all the better enabled to reach an intuitive grasp of the nature of those apparently strange relations existing between our two characters, the two imaginary "cosmonauts," and the objects surrounding them, which will finally seal their fate: no wonder, then, since they themselves, freed from the earth's gravitational pull, defy the laws of equilibrium—at one point, Ionesco tells us, "they look as though they are on roller-skates" (*Three Plays,* p. 38)—that those objects, those chairs, should whirl about on the stage-floor and end up "acting by themselves."[9] A science-fiction fan would not find it difficult to recognize those "things from outer space," half-spiritual, half-physical creatures, and to identify them as "mutants"—in other words, the imaginary products of some future evolution of modern man, reified by materialistic civilization. The ideological message (as is the case, in this respect too, in the best tales of science-fiction) is revealed without much difficulty: those "manless chairs," are they to be the latest offspring of today's "chair-men" who preside over the fate of our humanity? "What is irksome about society," explains Ionesco furthermore, "is the fact that man is mistaken for the function, or, rather, that man is tempted to identify completely with the function; it is not that the function shows its face, it is man, dehumanized, who becomes faceless" (*Entretiens,*

---

[9] Note to original French edition, not included in Watson's translation.

p. 17). No need here for this sort of explanation: the "chairs" speak for themselves. Ionesco was at pains to convince a fraction of the critics who, downright "realistic (in the pejorative sense given to this term by contemporary "poetics"), were completely put off by this kind of fiction. "The subject of the play," he wrote to Sylvain Dhomme, "is the chairs themselves." [10] "The Play," he told Claude Bonnefoy, "was: the chairs, first empty, then the arrival of the chairs and, lastly, the swirl of chairs being brought in, taking up the entire stage as if, as it were, a solid voluminous vacuum began invading everything and settling everywhere" (*Entretiens*, p. 84). "For *The Chairs*, I quite simply had the image of an empty room filled with vacant chairs. The chairs arriving at full speed and ever more quickly, formed the central image; this for me expressed an ontological void, a kind of eddying void . . ." (*Entretiens*, p. 96). Experience thus defined brings to mind, in our view, no longer science-fiction, but real scientific activity; that "empty room," in fact, bears a close resemblance to one of those evaporation-basins in which scientists, in atomic laboratories, create a vacuum and perform all sorts of experiments on matter, submitting it to various processes of scission, nuclear fission and polarization of corpuscles, following upon chain reactions at fast and slow speeds. We bring to mind, furthermore, other empty rooms, those decompression space cabins in which cosmonauts in space research centres carry out their preliminary training and get accustomed to their new environment, either in their space ships or on the moon's surface. We summon to mind those televised pictures of the incredible pantomime they perform on the moon . . . and we return to Ionesco's explanation: "*The Chairs*," he said, "should contain, at the time of the performance, some "ingredient of pantomime fantasia" (*Entretiens*, p. 112).

Must fiction, once the forerunner of science (*The Chairs* was performed for the first time in 1952), be forevermore outstripped by it, outstripped by the reality that it has revealed to us? Claude Bonnefoy believes that "what aggravates the crisis of literature—and of art in general—is the fact that the results of science (television, exploration of the cosmos) bring to life the wonders imagined by Jules Verne and, a good deal before him, by Cyrano de Bergerac" (*Entretiens*, p. 196). Ionesco, standing somewhat on the defensive, how-

[10] Letter from Ionesco to Sylvain Dhomme, quoted by F. Towarnicki, "Des 'Chaises' . . . vides à Broadway," in *Spectacles* 2 (July, 1958), quoted in M. Esslin, p. 100.

ever, objects firstly to Bonnefoy's belief by stating that "there are
in fact writers who try to imitate science, who draw their inspiration from it or utilize its methods. They are wrong. No world belongs to literature and poetry if not the world of the feelings"
(*Entretiens*, p. 196). "Everything is emotion," he continues. "We
could even say that if there were no emotions, desires, nostalgia,
there would be no science either" (*Entretiens*, p. 196). Do not let
us deduce from the existence of a certain complementary link between science and fiction that both systems might be brought into
relation with each other and purely and simply merged. For the
logic of science the poet substitutes the independent existence of
the logic of fiction. The novels of Jules Verne, for instance, *From
Earth to Moon* or *Twenty Thousand Leagues under the Sea*, do not
simply purport to be works of science-fiction: the author was not
content to "foresee"; he had to "see" by plunging deeper and further into the universe of the "inner vision" which is the universe
of human "emotion," of "desires" directed towards the future and
also of the "nostalgia" for a certain past. Thus the poet today who
contemplates the space exploits of the cosmonauts is exalted, like
each and everyone of us, by their fairy-like grace, but perceives at
the same time another visual effect which the television pictures
have moreover transmitted no less poignantly: is it not true that
those cosmonauts, awkwardly clad in their stiff space-suits, calcu-
lating every movement and every step, appear to us also, like cum-
bersome divers, advancing with difficulty in some sort of deep-sea
liquid element which restricts their movements? Is not therefore
the journey "from earth to moon" a mere voyage of "twenty thousand leagues under the sea?" Who will explain how this dream of
flight into space may be brought into relation with another dream,
which can easily end up as a nightmare (one slip on the moon's
surface and the cosmonaut might not be able to pick himself up
again), the dream of a fall into the oceanic depths? Pragmatic reason comes up against this insoluble contradiction of which the
poetic imagination, for its part, takes little stock. The latter un-
furls in a quite natural way, in fact, within a mental space given
over to this double postulation, the terms of which may be inverted
from top to bottom; imagination thus turns out to be confined once
more within a polarized field, in which the matter it produces, subject to continual change, turns immaterially, for example, from an

ethereal to a liquid state. This is why any such dream is associated consequently with a nightmare of sinking and drowning. This was explained by the pioneers of "dream interpretation," Freud,[11] Maeterlinck (*Entretiens*, pp. 30, 63), and Jung (*Entretiens*, pp. 41, 151), and the explorers of the universe of mythical thought, such as Mircea Eliade.[12] With Claude Lévi-Strauss, who, through the language of myth, has determined a certain "logic of sensitive qualities," and Gaston Bachelard, who has laid the foundations of a "physics of the imaginary," there may have been established an authentic "science" of "fiction." Ionesco acknowledges the debt he owes to most of these thinkers, while keeping his distance with respect to them: he would seem to have no intention of stifling his creative insights within the framework of a rigid system of thought. However, it is with considerable clearness and critical insight that, in indirect reference to them, he perceives two essential characteristics of his dramatic universe. "Two fundamental states of consciousness are at the root of all my plays," he writes. "These two basic feelings are those of evanescence on the one hand, and of solidity on the other." [13] If all his characters, he explains furthermore to Claude Bonnefoy, are subject to this dual attraction, it is because it "corresponds to one of my states. I feel either heavy or light, or else too heavy or too light" (*Entretiens*, p. 41).

From this standpoint, what emerges quite explicitly is that the dream constitutes a privileged experience for the playwright. "For someone whose job is the theatre," explains Ionesco, "the dream may be considered to be an essentially dramatic event. The dream is the drama itself. In the dream, man is always *en situation*. In short, I believe that the dream is both lucid thought, more lucid than in consciousness, that it is "thought conceived in images," that it is intrinsically theatrical and that it is always drama since we are always *en situation* in it" (*Entretiens*, p. 11). Let us emphasize here how far Ionesco, although drawing his inspiration from Freudianism,

---

[11] "Freud," said Ionesco, "has upset and revived our understanding of Sophocles and so many others" (*Entretiens*, p. 53).

[12] "I suffered from insomnia," Ionesco relates. "A friend advised me, to get to sleep, to imagine I was going up a mountain. . . . In fact, the ascent that my friend, Eliade, advised me to imagine was an archetypal dream" (*Entretiens*, p. 38).

[13] Eugène Ionesco, "My Plays and I," in *Notes and Counternotes* (New York: Grove Press, Inc., 1964), p. 162.

clearly diverges from it, as has been admirably pointed out by Serge Doubrovsky.[14] In fact, he does not accept the dream thought, the "thought conceived in images," as the result of a sort of decomposition of thought "in consciousness," rational and conceptual: it is quite simply based on a kind of perception different from the common vision, and it expresses, in a particular language the symbols of which harmonize with perfect logic and coherence (even if this logic is not Cartesian), a certain understanding of the universe, or at least of the inner universe of man. Why should we discredit this system of thought, for the sake of the debatable criterion of "truth" which we borrow from our concept of the "vécu," on the mere pretext that it is different? Scientific rationalization, after all, equally well "unrealizes" the universe, and its symbolic language is no less arbitrary. In fact, we might be able to establish many things in common between those two perhaps complementary activities of the mind, scientific research and dream interpretation. The logic of the dream, for instance, which is founded *inter alia* on the principle of the identity of opposites,[15] might easily be defined along the lines of scientific logic as a "generalized combinatory analysis." The science of dreams, from this standpoint, has thus conferred upon it a privileged status as a category of human knowledge, and Ionesco goes further than Sartre[16] in asserting that the dream is thought which is "more lucid than in consciousness." Be that as it may, it would be incorrect to characterize this thought as "unconscious," whereas for more than seventy years, since Freud himself founded the "science of dreams," poets and thinkers have not ceased in their efforts to catalogue and to decode its language; it appears to us today as an entirely conscious source of artistic creation: a "point of departure," says Ionesco.

The fundamental facts of the science of dreams are in effect, for Ionesco, indisputable *a prioris*. We have mentioned, for instance, that the various dimensions of space have been relativized within the universe of the dream. Let us add that time is subject to a sim-

[14] Serge Doubrovsky, "Ionesco and the Comedy of the Absurd," in *Yale French Studies* 23 (Summer, 1959), 3–10. See above, p. 11.

[15] We know that Ionesco contemplated writing a Ph.D. thesis on this subject.

[16] He thus joins hands with Gilbert Durand, denouncing in Sartre, Roland Barthes and Claude Lévi-Strauss, neopositivists who, when they try to elucidate "thought conceived in images" and "mythical thought," cannot help, in his view, reintegrating it within a "rational" framework which cannot be taken for granted to fit the "anthropological structures of the imaginary." Thus, whatever their original intentions, they would discredit both systems of thought.

ilar, corollary law; just as progression in "outer space" is associated with regression in "inner space," so projection into the future is matched by a turning back towards the past, towards the source. Let us go back for a moment to our two cosmonauts taking their first steps "on the moon"; when faced with those pictures forcing themselves literally on our minds, who has not pondered over the first steps trodden on earth by our mythical "primeval ancestors"? [17] Did they not resemble, in some more simple way, babies venturing for the first time into adult space fraught with dangerous objects? And the exit of those cosmonauts from the cabin of their space-ship might have enabled us to assimilate it, with a little more imagination, to the womb; did they not move about in it, like twin or triplet foetuses, stirring in the void as if in amniotic fluid, turning head over heels, in a word defying the laws of gravity? . . . Does this comparison seem somewhat farfetched? Let Ionesco have his say: "Paradise," he reveals to us, manifests itself to him in the shape of a "complete, spherical world," where "everything *is,* where there is neither finiteness nor infinity, where the finite-infinite problem does not arise" (*Entretiens,* p. 45). In *The Chairs* the Old Man exclaims: "Sometimes I wake up to find absolute silence around me. That's what I mean by the sphere. It's complete in itself. However, one has to be careful. The whole shape may suddenly disappear. There are holes it escapes through" (*Three Plays,* p. 43). Man cannot go back to this paradise lost; at most, he may, as he grows old, "sink back into childhood." It is "the most natural thing in the world," Ionesco tells us, that the Old Man "sits down [. . .] on the Old Woman's lap" (*Three Plays,* p. 9) and that he cries for his "mummy" (*Three Plays,* pp. 13, 14). It is "the most natural thing in the world," let us continue, that the Old Man and the Old Woman, who appear to us, moreover, as real acrobats, experience so much difficulty in moving about, walking, and dragging their chairs through the maze of their closed universe. The Old Man "trot(s) about" (*Three Plays,* p. 14), he "trot[s] round the Old Woman, with short, uncertain steps, like a child's or a very old man's" (*Three Plays,* p. 18). The Old Woman likewise "hobbles" (*Three Plays,* p. 22) and "clippity-clops" (*Three Plays,* p. 37). It

[17] Concerning every aspect of the myth of the "primeval ancestor" cf. Mircea Eliade, *Traité d'Histoire des Religions,* Préface de G. Durnézil, Paris, Payot, 1949, "Bibliothèque scientifique"; idem, *Cosmos and History; the Myth of the Eternal Return,* translated from the French by Willard R. Trask (New York: Harper & Row, 1959).

was because he had "holes in his feet," [18] Jean Cocteau recalled—
"Cocteau the discoverer" (*Entretiens,* p. 53) or rather the rediscoverer of myths—that Oedipus was thus called. Ionesco, also a poet, expresses "as [. . .] the most natural thing in the world" the invisible in terms of the visible in imaginary space. Let us mention one more significant image which also connects with the myth of the return to the ultimate source; at one point, the Old Couple "should [. . .] be behind the chairs, very close to each other, almost touching, but back to back" (*Three Plays,* p. 28). As Eliade says in his *Méphistophélès et l'Androgyne,* Man and Woman dream of going back to primeval Time, when they formed but one single androgynous being, when Adam and Eve, according to Judeo-Christian gnosis, were still conjoined, attached by their back like Siamese twins? [19] The Old Man who sits down "as [. . .] the most natural thing in the world" on the Old Woman's lap, will say later, welcoming his imaginary "guests": "The twins can use the same chair" (*Three Plays,* p. 36)! Dream perception, which here relates to matter, enables us to express in concrete terms, in the most conscious manner possible, the abstract components of the myth. As Ionesco asserts, the fundamental virtue of the dream seems to be to wrest us from the intellectual framework, circumscribed by the psychology and the logic of the "vécu," in which "common sense" has imprisoned us. The dream transcends it into a "psychological" relativized system of thought, which materializes the concepts into images, thus making them visible. In this system, science and fiction coincide "as [. . .] the most natural thing in the world," as is shown by the following "dream" account by Ionesco, which allows us to understand how his imaginary universe is based intuitively on these two categories of knowledge. "I dream," he relates to Claude Bonnefoy, "that I'm a cosmonaut. A strange cosmonaut. I find myself in a sort of celluloid cabin. I am bare, seated (almost the position of the foetus, isn't it?) with someone else in front of me who looks like me. I am at one and the same time foetus and cosmonaut. I know that I'm heading for another planet" (*Entretiens,* p. 39). Let us stop his story here: we shall resume it by immersing ourselves in the universe of *The Chairs.* Does it not in actual fact justify the theory that we have just outlined, according to which this work might be inter-

[18] Jean Cocteau, *La Machine Infernale* (Paris: Bernard Grasset, 1934), p. 13.
[19] Mircea Eliade, *Méphistophélès et l'Androgyne* (Paris: Gallimard, 1862), "Les Essais 103."

preted as an experiment of the "relativization" of science by fiction and fiction by science?

We still have to determine, before setting off on this exploration, that this experiment is a theatrical one. Undoubtedly the theatre itself, according to Ionesco, might be defined along with science and pure fiction as a means to knowledge of the universe. "I do not believe," he asserts, "that there is a contradiction between creative and cognitive activity, for the structures of the mind probably reflect universal structures." [20] "Logic and emotion join hands," he explains to Claude Bonnefoy, "and even mathematics is subjective since it is a structure of the mind" (*Entretiens*, p. 47); to the same extent, as we have seen, fiction, also a structure of the mind, would therefore be objective. Artistic activity, considered from the scientific point of view as an "invention," and from the point of view of fiction as a spontaneous creation of the imagination, would thus have no other function than to place both in a relationship of reciprocity on the epistemological level. A thinker who is both a writer, a poet, and a philosopher of science, Raymond Queneau, tells us that "all of science, in its completed form" might be conceived, "both as a technique and as gratuitous activity, in other words quite simply in the same way as the 'other' human activity, art, is conceived." [21] We can see, however, that both activities, although one and the same on the level of theory, of function of the mind (which remains to be proved), are quite clearly characterized by distinct "techniques." At this level, at any rate, art diverges from science and also from pure dream fiction, since it processes the material of its "experiments" in its own specific framework and with its own specific means. "There are the poets, the thinkers," says Ionesco, "and then there are the *gens de métier*" (*Entretiens*, p. 51). If it is the "medium," as McLuhan states, which is the "message," the difference could be fundamental. We know that Ionesco, at any rate, far from underestimating questions of technique, attaches considerable importance to them, insofar as they have some connection with his "métier" as a playwright. He does not seek to hide the fact, for instance, that the "medium" of the theatre at first seemed to

[20] Ionesco, "Le Coeur n'est pas sur la Main," in *Cahiers de Saisons* (Hiver, 1959), p. 264. Also quoted in Esslin, p. 82.
[21] Raymond Queneau, "The Place of Mathematics in the Classification of Sciences," in *Les Grands Courants de la Pensée Mathématique,* présentés par François Le Lionnais, Paris, Librairie scientifique et technique Albert Blanchard, 1962, "L'humanisme scientifique de demain," p. 395.

him unsuitable for the sort of "experiment" he wanted to perform: "It was the presence on the stage of flesh-and-blood people that embarrassed me," he told us. "Their material presence destroyed the fiction. I was confronted, as it were, by two planes of reality—the concrete, material, impoverished, empty, limited reality of those living, everyday human beings, moving about and talking on the stage, and the reality of imagination, the two face to face and not coinciding, unable to be brought into relation with each other; two antagonistic worlds, incapable of being unified, of merging." [22] It is the problem of conceptualization, that is, of "projection" into an unreal universe, that he had to come face to face with when he produced *The Chairs*; how was he to relativize, within the spatio-temporal framework and material environment of the theatre, beings and objects, "inanimate" beings—the Old Man, the Old Woman, and above all the Orator, who is defined as a "robot" (*Three Plays*, p. 53)—and "animate" objects—the chairs, which in his view formed the "subject" and not the "object" of the play—? The puppet theatre, which delighted him when young, might obviously have offered him further possibilities. The circus might have provided him with its acrobats and jugglers; let us bring to mind the favorite "act" of that king of clowns, the Swiss Grock, an accomplished acrobat, which consisted of confronting, against the law of gravity, an apparently ordinary, but nonetheless disarticulated, defunctionalized chair, now friendly, now hostile. Let us think, for a moment, of the part played in Ionesco by chairs and stools, essential elements of the setting. Let us recall, specifically, the fact that the vision of the two characters and their chairs is considered by him to be an "act":[23] "It's a *tour de force*," he exclaims. "It should have something circus-like about it." But the performance of *The Chairs* brings to mind mainly a third sort of vision, namely the projection of a cartoon film. The cinema, in general, fascinates Ionesco; he has even written a text for a film.[24] We find more than one reference in *The Chairs* to the cinema: the Old Man, for example, "scratches his head like Stan Laurel" (*Three Plays*, p. 10). But, as we can see, it is not the "talkies" which interest Ionesco, but the

[22] Ionesco, "Expérience du Théâtre," in *Nouvelle Revue Française* (February 1, 1958), p. 253.

[23] Note to original French edition, not included in Watson's translation.

[24] Barney Rossett, the editor in chief of Grove Press, once asked Ionesco, as well as Samuel Beckett and Harold Pinter, to write texts for a three-part film. Only Beckett's part was shot.

good old films from the time of the silent cinema, or at any rate comic films which derive their best effects from the repertoire of purely visual gags, in which, as we know, objects play the best part. The cartoon, in this sense, leaves the greatest possible freedom to the creator; the Canadian director Norman MacLaren, filming shot by shot the confrontation between "A Man and a Chair," has created a masterpiece equivalent in the history of the cinema to *The Chairs* in the history of contemporary theatre.

Ionesco seeks to revitalize space and time, mind and matter, men and things upon a stage-floor trodden by human beings—actors— and strewn with objects seemingly condemned to play insipidly utilitarian background roles. A true man of the theatre, Ionesco "depends to some extent upon the visible to reveal his deeper meaning." [25] In so doing, he hopes to achieve a geometrical locus governed by perfect symmetry; on both sides of the central axis which runs from the middle of the proscenium to "the great monumental double doors," doors and windows "face each other." The "two chairs," placed "side by side" on the front of the stage, determine a rectilinear axis which is extended to run parallel along the proscenium: this axis marks a definite and evidently impassable limit between, on the one hand, the imaginary universe as it is displayed on stage, and, on the other hand, the universe of real life—in other words the auditorium where the audience is seated. The spatial form, defined hitherto in terms of the intersection of rectilinear axes, takes us back to that conception of "cubic space" as we are told by Etienne Souriau has gained ascendancy in the modern theatre, whereas in the beginning, at the time of the "theatre of antiquity," it was the "spherical conception" which prevailed. The straight line, "the shortest distance between two points," which has allowed us to map the space of everyday life in order to get to know it better and to exploit it fully, would thus emerge as an authentic line of demarcation: the audience would on no account be able to "take part" in the play by "projecting itself" on stage. The two planes of the real and the imaginary, thus circumscribed by utilitarian thought, would at most be thrown back by some sort of mirror effect whose "reflection" would be purely passive and visual. Since Antonin Artaud's attempts to establish a dialectical relationship between these two planes, many departed from the "cubic

[25] Leonard Cabell Pronko, *Avant-Garde: The Experimental Theater in France* (Berkeley and Los Angeles: University of California Press, 1966), p. 77.

form" by breaking up or curving their demarcation line, such as the directors who returned to "theatre in the round" or open-air circus performances enveloping the spectators. Ionesco seems to aim for some such effect. In the presentation of the setting, he specifies that the stage should be bare. With the curve of the "circular walls" enclosing the back of the stage, the latter acquires a semi-circular shape, and the axes may be compared to spokes which converge on a central point, situated somewhere between the two chairs which originally occupied the front of the stage.

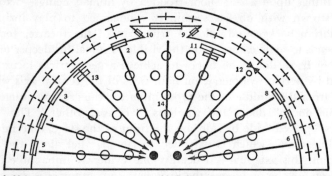

1: Main double door.
2, 3, 4, 5: Side doors on the right.
6, 7, 8: Side doors on the left.
9, 10: Two doors hidden in the recess.
11: Dais and blackboard.
12, 13: Windows, with stools, left and right.
14: Empty chairs.
XXX Corridor, in wings.

Looking like half of a wheel, the stage-floor would, were it to revolve around a central point, describe a circle, absorbing the audience. The proscenium, subjected to this rotational movement along its entire length, loses all reality, being transformed into a sort of abstract diameter. The real and the imaginary coincide in a single swirl, and, as a result of gravitational pull acting upon the rectilinear planes, cubic space become curved can be embodied in a sphere or cosmos.

To create this optical illusion an imbalance, a rocking motion, would have to exist. Yet, the Old Couple and the pairs of objects (chairs, doors, windows) form relational systems similar to pairs of scales whose trays balance each other evenly. The equilibrium, however, is not as perfect as may appear at first glance. Standing on a step-ladder to look out the window, the Old Man succumbs to a fit of dizziness—not his own, but that of his wife, who cannot bear to watch him lean out. As to the Old Woman, it is by turning up "the green light" of the gas lamp that she sets off the kaleidoscope of fantasy. But the two chairs, standing as they do at the front of the stage, summon the characters to take their positions in the outside world, both feet solidly on the ground.

This is where Ionesco has a *coup de théâtre* in store for us: the Old Woman pulls the Old Man forward, and he "sits down in her lap as though it were the most natural thing in the world." The chair supports the Old Woman, who, in turn, is transmogrified into a sort of armchair, providing her husband-son with a comfortable seat. The latter ends with his feet dangling in mid-air, like those of the strollers "in the air" beloved by Ionesco. Part foetus, part cosmonaut, the Old Man can now rise to the heights of imaginary existence. His spouse "blasts him off": "Ah! yes, you've certainly a fine intellect. You are very gifted, my darling. You could have been head president, head King, or even head doctor, or head general if you had wanted to, if only you'd had a little ambition in life." There goes the Old Man, the nose-cone of a three-part rocket fired into the spaces of unreality: "I've a message . . . a mission." Although he wants to formulate his message, the Old Man will not turn to his companion, for she merely echoes his words. Their dialogue is a two-way monologue dictated by a mechanical speaker, the *deus ex machina* of Occidental civilization. A bit of Villon sprinkled with Ronsard, the clichés of love, the same stories endlessly repeated make up what passes for conversation. The language of love yields to the love of language! "Shared loneliness—that's the worst kind," declares Ionesco in his *Entretiens* with Bonnefoy.

Superimposed one on top of the other, the Old Man and the Old Woman lose all individuality; they form a kind of infernal machine which must begin the process of scission. We learn from Abellio that "every pair of oppositions is always divided . . . into a pair of pairs." In the terminology of physics, we might say that the initial scission of the nucleus reproduces itself by a chain reaction throughout the entire universe of the imaginary, subjecting it to a bi-polarization which controls the inter-relations of the particles (or "guests") created by the process. This is concretized upon the stage by the phenomenon of the reproduction of the chairs. As Jacques Guicharnaud points out: "Not only is a mathematic rigour imposed on human phenomena, but it is completed by a process of geometric progression or acceleration." [26] The pair of chairs initially

[20] Guicharnaud, pp. 183-84.

placed on the stage undergoes the same ordeal as the couple; it is the victim of an inner eruption which brings about the increase in the number of its elements. Condensation—in this case the fusion of the two bodies as the Old Man sits in his wife's lap—produces eruption. Gone is the myth of the Oneness of original matter.

The carrying in of a third chair shatters the spatial dimension of Euclidean geometry, opening the stage, and thus the world, to the possibilities of reproduction *ad infinitum.* The positive and negative elements composing what Plato calls in his *Timaeus* a "series of doubles" are both attracted and repulsed as they follow the trajectory of an ideal and material disintegration chain. In this polarized field, the presence of the chairs concretizes the absence of "guests," and vice versa.

Let us examine, for instance, the introduction of the first "guest," the Lady. She is a mere idealized projection, in the Old Couple's imagination, of what the Old Woman was, or might have been, when she was younger, many years before. Her "arrival" in a boat "slipping through the water" (*Three Plays,* p. 18) is a dream occurrence; the "bell" marks the beginning of the "illusion." The pseudo-dialogue clearly shows that the Lady who is presented as an "ideal of self" is imposed upon the "ideal self" of the Old Woman. The following chart, in which we have regrouped and correlated the main "cues" of the Old Man and the Old Woman, allows us in fact to detect easily the antithetic relation (positive-negative, active-passive) binding them together within the same antinomic system:

THE OLD WOMAN	THE LADY
My hair must look a sight *(She tidies her hair.)*	*(Voice of Old Woman opening the door for someone.)* Take care, don't ruin your hat. You might take out the hatpin, that will be more comfortable. Oh! no, no one will sit on it.
I'm so badly dressed . . . I'm wearing an old gown and it's all rumpled. *(The Old Man grumbling to the Old Woman:)* You should have gotten ready before . . . you had plenty of time.	*(Voice of Old Man addressing the Lady:)* Put your fur down there. Let me help you. No, nothing will happen to it. *(Voice of Old Woman addressing the Lady:)*

Oh! What a pretty suit!

(*Old Woman to the Lady who, though invisible, seems to have come in:*)

What a charming fan you have! My husband gave me one very like it, that must have been seventy-three years ago . . . and I still have it.

(*Loud ringing of the doorbell. The Old Woman hobbles towards the concealed door on the left.*)

(*Old Man to the Lady:*)

Old age is a heavy burden. I can only wish you an eternal youth.

With respect to this ideal Lady, both characters gradually adopt an ambivalent attitude; admiration is tempered, in the Old Woman, by a modicum of envy and, in the Old Man, by a shade of spite. For the sight of youth, graciously endowed, puts them face to face inevitably with their own decrepitude. Whereas it should have enabled them to recapture, by going back "seventy-three years" in time, some of the freshness of their original feelings and the warmth of their original passion . . . it draws them further away from that idyllic period. In their attempt to draw closer to each other through the medium of memory, they merely extend the void between them. This void will in fact be given concrete form in the shape of the third chair. The mediation is thus "objectivized" and Ionesco literally projects it on stage. Let us therefore follow his stage directions closely. It is the Old Man, unexpectedly gallant and solicitous, who "goes off left" (*Three Plays*, p. 20) to fetch this chair for the Lady, but it is the Old Woman who meanwhile offers her a seat by her side: "She points to one of the two chairs and sits down on the other one, on the right side of the invisible Lady" (*Three Plays*, p. 20). At this point, the antithetic relation binding the two characters, the visible and the invisible, is materialized by the fact that they occupy a "pair" of chairs. It turns out, following the same principle, that the invisible Lady has settled herself on one of the two chairs that the Old Couple had left vacant at the beginning of the play: the imaginary thus becomes embedded in the real. The Old Man then "re-appears [. . .] carrying a chair" which he "sets . . . down to the left of the invisible Lady" (*Three Plays*, p. 20).

Ionesco gives us the following stage direction: "The Old Man sits
down on the chair he has just brought, so that the invisible Lady
is in the middle. The Old Man looks at the Lady, smiles at her, nods
his head, rubs his hands gently together and appears to be following
what she is saying. The Old Woman does the same" (*Three Plays,*
p. 20). He adds further on that it is "in profile" (*Three Plays,* p. 21)
with respect to the auditorium that the Old Couple "look at the
Lady." Any comment here becomes more or less superfluous; we
have moreover already given some theoretic outline to this notion;
the Lady is indeed a potential image formed from the two focal
points projected from their imagination; it is materialized, if at all,
into a chair, placed between them, which keeps them irremediably
apart. The playwright by "conceiving thought in images" thus suc-
ceeds in manipulating abstractions concretely! It remains merely to
be shown, with respect to this scene, how the notion of the "ambivalent relation" between the individual and its "idols" is established via mimicry. Confronted with the invisible Lady "the Old
Couple smile. They even laugh. They look as if they are enjoying
the story the Lady is telling . . ." (*Three Plays,* p. 20). At the same
time, they are afraid: "A pause: a lull in the conversation. Their
faces have lost all expression . . ." (*Three Plays,* p. 20). It is within
the non-linear time of logic that the contradiction which governs
the "two-facedness" of the characters is formulated. During the
course of the play, it is displayed in a rotatory movement which allows us to alternate successively the positive and the negative, the
active and the passive, affirmation and negation, and to cancel them
out by each other. An Ionesco dialogue, sometimes called absurd,
reveals the perfect logic of this system:

> *Old Man.* [. . .] Oh yes, you're perfectly right . . .
> *Old Woman.* Yes, yes, yes . . . Oh, but no!
> *Old Man.* Yes, yes, yes. By all means.
> *Old Woman.* Yes?
> *Old Man.* No! (*Three Plays,* p. 20).

Let us move to the following scene. Again a bell rings. Then,
"the sound of an approaching boat" (*Three Plays,* p. 22) is heard.
The Old Man orders the Old Woman to "go and fetch some chairs!"
(*Three Plays,* p. 22.) Just as the Old Woman was found to be projected into the image of a Lady younger than herself, in elegant
array, so the Old Man is portrayed in the guise of the "Colonel,"
he, too, obviously invisible. The "pair" composed of the Old Woman

and the Lady therefore corresponds to the "pair" formed by the Old Man (a quartermaster, we recall) and the Colonel. With respect to this imaginary figure, the Old Man naturally adopts an ambivalent attitude; he is complimentary—"Good evening, Colonel! . . . This is indeed an amazing honour for me . . . I . . . I . . . I never expected . . . Although . . . and yet . . . well I'm very proud to see you in my humble abode, such a distinguished hero . . ." (*Three Plays*, pp. 22, 23) and anxious not to be underrated in his own eyes: "Nevertheless, without false modesty, may I confess that I do not feel myself entirely unworthy of your visit! Proud, yes . . . but not unworthy . . . !" (*Three Plays*, p. 23.) The Old Woman, similarly, is wonderstruck: "Oh! What a fine uniform! What pretty decorations!" (*Three Plays*, p. 23.) Then, having realized the link between this character and her husband, she attempts a revaluation of the latter in this new light: "You are an old friend of my husband's, he's a General . . ." (*Three Plays*, p. 23)—"Quartermaster, quartermaster," rectifies the Old Man, "displeased" at the sight of his "idol" being underestimated. The Old Woman waxes sentimental—"Oh! What a polite man . . ." (*Three Plays*, p. 23)—and yields in deference: ". . . anyone can see that he's out of the ordinary, really superior!" (*Three Plays*, p. 23.) She accepts the introduction of a new medium between herself and her husband: "This chair is for you . . ." (*Three Plays*, p. 23) she tells the Colonel. Henceforth she is attracted by their "good friend [. . .] renowned in military circles" (*Three Plays*, p. 24). She tries to get him to sit down beside her; she "places her chair on the right" (*Three Plays*, p. 23) and, "indicating the chair she has brought up for the Colonel" (*Three Plays*, p. 24), she invites him resolutely to sit down: "Do take this chair . . ." (*Three Plays*, p. 24). Why is she so insistent? Will she encounter a hitch? Yes indeed. . . . The Colonel is obviously more interested in conversing with the Young Lady!

At this point, it is important to recall that the Colonel moves on a different plane from that of the Old Couple, namely on the a-temporal world of the "invisible," the universe of fantasy. For the two levels to be brought into relation with each other, a process of duplication must occur: the pair composed of the Old Man and the Old Woman will subdivide into its mirror image in the realm of the imagination, the Colonel and the Lady.

The similarity between the movements of *dramatis personae* on the stage-floor, and those of pawns, rooks, or other pieces across the chess-board has struck a number of contemporary critics. Hugh Kenner, in his *Samuel Beckett, A Critical Study,* pointed out the connections in *Endgame.* Contemporary philosophers and philologists have demonstrated their interest in exploring the theory of chess, applying the structural relations which govern the various moves to their own line of inquiry—I am thinking in particular of Ludwig Wittgenstein's *Tractatus* and of Ferdinand de Saussure's *Cours de Linguistique Générale.* In the same line of thought, the mathematician Klein embodies geometrically, in the form of a quadrilateral, every possible algebraic operation. If, in turn, we apply the laws which govern the correlations (whether of opposition or inversion) within "Klein's square" to the "pairing" in *The Chairs,* we will discover the fundamental necessity dictating these relations.

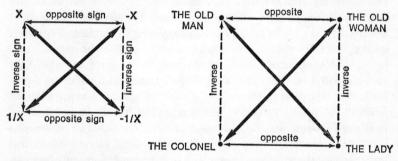

Clearly dual and ambivalent correlations define the network of associations combining each of the following pairs of characters:

> The Old Man and the Old Woman,
> The Old Woman and the Lady,
> The Old Man and the Lady,
> The Old Man and the Colonel,
> The Old Woman and the Colonel,
> and, finally . . . The Colonel and the Lady.

On the stage two "guests," in other words, two chairs, now stand between the Old Man and his wife; the gulf between them grows proportionally wider as the mediation becomes more intense. They are being gradually inched away from the center of the stage that they originally occupied and wafted each to one side by a sort of centrifugal force. This force causes them almost to levitate.

Having projected their desires into the universe of mediation in which a veritable amorous fantasy is let loose (the Colonel does violence to the Lady: "Invisibly, something not quite respectable is happening"), the Old Couple is suddenly helpless and dispossessed. As pointed out by Jean-Hervé Donnard, "the assumed presence of a soldier beneath their roof kindles in Semiramis and her husband those two basic instincts long since buried beneath the snow of years: eroticism and aggressiveness, interdependent and merged together" (p. 160). As their idols fall, the Old Couple is forced into a reassessment of their status: "I know we're very old, but we are respectable people." Although the Old Man brags "I'm not yet past the age when I can carry arms," he is clearly unable to provoke the Colonel to a duel. He does, however, knock over the Lady's chair, thereby withdrawing her from the latter's advances. This action, due on the surface of things to a "clumsy movement," constitutes in fact an act of aggression. (We know that "abortive attempts" are particularly significant.) This reveals the fundamental workings of the machinery of the imaginary: the dialectical relationship between active and passive which governs the reversal of situations and brings the characters to act and think in absolutely contradictory fashion. Each of them has a "double personality" conferred upon him. The Old Man is "active" (soldier, "cosmonaut") while the Old Woman as "passive" (admiring spouse), and in turn he is "passive" (wailing "foetus," inarticulate writer) and she "active" (protective "mother"). There is always something active behind the passive, and passive behind the active. Thus, the negative polarity and the positive one are revitalized and may be inverted in the world of the imaginary. The Colonel, therefore, represents in all likelihood an intensification of the active polarity of the Old Man, whereas the Lady stands for an intensification of the passive polarity of the Old Woman.

Let us pursue the analysis of this "system" in compliance with its "movement" and with the "dynamism" of its "forces." It is by a sort of phenomenon of physics, in fact, that the cells constituting the psychological "make-up" of the characters are split by the bipolarization of the (invisible) world of the imaginary and emerge as being engulfed as if by the mass of an irresistible sound-wave which advances in a linear direction, throughout the space of the text, from one word, from one "cue," to another, and, throughout the space of the stage (concretely this time), from chair to chair. In the terminology of psychoanalysis, we might say that they are all bound together, by means of a "symbolic chain," like so many links.

A specialist in the study of myths might explain, furthermore, how everything may be integrated into a system analogous to a braid being slowly interwoven. Finally, a linguist would, no doubt, in his attempt to define this process, resort to the notion of "sentence embedding" in his transformational system. . . . We detect obvious correspondences, on the theoretical level of epistemology, between the various structural representations provided by the various human sciences. Let us portray by means of the following diagram the system which we consider to govern likewise the projection of imaginary characters on the basis of the initial "split" in the personalities of the Old Man and the Old Woman:

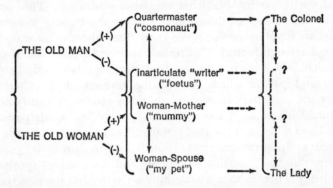

We can see in this diagram that, in order for it to be balanced, the system should be completed by the appearance of two additional characters; one will be superimposed, antithetically, on the character of the Colonel and will thus continue the passive, negative postulation of the Old Man by intensifying it; it will be "coupled" organically with a female character who, being antithetically related to the character of the Lady, will represent an intensification of the "maternal," active, positive postulation of the Old Woman. Let us see how this hypothesis, formulated in such abstract and sketchy terms, is verified in the play.

A bell rings again, but this time we do not hear any boat slipping through the water; the movement of the play grows faster. Indeed, the two characters making up the new "pair" appear simultaneously: they are Mrs. Lovely and the Photo-engraver.[27] No need to state that

---

[27] It is considered imperative for the purpose of our analysis to translate "photograveur" as "photo-engraver" and not "photographer" as it appears in Donald Watson's translation. The term "photo-engraver" will be maintained throughout.

these two characters are every bit as invisible as the Colonel and the Lady. They, too, are projections of the imagination. The above diagram would thus be completed in the following way:

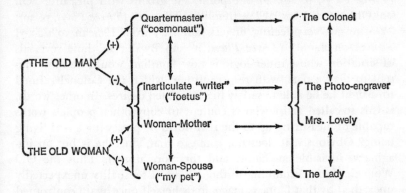

Let us comment upon the system of relations outlined above. The Photo-engraver, in all probability, is yet another projection of the imaginary personality of the Old Man, or at least, as we have suggested, of his passive postulation; the inarticulate writer unable to express his "message," the "reminiscer" at pains to regain his memories, is transcended by an artist who does have, to his credit, the advantage of being able to dispense with language and with words, but who is nonetheless condemned to barrenness as a creator. The Photo-engraver, indeed, can merely reproduce, via a largely technical and mechanical process, the works of other artists, who themselves would be considered the true creators. From this point of view, he seems confined to performing an activity that we might qualify, in relative terms, as passive, since his own works—which are exposures—are, strictly speaking, merely the "negatives" of pictures which he has not processed himself. This notion of "helplessness" is brought out clearly if we compare him to the evidently all-powerful character of the Colonel;[28] whereas the Colonel, a true soldier, an old trooper, does not hesitate to precipitate upon himself the Lady to satisfy his lust, the Photo-engraver must indeed emerge as the victim of aggression before his own sensuality can be aroused. It is, in actual fact, the Old Woman who has to provoke him from his entirely passive contemplation—she takes him to be a "doctor!"

[28] Cf. Ionesco's short story entitled "La photo du Colonel." Did he not dream, as a child, of becoming either a great soldier or a great artist (*Entretiens*, p. 28)?

(*Three Plays*, p. 27)—of her body. "Hands on hips," she "throw[s] her head back [. . .] uttering erotic cries," she "thrust[s] her pelvis forward, standing with legs apart, she laughs like an old whore . . ." (*Three Plays*, p. 29). At one point, she groans with pleasure: "Oh no! Oh! No, oh! La, la! I'm trembling all over" (*Three Plays*, p. 30); "You've got very feeling fingers, ah! . . . well, I mean to s-a-a-y! . . . oh-oh-oh-oh!" (*Three Plays*, p. 30.) By one of those reversals of situation whose inner logic is now familiar, would he now consent to play a part, with respect to her, which the Colonel refused to? Might he be able to satisfy her frustrated desires? In other words, is this so-called artist who is content to copy other people's works capable of measuring up to the real world by possessing a real living being? Obviously, it does not come to that, since he is but an imaginary, invisible mediator, and therefore unreal. Thus the Old Woman, after succumbing to the delight of sensuality unexpectedly unearthed by that fantasy image, finds herself once again confronted even more dramatically with the problem of the flesh, which is, for her, the vexing problem of procreation: "You really, really believe," she asks the Photo-engraver, "that you can have children at any age? Children *of* any age?" (*Three Plays*, p. 30.) This should help us to realize more poignantly, if it were still necessary, what the Old Man means to her.

Consequently, we may determine more fully what she means to *him* by examining the attitude he adopts with respect to the new "Lady," Mrs. Lovely. Through this imaginary character he obviously sublimates his sensual desires, which have been transformed into a deep need for affection, tenderness and protection. Whereas he behaved in a rather condescending fashion with respect to the other Lady, he seeks protection beside Mrs. Lovely as he might in the arms of a "mother-spouse" who could console him, better than the Old Woman, over life's disappointments, and dispel his anxiety by offering him the pure joys of an ideal love. Mrs. Lovely in fact extends the active, positive postulation that we have discovered in the character of the Old Woman and, in more than one respect, she intensifies it. She is also described by the Old Woman as "a friend of [her] childhood days" (*Three Plays*, p. 27), but she is much older than the Old Woman (she is "bent double" and "her hair is white") (*Three Plays*, p. 27). Indeed, the Old Man used to love her long before losing his heart to his spouse, in some remote past which goes back to his childhood days and, even beyond, to the period before birth; "I was in love with you a hundred years ago . . ." (*Three Plays*, p. 28) he reminds her. His heart melts at the image of this fairy-tale character, fresh from the night of mythical childhood: ". . . Lovely Miss Lovely, that's what you were called . . ." (*Three Plays*, p. 27). At that time she was still a miss, a child even, like him —"we were only children"—(*Three Plays*, p. 29) and her hair was still "blue" (*Three Plays*, p. 27). Indeed, outside the context of time she was beautiful, as beautiful as a fairy, a goddess, or a queen; she was as beautiful as that most beautiful of queens, Cleopatra, against whom Semiramis would be but a poor reflection. But the pure flame of dawn blazing forth in all its glory from the East soon gives way to a stark light, as despairingly white as the Old Woman's hair, which brings out cruelly the lines on their faces fossilized by History. "Your nose really has got longer," laments the Old Man, "it's filled out, too [. . .] terribly long . . . ah! what a pity!" (*Three Plays*, p. 26.) He may cite with impunity François Villon's refrain from the "Ballade des Dames du Temps jadis": "Where are the snows of yesteryear?" (*Three Plays*, p. 28.) He may exclaim like a hero of the medieval legend: "May I play Tristan to your Isolde? . . . We could have had our share of bliss, beauty and eternity . . . eternity . . ." (*Three Plays*, p. 30). He may attempt, like Proust's hero, "to live those long-lost days again" (*Three Plays*, p. 29). These days can never be recaptured, however, and the "ladies" who were alive at that time can be no more than invisible dream characters. The Old Man vainly cherishes the illusion that he might rid himself of his obsessions by getting his wife to play the part of one of these ideal "ladies." "My worthy spouse, Semiramis, has taken the place of my mother" (*Three Plays*, p. 30), he explains to Mrs. Lovely. He is more than ever the victim of the imaginary mediation which unrealizes all his desires. But it is obviously not Mrs. Lovely who allows him to free himself from this trap: ". . . everything is lost to us, lost, lost" (*Three Plays*, p. 30), he admits, snivelling.

The proliferation of imaginary characters is matched on the stage by that of the chairs. As they accumulate, the couple is prevented from meeting and embracing. The break between the original two is absolute: their minds and bodies will not be reconciled again, even when they themselves are once more brought together. Ionesco tells us: "The Old Couple should be . . . behind the chairs, very close to each other, almost touching but back to back." They address their remarks to the imaginary guests, while the newcomers are invited to be seated on two of the six chairs which now stand in a row along the front of the stage.

We have by now reached a turning point: the six chairs and the visible and invisible characters occupying them form a set, all the elements of which, hitherto defined, are relativized. We are confronted with an evidently closed but self-regulating system. After the six-character scene, the guests will suddenly turn up *en masse*, creating a hubbub which upsets the linear movement described above. At this point, the Old Woman "arranges the chairs, their backs to the audience." With the stage transformed into an auditorium, the audience is now invited to take part in the "experiment."

It is now that the "family story" related by the Old Couple will be presented to the "guests" and to us, the spectators. Pieced together from two contradictory accounts, the story remains enigmatic. The logic of relativity, however, reveals that the contradictions themselves are meaningful, suggesting a fundamental duality. The dialogue, presenting the same story from two opposite points of view, becomes a two-way contrapuntal monologue in which the themes are antithetically related.

A certain number of elements in this strange story about the classical triangle of Father-Mother-Son relate it directly to the myth of Oedipus. The Old Woman asserts that they had a son. His memory is brought to mind in loving terms. The boy, however, is said to have arraigned his parents: "You kill the birds! Why do you kill the birds?" He speaks of streets full of dead birds and dying children. "He had a heart of gold," says the Old Woman, refusing to turn against her son. As for the Old Man, he denies ever having had children, and explains: "Perhaps it was better this way. I myself was an ungrateful child." It is with respect to his mother that he is smitten with remorse. He left her "lying in [the] ditch."

If we examine the text of the Old Man, which corresponds "inversely" to that of the Old Woman, we understand why the latter is so much at pains to justify her son: this son might indeed be her husband as she pictures him in her psychic universe. The Old Man, in turn, justifies the part she plays in respect to him by acknowledging his crime towards his own mother. Thus is formed the "usual" but nonetheless strange pair of motherly wife and childlike husband, the very pair which comprises the Oedipus triangle.

A world order emerges from the story: Behind the Father, there may be a God, or at any rate a Heaven, now "blue," now "red with blood"; behind the Mother, there is Mother Nature, Earth (the ditch), in whose depths we may attempt to recover our lost childhood. This is the dual postulation—the same one that Baudelaire, Ionesco's favorite poet, describes in his intimate journals—towards high and low. Both "bird" and "cosmonaut," the Old Man takes flight into the "blue" sky, only to discover that it is illuminated by a destructive light, "red with blood"; he plummets back to earth, blinded, his eyes "put out" (the birds, Oedipus). On earth, he sets out on the quest for his origins, in the hope of becoming a "foetus" once more, and scratches about on the surface like a "little chick" (his nickname) to find his "mummy." After scratching fruitlessly, the chick will become a "bird" again and take flight towards the sky. "Life is like that," life symbolized by the "lily of the valley" held by "the mother" buried in the ditch according to the Old Man's story. Is not this spring flower the symbol of the eternal cycle of Nature, the rebirth after death?

The "infernal machine" of the imagination is now let loose. The dialogue becomes "completely disconnected." Those who arrive, announced by a bell ringing ceaselessly, are apparently so tall that the Old Man has to stand on tiptoe (visibly leaving the ground) to shake hands with them. The proliferation of guests goes together with their growth in stature. The Old Woman, meanwhile, arranges the chairs as though "for a show," and the authentic members of the audience are invited to project themselves, in their imagination, onto the stage, to settle down in the empty chairs, to become the "doubles" of the missing actors as Antonin Artaud would have wished. During this time, the invisible but all-powerful force which has "split" the two protagonists, drawing them further apart, births "guests" in such numbers that they threaten to take up the whole floor, driving their hosts out, permanently. The latter have arrived at their final position, "each one near a window." It is through these that they will jump to their end.

Before their death, however, a great event will take place: the door at the back opens wide while fanfares trumpet forth, and the highest conceivable mediator, higher than the Colonel, higher even than the General, enters. He would be the perfect Father-surrogate . . . were he alive, and not invisible like the rest. The Emperor, for it is he ("Oh! Majesty! Oh! Blazing sun!"), grows impatient, and appears ready to leave, for he, like the rest of the audience is expecting the Orator who will be able to express the "message."

Hailed by a chorus, the long-awaited Orator finally materializes. We are surprised to find that he is "a real person." The Old Couple is dumbfounded by the intrusion of a man of "flesh and blood" into their fantasy universe. The Old Woman "touches his arm to make sure he is really there." The Old Man exclaims: "It's not a dream!" and his wife echoes: "It's not a dream, I told you it wasn't." As it emerges, the Orator might easily fit into the symbolic chain of characters which we have thus far examined. He might find his place as another link in the chain extending the Old Man's negative and passive postulation, coming after the Photo-engraver and facing the Emperor, who illustrates the highest degree of the other postulation. Our diagram would thus have to be completed in the following way:

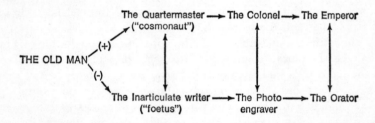

Ionesco in actual fact was at pains to cushion to some extent the impact liable to be produced by the unexpected appearance on stage of a third flesh-and-blood character who might have suddenly driven all the rest into the background. "If the invisible characters should appear as real as possible, the Orator should look unreal" (*Three Plays,* p. 53), Ionesco points out. The real is therefore relativized by the unreal. Thus, the Orator moves about on stage, from the first, as if he were some grotesque creature drifting with the watery current which permeates the space of dreams. "[. . .] slipping along the right-hand wall," Ionesco writes, "he goes quietly to the back of the stage, in front of the great door, without moving his head to right or left; he passes close to the Old Woman, without seeming to notice her . . ." (*Three Plays,* p. 53). The description of his dress confirms our impression that he does not belong entirely to the Old Couples' universe: "He looks like the typical painter or poet of the last century: a wide-brimmed black felt hat, a loosely tied cravat, an artist's jacket, moustache and goatee beard, rather a smug-pretentious look about him" (*Three Plays,* p. 53).

Like the Old Man, whom we might consider a typical "poet," or the Photo-engraver, an "artist" in his way, the Orator emerges in Ionesco's brief description as the portrait of the sterile creator, the failure, the unsuccessful actor. He is a negative, passive character, one who will clearly not fulfil the role entrusted to him. According to the "pairing" scheme of the play, the Orator falls under the sway of the Emperor—symbol of omnipotence—and is crushed beneath the weight of his "imaginary" presence. Even the autographs he signs are in his father's name: "Adieu, Papa."

With these final words scribbled on the blackboard by an aphasic orator, we return to the Oedipus myth. We saw that the Old Man was projected into the *dramatis personae* of Father and Son. The Emperor and the Orator are two new terms of this dual relationship. As the Old Man bows to the Emperor, as to a long-lost father, so the Orator, the Old Man's mouthpiece, could be that very son whose existence he had previously denied. This would account for the surprise and emotion of the Old Couple at the appearance of this "flesh and blood" character, *their* flesh and blood. Indeed, the Old Couple and the Orator are separated in age by one generation: the Old Man is ninety-five, his wife, ninety-four, and the Orator is between forty-five and fifty. In a previous scene, the Old Man explains to the Emperor that he was approximately that age ("I was forty years old . . .") when torn from his father's arms. The correlation between the symbolic father and son is situated outside historical time and may be included within the temporal framework of fiction and logic, which relativizes and even inverts the chronological facts of the narrative. Thus the Old Man explains that when he had the revelation—when he finally became conscious of paternal mediation—he was older than his father ("my moustache was bigger than his, and more pointed . . . my chest more hairy . . . my hair already turning grey . . . while his was still brown).

Let us relate the various stage directions and attempt to integrate them into Ionesco's Oedipus theory in order to be able to deduce that the double chain of mediation which we have already analyzed, the terms of which we have qualified as positive or negative, active or passive, also places the characters within the two relative categories—that of the Father who is all-powerful, and of the Son who is a slave to his mediatory role. Thus the artist is paralyzed or even annihilated by the destructive force of the warrior or leader.

In a wider perspective we have the image of modern man, *homo duplex,* confronting us in the guise of a foetus cosmonaut! To verify this hypothesis we would have to return to our classification of the foregoing characters and show, in particular, how the Colonel and the Photo-engraver play the part of symbolic father and son with respect to each other. We should point out further that the female characters are likewise divided, through substantially complex processes of reproduction, duplication and polarization,

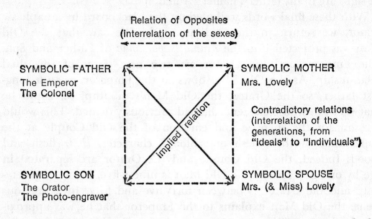

into the two categories of the very old Woman-Mother and the relatively quite young, almost girl-like, Woman-Spouse. We might therefore depict, graphically, the system of relationships existing between all these characters—while reproducing some of them in our attempt to isolate more fully the terms of the relations—within the framework of Klein's square, which may serve as a model both in logic and in fiction.[29]

In the above ideogram[30] we see all the logical correlations which

[29] Let us point out here that this model, as previously stated, has already been used in various human sciences and has, furthermore, enabled A.-J. Greimas, working in semiotics, to depict ideogrammatically. Cf. "Game, Play, Literature," *Yale French Studies* 41 (1968), reproduced in *Du Sens-Essais sémiotiques* (Paris: Editions du Seuil, 1970). We have adopted a number of general ideas from this study which, in a predominantly linguistic analysis, might be applied to the language of the theatre.

[30] No importance will be attached in the diagram to the orientation of the axes or to the specific position of the various terms of the relation (symbolic father, etc.). They are completely arbitrary and highly questionable in the present state of research. In fact, should we be referring to the diagram which outlines the spatio-temporal structure in physics, the horizontal axis would be the time axis

we might establish between the various characters representing the imaginary postulations of the Old Man and the Old Woman: this enables us in fact to gain a fuller insight into the scheme governing their structure throughout the play. We can understand more clearly, for instance, why the Old Woman, after brushing aside the Colonel, should indulge in her erotic pantomime. Did not Jocasta after the disappearance of Laius, seduce Oedipus and does not Phèdre, during the departure of Theseus, covet Hippolytus with an incestuous passion? Thus the Colonel and the Photo-engraver, by the very attitude they adopt with respect to the Old Woman, find themselves once more, logically, and vis-à-vis each other, in the positions of symbolic father and son. The Emperor and the Orator do no more than supersede them as the ultimate symbols of the Old Man's dual imaginary projection. It follows that the Orator, as we have suggested, emerges also as the Son whose story the Old Couple had begun to relate. His appearance on stage is highly dramatic since he is a flesh-and-blood character (the classical triangle of Oedipus is thus concretized) and cannot fail to remind us of the traditional image of the return of the prodigal son. Hence their emotion and, especially, the Old Man's pride. Now that he has an heir, he is liable to believe that the mission he had been charged with by the Father has been faithfully accomplished and that he therefore deserves His eternal and infinite gratitude: "We shall not be forgotten," he shouts to the Old Woman. "The eternal Emperor will always remember us, always" (*Three Plays*, p. 57). Little does he care that the Emperor's armchair (for the latter is entitled to an armchair in which he "so softly nestles") (*Three Plays*, p. 55) may be empty while the Orator remains standing, as stiff as a robot, unable to sit down and thereby take root in the universe of reality. Beside himself with joy at the idea that he has succeeded, in his imagination, in transcending the opposition between the generations, he exults: "No man can ask for more" (*Three Plays*, p. 54).

Then the final "celebration" (*Three Plays*, p. 55) begins. The Old Man thanks all those who have helped him perform the miracle and, especially, "[. . .] the joiners who made the chairs . . ."

(interrelation of the generations) and the vertical axis would be the space axis (interrelation of the sexes, i.e., non-temporal). This specific orientation gives rise to many difficulties which we prefer not to bring up within the scope of our study. Our main concern is to show that all the elements are relativized as from a central point which might be taken to be centre of projection.

(*Three Plays,* p. 55) the guests are sitting on, "[. . .] the skilful craftsman . . . who fashioned the armchair" (*Three Plays,* p. 53) belonging to the Emperor, the technicians, mechanics, electricians— in short, all those who have enabled him to realize his dream and to accomplish the impossible mission he was entrusted with, by conquering the spaces of the imaginary. "My mission is accomplished," he says, in the language of a safely returned astronaut.

Glory, however, is achieved at a high price. Separated from his wife "by a pitiless mob," he addresses her over a great distance in the elegiac style which reveals him to have been, indeed, a poet:

> And yet I would
> Have found it good
> That you and I
> As one might lie
> Each bone to bone
> Beneath our stone.
> Our own flesh breeding
> The same worms feeding
> Mouldering together . . .

The poet-cosmonaut would have liked to return to Mother Earth to be buried among men. Another death is in store for him: he will drown in the waters which inundate the universe of his dreams ("We shall rot in watery solitude"). As the Old Couple jumps out, each from his window, "a brilliant light, as from fireworks," fizzles out, and the dim, glaucous atmosphere of the play's beginning is reestablished.

Sunk in the waters of dreams, moving through air-sealed space, the Orator, now alone upon the stage, is equally condemned to death and asphyxiation. His mouth opens, as though he is gasping for breath, and he courageously tries to express something. What comes out are the gurglings and rumblings characteristic of deaf-mutes. "The message of the play is an anti-message," according to Rosette Lamont. "Speech, art, communication of any sort, are the illusions man needs while there is breath." [31] Like the two windows, now empty and gaping, the doors at the back are "open, gaping black."

Reality returns to the stage as the sound effects reproduce human noises seeming to come from the invisible crowd. These last long

[31] "The Metaphysical Farce: Beckett and Ionesco." *The French Review,* vol. XXXII (February 1959), p. 319.

enough for the visible public to rise from their seats, making the same whispers, tiny sarcastic coughs. Thus, the imaginary space, which is also the space of death, fades into the very spaces of reality, in life. It is therefore the real, visible public which has the last word. Science and fiction are both transcended, by means of a catharsis which reinstates man at the centre of the universe. Must we conclude that the final catastrophe is inevitable? Are writers, poets, playwrights and artists, like the Photo-engraver and the Orator no longer to be anything other than mere foetuses condemned to speechlessness and inertia by the omnipotence of Colonels, Emperors and cosmonauts? It would in our opinion be giving an oversimple view of Ionesco's thought if we considered it as a mere banal impeachment of science and technology in the name of art and poetry. Let us stress, indeed, that he does not for one moment think of denying that scientific progress and, above all, the conquest of space have enriched man's imagination to an extent still difficult to estimate. "Since the beginning of the science of space and the remarkably wide view opened up to cosmonauts" (*Entretiens*, p. 193), he explains with admiration, our intuition and apprehension of the universe have been turned upside down and we have embarked upon the road to inevitable mutation. The problem, here and now, is to take stock of this rift, which is of a veritable epistemological nature, in order to assure the continuity of our history and destiny. It is the job of thinkers, poets and artists to take up this task, since their mission is to explain the unexplainable and to reveal the invisible. Until relatively recently, this mission had been accomplished to perfection, according to Ionesco. He adds with reference to French literature that Descartes, Pascal, Diderot, Balzac, Hugo and Proust were "visionary" thinkers who mastered and transcended the scientific thought of their day. "With respect to the psychology of his time," he writes, "Proust was a forerunner" (*Entretiens*, p. 193). Freud would not have proved him wrong! But since Proust, at the beginning of the twentieth century, philosophy, literature and art have fallen behind science. Can this loss of ground be made up?

According to Ionesco, "the theatre ought to be a concrete exploration or experiment; it should provide the opportunity to use our imagination to better advantage; it could be the unforeseen. I am thinking of the new American theatre, of the "happening," in which people appear suddenly on the stage and begin not only to imagine something but to live what they have envisioned, creating wholly unexpected events both for themselves and the audience" (*Entretiens*, p. 197). Thus, the playwright cherishes the ambition of modifying and enriching the inner vision we have of ourselves and of the universe by enabling us to enter the experience of intersubjective communication. We see in the mirror he holds out from the stage our "double." A new pair is formed—actor-spectator—which embodies all pairs, and all pairs of pairs glimpsed in the abstract mirror of the play. Hence the overwhelming joy when it whirls round in the oneness of Eros, freed from the burden of material reality, wrested from the destructive forces of nature and history in the completely coherent and fundamentally integrated universe of the theatrical performance. We also discover the innocent joys of our childhood when we used to climb on the merry-go-round, or ride the Ferris wheel tasting the exhilaration of space high above the fairground. Re-creation and recreation are corollary activities. Dramatic play-acting, like all human entertainment, aims at liberating us from the pressures of society, and from the stereotyped thoughts and conventions which become acquired reflex actions. Thus, it may well be that science, forced at the present moment into a utilitarian role, will appear in its complete form as a supremely imaginative and gratuitous activity of the mind.

By creating a confrontation of science and fiction within a dramatic experiment which is something of a gamble, Ionesco has in effect indulged in an intellectual activity which must be viewed as one of utmost earnestness.

Eugene Ionesco:
The Existential Oedipus

by Hugh Dickinson

> Even I cannot say whether I am a Christian or not, religious
> or not, a believer or not, a mystic or not; I can only say that
> my upbringing was Christian. The title of the play *Hunger and
> Thirst* is, in fact, biblical. We all hunger, we all thirst. Our
> hungers and thirsts are various: for the fruits of the earth, for
> water, for whisky, for bread; we hunger for love, for the abso-
> lute. The bread and wine and meat for which the hero Jean
> thirsts are only substitutes for what could have gratified a hun-
> ger and thirst for the absolute.[1]

I

The comic-tragic world of Eugene Ionesco is thoroughly, dev-
astatingly, modern—the last place we should look for myths. It is
filled with clutter and debris, yet it appears to bear no relation
to a living past. It is an enclave in time, cut off from the past and
also leading to no future other than an indefinite extension of its
dreary, and sometimes horrifying, self. The characters who people
it may each have had a past, yet they seem to come from nowhere
and to be going nowhere, although they are of course going to die.
They are prisoners of the present, so much so that it dominates
their lives, even to the point that they may come to wish for no

"Eugene Ionesco: The Existential Oedipus" by Hugh Dickinson. From *Myth
on the Modern Stage* by Hugh Dickinson (Urbana: University of Illinois Press,
1969). Reprinted by permission of the publisher.

[1] Eugene Ionesco, quoted in Simone Bemussa, *Eugène Ionesco* (Paris: Éditions
Seghers, 1966), pp. 8–9 (my translation).

I have borrowed for this chapter the title of the chapter on *Oedipus Rex* in
Richmond Y. Hathorn's excellent study, *Tragedy, Myth, and Mystery* (Bloom-
ington: Indiana University Press, 1962).

more than its indefinite continuance. Such a world is uncongenial to myths because myths give the present meaning by explaining the past and the future. Yet Ionesco's plays might serve as illustrations of what Antonin Artaud sought for the "theatre of cruelty": a way to extract from classical myths the powerful forces still struggling within them, while discarding their "defunct images."

From his earliest plays Ionesco has seemed intent on devising his own myths—myths based on his own experience of life—for his highly confessional theatre. The last thing one would expect him to do would be to dramatize classical myth. Take *Amédée; or, How to Get Rid of It*. It creates an original image to express marital guilt over the death of love, or to express "the ever greater and greater encroachment of death on our lives" [2]—that of a corpse in the bedroom that grows and grows until it shatters the door and fills the flat, while husband and wife accept its presence and try to carry on life from day to day. A playwright of such originality could well dispense with tales, however perdurable, handed down from distant times and places. He cannot, because he thinks mythically, entirely avoid resemblances to them. *Rhinoceros* evokes the myth of Ulysses resisting the spell of Circe while his men are transformed into swine. But Ionesco was writing from personal experience of fascism, and the evocation is incidental. *Exit the King* may remind us of *Everyman,* but only to make us aware of the distance separating medieval and modern man and their respective theatres. Again Ionesco's source was personal: "I wrote that work that I might learn to die." [3] Having contemplated the unthinkableness of death for insatiable man, he recreates the Faust legend in *Hunger and Thirst* and lets man satisfy his infinite longings—only to confront him with the same horror, now in the guise of eternity, that he faced when it was called extinction.

Writing directly from experience and his own responses to life, he developed a symmetry in his works that became more and more apparent as he systematically explored the dialectic of man's absurd condition. There is no solution; but there is an answer, and it is the same in both cases: "One can do nothing. One can do nothing. One can do nothing. One can do nothing." [4] If *The Pedestrian in Air* seems to rework the myth of Icarus almost by inadvertence, it

    [2] George E. Wellwarth, *The Theater of Protest and Paradox* (New York: New York University Press, 1964), p. 63.

    [3] Eugène Ionesco, *Journal en miettes* (Paris: Mercure de France, 1967), p. 167.

    [4] *Ibid.,* p. 39.

leaves it broken, truncated, without the clean shape of the catastrophe in which the young overreacher, having soared too near the sun, plummets to his death. His Icarus, Bérenger, takes a flight of the imagination only and returns "safely" to earth; but what he has seen of the infinite waste spaces of the universe leaves him a broken man within, one who can only return to the unutterable mystery of mundane existence. Given the paradox of existence that is Ionesco's beginning and ending, it seems unavoidable that any classic myth in his hands would break off, remain incomplete. However, the fourth play he wrote, *Victims of Duty* (1953), consciously borrows one of the most famous of all classic myths, that of King Oedipus, to embody the existential dilemma of modern man and also to exemplify the kind of theatre that Ionesco believes must supplant the theatre of the past.

Choubert, the anti-hero of *Victims of Duty*, voices Ionesco's critique of that theatre: "All the plays that have ever been written, from Ancient Greece to the present day, have never really been anything but thrillers. Drama's always been realistic and there's always been a detective about. Every play's an investigation brought to a successful conclusion. There's a riddle, and it's solved in the final scene. Sometimes earlier. You seek, and then you find. . . . The police arrive, there's an investigation and the criminal is unmasked. It's a thriller. A naturalistic drama, fit for the theatre of Antoine." [5] And the classics? "Refined detective drama. Just like naturalism." It is no accident that we think at once of Sophocles' tragedy, *Oedipus Rex*, that splendid thriller with its distinguished detective, its successful investigation, its solved riddle, and its unmasking; we are meant to do so. So far as the tragedy itself is concerned, it is easy to dispose of Ionesco's disparaging polemic. It is, as Richmond Hathorn points out, "only externally a crime-and-punishment play; internally it is a moral drama of self-recognition." [6] We can also exonerate it from any charge of being blood-and-thunder melodrama. Sophocles, in keeping with the law of decorum, relegates all violent deeds to the antecedent action or to the wings; whereas Ionesco, availing himself of the freedom of later theatre, which he also condemns, climaxes his play with an almost gratuitous murder committed on stage. What are the playwright's

---

[5] This and subsequent quotations from *Victims of Duty* are from *Three Plays by Eugène Ionesco: Amédée, The New Tenant, Victims of Duty,* trans. Donald Watson (New York: Grove Press, 1958), pp. 117–66.

[6] Hathorn, *Tragedy, Myth, and Mystery,* p. 90.

real objections, and what kind of drama would he have take its place?

His objections have to do with an Aristotelian emphasis upon plot, and a certain kind of plot, at that, and with style or method, which he labels "refined naturalism," by which he appears to mean pointless imitation of physical or external reality. He exaggerates grossly for polemical purposes: the theatre of Sophocles depended upon nonillusionistic conventions of playwriting and staging to an even greater degree than Ionesco's. What he does not state explicitly here is his objection to the Greek use of distinct genres, comedy and tragedy, and their strict maintenance. It is based upon his desire to realize in theatrical terms his personal view of life, which is that "the comic is tragic, and that the tragedy of man is pure derision." [7] He has explained this elsewhere: "In *Victims of Duty* I tried to sink comedy in tragedy: in *The Chairs,* tragedy in comedy or, if you like, to confront comedy and tragedy in order to link them in a new dramatic synthesis. But it is not a true synthesis, for these two elements do not coalesce, they coexist: one constantly repels the other, they show each other up, criticize and deny one another and, thanks to their opposition, thus succeed in maintaining a balance and creating tension. The two plays that best satisfy this condition are, I believe: *Victims of Duty* and *The New Tenant.*" [8]

There lies behind these esthetic objections a different metaphysic, a different view of man and existence. In Ionesco's "tragic farces" there is no place for the traditional hero or a heroic view of life. Greek tragedy pushed the exceptional man to the limits of his nature, simultaneously exalting the godlike in him and warning him of the dangers of self-intoxication, by centering his being in the active will. Just as Ionesco will not adopt alternatively two ways of looking at man in drama, tragedy and comedy, but insists on juxtaposing them in permanent clash, so he will not permit the magnification of man, or accept a belief in supernatural powers that influence or control his destiny; thus he gives us man suffering, rather than man active.

There is a further objection, especially pertinent to *Victims of Duty.* Even as it placed the tragic hero in high relief, Greek drama

    [7] Eugène Ionesco, "Experience of the Theatre," trans. Donald Watson, in Robert W. Corrigan and James L. Rosenberg, eds., *The Context and Craft of Drama* (San Francisco: Chandler, 1964), p. 286.
    [8] *Ibid.,* pp. 286–87.

bound him to the community; for the ongoing life of the group, its spiritual and physical health, were its basic concern: that was what it existed to celebrate. If the tragic hero was his people's redeemer, it was by becoming a sacrificial victim offered to restore health to man and the earth. Ionesco has no such faith to sustain him. Man's suffering and sacrifice can only appear meaningless to him. The Sphinx propounded the riddle of life to Oedipus. Ionesco's anti-hero will face the same riddle. His answer will be the same: man. For Ionesco, what else is there? But with what a difference! For he must also add: "One can do nothing." It is the anti-thesis of Gide or Sartre.

II

Victims of Duty is a five-character play that lists a sixth character in its *dramatis personae*—"MALLOT *with a t.*" This is a clue to the objective of the play's action, which is *to find Mallot*. The parallel with *Oedipus Rex* is close: "To find the slayer of Laius and lift the plague from the city of Thebes." The dramatic question the action raises is thus: Who is Mallot—what is his crime, and where shall we find him? Although a murder occurs later on in the play, no identifiable crime, plain or hidden, appears to be involved at the outset. We might expect the quest to be pointless, but it will not be: there *is* a Mallot. What seems pointless, yet is as unavoidable as it is inexplicable, is the fact of his guilt.

In proceeding in this fashion to examine *Victims of Duty*, I am making certain assumptions about drama and proposing to hold Ionesco's theory of drama to them. Theatre is the most human, and the closest to life, of all the arts. "It is based upon a pretense and its very nature calls out a multiplication of pretenses," says Thornton Wilder; hence, it invites the audience to use to the full its imagination, its powers of make-believe; and because of its very closeness to life, it not only permits but encourages an extreme degree of distortion on the playwright's part. It achieves all this through the frank employment of conventional, rather than naturalistic, devices.[9]

Ionesco seems to have been born knowing this, or to have learned

[9] Thornton Wilder, "Some Thoughts on Playwriting," in Corrigan and Rosenberg, *Context and Craft of Drama*, pp. 231–41.

it early and well as a child, watching the deliberate distortion of
life through fantasy that he found in Punch and Judy shows, with
their maximum demands upon the spectator's imaginative acceptance. (Behind every Ionesco play, whether or not it explicitly involves domestic squabbles as does the archetypal booth-show, is a
Punch and Judy scenario.) Regardless of what else we encounter in
Ionesco's theatre, we shall not be limited by realism; and *Victims
of Duty* is an outstanding example of the dramatist's innate ability
to break out of the bounds of time, place, and verisimilitude, and
yet to do so within the standard box-set of tables and chairs with
only, but appropriately enough, the addition of a toy stage.

Now, by all means let the playwright have as much freedom as
he needs, and let him depart as far from realism as he wishes, in
order to capture the particular sense of reality that it is his to give.
But the one thing without exception that he must be held to is that
his work constitute an action—and yes, that the imitation of that
action consist of a beginning, a middle, and an end. The playwright
may develop his plot on thematic principles or otherwise disregard
strict logical coherence to achieve his particular aim. He may prefer an entirely internal drama or one as full of external tussle as he
wishes. His play may, by design, be far more "theatrical" than it is
"dramatic," [10] or its action may be merely flaccid or attenuated because he could do no better; but a plot of some kind it must have.
Regardless of how disdainful of it Ionesco may claim to be, this
much resemblance between traditional drama and his own plays he
must allow.[11] A play that cannot be defined by its action is either
a poor play or not a play at all. This goes for Ionesco as for anyone
else. In assuming that *Victims of Duty* can be so defined, I have

[10] This distinction, a very useful one in dealing with existentialist drama and
the "theatre of the absurd," is made by Eric Bentley in his review of *Waiting for
Godot,* the *locus classicus* of the "theatrical" play, because its frame of action
consists of waiting, which by definition suspends the will and kills time.

To me "theatrical" is anything which achieves its desired effect through performance; "dramatic" involves consequential action, that is, significant change
directed to some aim or end. See Eric Bentley, *What Is Theatre?* (Boston: Beacon
Press, 1956).

[11] Kenneth Thorpe Rowe proceeds on the same assumption in *A Theatre in
Your Head* (New York: Funk & Wagnalls, 1960). He demonstrates that Ionesco's
The Chairs affirms "plot structure as the foundation of drama," despite Ionesco's
assertion: "I detest the reasoning play, constructed like a syllogism, of which the
last scenes constitute the logical conclusion of the introductory scenes, considered
as premises." Rowe says of *The Chairs:* "Never has a play moved with more relentless syllogistic logic from scene to scene . . ." (p. 109).

looked for it to pose a dramatic question (formulated above), and further assumed that it will answer it by providing the action with a crisis or turning-point that leads consequentially to a relevant climax.[12]

Ionesco believes that the surest way to achieve the universal is to concentrate to an extreme degree on the individual. We may therefore expect him to be highly subjective in his treatment of the Oedipus myth, and we shall waste our time if we insist on point-to-point correspondence. Despite his polemic approach, we should not expect him to satirize Sophocles by direct parody. With these allowances in mind, we may ask: how much of the myth will he reconstitute in his own work, how well will it serve his view of life, and will that work contain the essentials of drama?

At rise, we are in another of those *petit bourgeois* interiors, with the middle-aged Choubert reading the newspaper and his middle-aged wife Madeleine darning socks, just as Mr. and Mrs. Smith were doing at the opening of *The Bald Soprano*. But such placid domesticity in an apparently realistic style is disarming, a booby-trap for the unwary. Ionesco will shatter the placidity and the realistic illusion as soon as possible. We begin with a leap from the cosmic to the cloacal: "Nothing ever happens," says Choubert. "A few comets and a cosmic disturbance somewhere in the universe. Nothing to speak of. The neighbors have been fined for letting their dogs make a mess on the pavement. . . ." Very soon, and without quite knowing how, the unoffending Choubert is trying to help a shy young man (the Detective) locate a former tenant—by name Mallot, but whether with a "d" or "t," both Choubert and the Detective are uncertain. The whole action hinges on this apparently trivial question. Mallot has evidently become a criminal, but the detective begins to treat Choubert as if *he* were the guilty party.

The Detective's questioning of Choubert turns to bullying, then to brainwashing. Madeleine treacherously aids and abets the young man in this. Was it Mallot with a "d" or a "t"? From the outset, Choubert cannot remember. His attempt to do so turns into an effort to recapture the past, and this in turn plunges him into his own depths. The trail of memory that he follows under the Detective's interrogation becomes the way into his unconscious, his hidden emotional life. Time dissolves into an eternal present (there is

[12] Crisis and climax complete the "plot structure as the foundation of drama."

no past or future for the unconscious, only *now*), where all that Choubert has known and felt is stored up to be relived as keenly as if it were happening for the first time. (Choubert at one point even travels ahead in time, foreseeing his own old age and Madeleine's.)

The descent into the past and to the center of the self reveals terrible quarrels that took place between his parents while Choubert as a child looked on helplessly. His mother threatens suicide by poison; his father first tries to prevent her, then forces the poison on her. Madeleine appears as Choubert's mother in the flashbacks; in her own person she alternately joins the Detective in forcing Choubert to go down deeper and hesitates to go on with the interrogation, fearing that when he does so, she may lose him. Similarly, the Detective becomes Choubert's father in the flashbacks, while in his own person he keeps hammering at the helpless man: "You must never stop." At the same time, both Madeleine and the Detective are curiously detached, even calloused, observers of Choubert's agonized inward journey—a point which is explicitly acted out later in the play when they take seats as spectators while Choubert exposes his sufferings on the tiny stage.

Dying, his mother speaks to Choubert of his father: "*You must learn to forgive, my child, that's the hardest of all. . . . The time for tears will come, the time for repentance and remorse.* You must be good, you'll suffer for it if you're not and you never learn to forgive. When you see him, obey him, kiss him and forgive him." [13] We have already witnessed the tears she predicted. Now the theme of repentance, remorse, and forgiveness invests Choubert's quest with a wearisome burden of guilt that must be lifted: "*Who will have mercy on me?*" he cries. "*I could never forgive myself.*" For what? For his hatred of his father, for his hatred of his father's selfishness and violence; for his own pitilessness towards his father's frailties; most of all, for his own contempt: "You used to hit me, but I was stronger than you. My contempt hit you much harder. *That was what killed you, wasn't it?*" He defends himself: "Listen . . . I had to avenge my mother . . . I *had* to . . . What *was* my duty? . . . Did I really *have* to?" He has already asked his father to "forgive us as we forgave you." But his father has not answered: father cannot hear son, as son in turn cannot hear father; and he

---

[13] Here and below I have taken the liberty of underscoring those parts of the quoted passages of the play that stress the theme of guilt and forgiveness.

cries out again: *"Who will have mercy on me, I who have been unmerciful! Even if you did forgive me, I could never forgive myself!"*

Then, in an ironically counterpointed *tirade,* we hear the father's lament for all he felt, but never said to his son—the son who would be his murderer: "I lived in a perpetual state of rage. . . . The good I did turned into evil, but the evil done to me never turned into good. . . . I had a horror of mankind. . . . You were born, my son, just when I was about to blow our planet up. It was only your arrival that saved it. At least, it was you who stopped me from killing mankind in my heart. *You reconciled me to the human race and bound me irrevocably to the history, the crimes and hopes, despairs and disasters of all men. I trembled for their fate . . . and for yours."* The speech foreshadows the crisis of the play—that moment when Choubert elects to stay on earth and live his life in society. There is further irony in that the thing which his father had wished to communicate but could not was the very thing that proved crucial in his son's life. (Unheeded, Choubert had told his father: "If you would look at me, you'd see how alike we are.")

The father, like Laius of old, had tried to kill his child: "My head," he says, "was spinning with unspeakable remorse to think I'd not wanted a family and had tried to stop you coming into the world. *You might never have been, never have been!"* This last idea is fundamental to Ionesco's thought. In a journal entry, meditating his own death, he says of his life: "Yet this will have existed. No one can prevent this from having existed." [14] Two men meet and come to blows: the father who had rage in his heart until his son's birth "justified and redeemed all the disasters of history," and the son whom he once tried to kill. They meet and come to blows—not once and fatally as stranger on a roadway, but often as strangers in the same house where the son felt the father's presence to be a barrier on his own road to life.

Where is Jocasta in all this? Richard Coe says *Victims of Duty* may be interpreted as "a dramatic illustration of Freud on dreams, or a satire on the Oedipus-complex." [15] If so, we have to do not only with the Oedipus myth and the Oedipus tragedy, but also with the Oedipus-complex! In which latter case, the figure of Jocasta becomes

[14] Eugène Ionesco, "Selections from the Journal," trans. Rosette C. Lamont, in *Yale French Studies,* No. 29 ("The New French Dramatists"), n.d., p. 4.

[15] Richard N. Coe, *Ionesco* (New York: Grove Press, 1961), p. 108.

even more important. Wallace Fowlie, speaking of *Victims of Duty,* ascribes to dream and mythology the figure of "the son in the dual role of slayer of his father and of redeemer" and stresses the influence of the mother: "Under the power of the maternal force in this household, both father and son attempt to justify their existences." [16] Dramatically speaking, Ionesco is nowhere explicit; if incest and oedipal conflict are there, they are so obliquely and by inference. Theatrically, however, the answer to the question is plain: Jocasta is there before our eyes, embodied in the actress playing both *wife* and *mother.*

In the first episode of Choubert's journey backward in time and downward into himself, Madeleine changes markedly from the humdrum housewife to the seductive woman she once was and uses her allurements to beckon him onward: "Hold tight the handrail . . . Down . . . go on down . . . if it's me you want!" In middle-age she is bossily maternal but never affectionate: she shows no love for her husband. In both stages of her husband's quest—the descent into the unconscious and the ascent into the empyrean—she is like Jocasta in first urging him forward to find Mallot, then trying to stop him when she thinks she may lose him; similarly Jocasta sought to dissuade Oedipus when she saw that what the oracle foretold had come true.

Her alliance with the Detective is evident from the outset. It is she who invites him to enter their flat and she who induces her husband to help him find Mallot. The Detective represents law and authority, which in the play are totalitarian. Madeleine subscribes to the government's propaganda about practicing renunciation and detachment, which are euphemisms for individual irresponsibility in letting the government take over and invade the citizen's private life. In any situation involving her husband and authority, Madeleine sides with the latter. It is interesting to consider the role of Madeleine-Jocasta in the light of Erich Fromm's interpretation of the myth, where the myth is seen as having as its central theme "one of the fundamental aspects of interpersonal relationships, the attitude toward authority";[17] for this theme is central to *Victims of Duty* also.

[16] Wallace Fowlie, *Dionysus in Paris: A Guide to Contemporary Theater* (New York: Meridian Books, 1960), p. 234.

[17] Erich Fromm, *The Forgotten Language* (New York: Rinehart, 1951, pp. 195–96, 202 *et seq.*

The myth, says Fromm, symbolizes "the rebellion of the son against the authority of the father in the matriarchal family"; and the roots of the struggle go far back into the ancient fight between the patriarchal and the matriarchal systems of society. The matriarchal system with woman as lawgiver in both family and society emphasized sexual promiscuity, ties of blood and of soil, and passive acceptance of all natural phenomena. It held that all men are equal, that the happiness of man is the aim of life, and that human life and existence represent the supreme value. By contrast, the patriarchal system invested in the father the final authority in the home as well as the dominant role in a hierarchically organized society that gave predominance to rational thought, undertook to change or control natural phenomena, and stressed respect for manmade law. In fact, it made obedience to authority the main virtue of life. Jocasta, says Fromm, in consenting to the killing of Oedipus, performed an act that, although legitimate from the patriarchal view, constituted the unforgivable crime from the standpoint of matriarchal ethics. She was betraying the role of woman as wife and mother, the life-giver and life-nourisher. And since human life and happiness are the aim of matriarchal society, it follows that capitulation to the hard, abstract reign of force imposed by the patriarchal system was treachery to the child and to woman's own nature.

Madeleine's turning against her husband is unconsciously done because it is habitual. She treats his sufferings with annoyance and nagging or, worse, with calloused detachment that would be impossible if she loved him. Richard Coe, recalling "the horrifying sadistic glee of Madeleine as she watches her husband tortured" in the brainwashing episode at the center of the action, remarks: "In this deliberate destruction and betrayal of the inner life, for fear 'of what the neighbors say,' woman, in Ionesco's world, is guiltier far than man. Adam is betrayed by Eve. Choubert is betrayed by Madeleine . . . and betrayed in the most cruel and sordid manner, to the police." [18]

Who is the Detective? What does his menacing figure represent? Since Ionesco is nothing if not a metaphysical writer, we might expect him to make the Detective the equivalent of Tiresias, with more than human power. But he does not. Theatrically, the role, like Madeleine's, provides a double image not merely in that the Detective is shy and polite at first, then cruel and brutal, but also

in that he is young enough to be Choubert's son, and therefore in
the scenes of father-son conflict, the ages of the actors are reversed.
An entry in Ionesco's journal may ultimately help us identify this
representative of the police. Ionesco, describing therein an erotic
dream he had, tells how he tried to interpret it to his friend Z. He
had wished to make love to an unknown woman, but everything
conspired to foil him. Police shadowed him. He had to catch a train.
He lost his luggage. People blocked the corridors. And so on. "The
police are my conscience, of course," said Ionesco. "I wanted to
leave, but my luggage prevented me. I wanted to take my luggage
with me." *"No,"* replied Z., *"in reality you did not wish to be free.
Your luggage was an excuse, a pretext. It is precisely your luggage
you would have to give up if you truly wished to be free."* [19]

Shall we see the Detective as conscience, that is, as Choubert's
own moral sense, originating with him? Or shall we take him to be
a kind of Freudian super-ego, the representative of public opinion,
the censure of The Others? If the latter, then we have a standard
of custom imposed upon the person from without but regarded by
the unquestioning citizens as an absolute standard of right and
wrong. And does such a standard reflect a metaphysical order of
good and evil? It will not do so in Ionesco's play. So it raises a question as to whether the guilt Choubert feels has a rational basis, or
whether it is irrational only.

In Sophocles' play, the king's unseen antagonist is Apollo, and
it is the victory of the god that is signalized in the catastrophe. (Tiresias, his representative, warned Oedipus away from undertaking the
quest and so did just the opposite of the relentless Detective.) But
there is no God in Choubert's world, or in Ionesco's either; and the
playwright cannot make the Detective stand for anything more than
human. Unlike Apollo, the antagonist is there before our eyes
throughout. But he is not alone. Madeleine and, later, Nicolas d'Eu
and the Lady are antagonists also, because they are his allies. He
represents the state, an abstraction that stands for society, for The
Others, without whose consent he could not do what he does. But
Choubert is also his own antagonist, for there is something in him
—Ionesco cannot name it or explain it—that makes him a party to
the crime of the Many against the One, even when he is that one;
hence, he is a sharer in the universal guilt by which the state and
The Others impose their will.

      [19] Ionesco, *Journal en miettes*, pp. 107–8 (my translation, emphasis added).

Choubert appears on the toy stage, groping his way like a blind Oedipus to find out who he is. Madeleine and the Detective sit to watch him, like unsympathetic playgoers. As he journeys toward the center of himself, Choubert sees in the distance a magical city, "fountains and flowers of fire in the night . . . a palace of icy flames, glowing statues and incandescent seas, continents blazing in the night, in oceans of snow!" Conflicting emotions that both rend and heal overwhelm him: "I feel strong. I feel weak, I feel ill, I feel well, *but I feel, above all, I feel myself, still, I feel myself.*"

But at the very center, the magical world of light vanishes and night surrounds him, "only one butterfly of light painfully rising. . . ." The curtains of the toy stage close and Choubert vanishes, to reappear only after he has begun to surface. At the supreme moment of self-assertion, he drew back from the brink of death: extinction. This is the crisis of the play, or rather its first main crisis. *Victims of Duty* may be structurally unique in requiring two crises, each the equal of the other metaphysically and hence as indispensable as the other in depicting the dialectic of human absurdity. At the second and final crisis, the same fate will confront him: death, extinction. And again he will have to choose.

In inducing Choubert to retreat and try a new tack, the Detective makes a significant appeal:

> You must realize Mallot's got to be found again. *It's a question of life and death. It's your duty. The fate of all mankind depends on you.* . . . Remember and then everything will come clear again. . . . [*To MADELEINE*]: He'd gone down too far. He's got to come up again . . . A little . . . in our estimation.

One might expect that Choubert, having recovered his essential self, would break free of the Detective's domination when he comes back to the surface, but he does not. Instead, influenced by that appeal to duty, he continues to turn over his memories, trying to share them with Madeleine. He remembers Mallot's nickname: Montbéliard. "Why yes, good Lord, yes," he exclaims. "It's true . . . it's funny, it's true." And with this, the direction changes: Choubert goes off in search of him above ground, across oceans, forests, the mountains of Europe. He begins a mystic ascent, a painful, exhausting climb up sheer walls of rock. "He mustn't rise too high above us," says Madeleine, beginning to vacillate at the danger of this new course. But the Detective, adamant, drives him on: "You must be a man to the

bitter end. . . . Come on now, one last effort." When Choubert
reaches the mountain peak and can see right through the sky, however, there's no sign of Montbéliard. Here again, at the opposite
pole, are freedom and affirmation: "I'm alone. . . . I can run without walking! . . . I'm not dizzy. . . . *I'm not afraid to die anymore.*"

Now the Detective realizes that Madeleine was right: "I've driven
him too far. Now he's getting away from us. . . . My dear old chap,
we've both got on the wrong track." They redouble their appeals to
Choubert. Madeleine plays on his sympathy: "It's not good to be
alone. You can't leave us. . . ." She pretends to be an old woman
starving for bread: "Have pity, pity!" They solicit Choubert with
"all the advantages of everyday life in society": sensual pleasures,
wealth, position, security, patriotism, revenge, fame, power, a second
chance at life. "If you like," says the Detective, "you can start life
afresh, learn to walk again . . . fulfill your ambitions." And always
there is the appeal to duty.

But Choubert appears unheeding. He is transformed, bodiless. He
can fly. "I'm bathing in the light. . . . The light is seeping through
me. *I'm so surprised to be, surprised to be, surprised to be.*" But
suddenly, mysteriously, distress overcomes him. He feels ill. He cannot bear it—and he jumps. This is the second and final crisis.

"The act of climbing or ascending," says Mircea Eliade, "symbolizes *the way towards the absolute reality;* and to the profane consciousness, the approach towards that reality arouses an ambivalent
feeling, of fear and of joy, of attraction and repulsion. . . ." [20] Choubert had been ecstatic. "I no longer fear death!" he had cried. But
when it seemed that the moment of deliverance was at hand, he
could not, or would not, break free; instead, he jumped.

Choubert awakes, presumably "himself" again. "Where am I?" He
finds it strange that Monsieur Chief Inspector is still there, even
stranger that the Detective found his way into his memories. *"A new
character, a LADY, who takes no notice at all of what is going on,"*
has appeared and sits to one side. The Detective resumes his bullying and takes all credit for having rescued Choubert, while insisting
that the search continue. Madeleine, too, resumes her badgering.
From here on, Choubert regresses outwardly, becoming more and
more babyish.

[20] Mircea Eliade, *Images and Symbols: Studies in Religious Symbolism,* trans.
Philip Mairet (New York: Sheed & Ward, 1961), p. 51.

Again the moment has passed when we feel that Choubert might have asserted himself. But the reversal does not take place. On the downward journey, he had found himself; in the empyrean, he had lost his fear of death; but the fall to earth returns him to the bondage of the waking world and to life in society. A change of sorts occurs, nonetheless: there enters a preposterous but formidable figure, a writer named Nicolas d'Eu. At once the Detective finds himself on the defensive, even contemplates flight. But he is reassured when Nicolas says: "Carry on, carry on, don't let me interrupt you!" Madeleine, meanwhile, returns to her original character, and at the Detective's barked request races back and forth from kitchen to living room, bringing cups of coffee until all the surfaces are covered with them.

The Detective continues his hypnotic domination of Choubert: "I'll give you back your strength. You can't find Mallot, because you've got gaps in your memory. We're going to plug those gaps!" He forces bread on Choubert, who begins to stuff himself like a reluctant child. The Detective tries to win over Nicolas d'Eu, who asks him his attitude toward renunciation and detachment. "My duty, you know, my dear Sir," says the Detective, "is simply to apply the system." Nicolas also chats incongruously (if anything is incongruous in this chaotic world) about theatre, and we come back to the idea proposed earlier: "I've thought a great deal about the chances of reforming the theatre. Can there be anything new in the theatre?"

Nicolas wants a theatre that reflects the tone of the age, utilizes a new kind of psychology, a different logic, based on contradictions: "We'll get rid of the principle of identity and unity of character and let movement and dynamic psychology take its place. . . . We are not ourselves. . . . Personality doesn't exist." As I see it, Nicolas here plays the devil's advocate and is not straightforward spokesman for the dramatist, even though he asserts: "We've got Ionesco and Ionesco, that's enough!" There is ambiguity in the statement: "We'll get rid of identity and unity of character." It sounds like faded Pirandellism or a totalitarian slogan. Choubert's twofold quest, surrealist and oneirical as it may have been, affirmed the existence of self at opposite extremes. That self persists beneath all the distortions and confusions that society creates in a person's consciousness. Its essential awareness is that of surprise: "I'm so surprised to be, surprised to be, surprised to be. . . ."

The tension increases as Nicolas challenges the Detective and the latter defends himself while continuing to force bread into the babyish Choubert: "Why Monsieur Nicolas d'Eu, I'm only doing my duty! I didn't come here just to pester him! I've really got to find out where he's hiding, Mallot with a t at the end. There's no other way I can do it. I've no choice. As for your friend (Choubert)—and I hope one day he'll be mine. . . . I respect him, sincerely I do!" Duty, regardless of what action it may require, becomes a categorical imperative. Everything one does can be justified by appeal to authority. Conscience has abdicated. Renunciation and detachment have won. The state is supreme. Nicolas' manner becomes more dangerous as the Detective weeps and protests: "I didn't want to upset your friend! . . . I swear I didn't! . . . It's he who forced *me* to come into this flat. . . . *I* didn't want to, I was in a hurry. . . . They insisted, both of them. . . . I'm only a pawn, Monsieur, a soldier tied to his orders. . . ." Suddenly, Nicolas brandishes a knife and thrice stabs the Detective, who dies crying: "I am . . . a victim . . . of duty!" Madeleine, impervious to the violent death except as a nuisance, takes out her annoyance on Nicolas: "It's such a pity it had to happen in our flat! . . . Who's going to help us find Mallot now? . . . We've got to find Mallot! His sacrifice [*indicating the DETECTIVE*] shall not have been in vain! Poor victim of duty!" Echoing her, Nicolas now assumes the Detective's role and badgers Choubert: "Come on, eat, eat, to plug the gaps in your memory!" Choubert protests: "I'm a victim of duty, too!" And Madeleine: "We're all victims of duty! . . . Swallow! Chew!" Now they are all at it, including the Lady, who up to now had simply looked on. "[*While all the characters are ordering one another to chew and swallow, the curtain falls.*]"

A beginning, a middle—and an end of sorts, although the process may be assumed to continue indefinitely in this surrealist nightmare of man in society. Because Ionesco wishes to show Choubert as victim to the end, he introduces Nicolas to provide a climax by killing his antagonist, only to become his persecutor in turn. But then, as Madeleine says, "We are all victims of duty." Or as Sartre, Ionesco's *bête-noire*, might say: "Hell is the others." The conclusion seems to be that each of us is Choubert, *but also one of The Others.* Conceivably, Ionesco could rewrite his play with Madeleine as the central figure, or the Detective, or Nicolas, or even the Lady, and repeat the essential action with variations to suit the particular person. It is merely a matter of point of view. For this is another parable about Everyman and the inescapable experience of man's existence among his fellows. The dialectic of downward and upward, of the subjective and the objective, of the self and others, carries throughout. The action ends, as it must, in an impasse of paradox and surprise, because this is Ionesco's existential or metaphysical view. And the form and tone of the play extend its dialectic, with the comic and tragic, the frightening and the funny, seen as coexistent and coextensive. Life is not an alternation of the tragic and the ridiculous; it is both things at once, or the same thing viewed simultaneously in its two aspects.

As Ionesco's theatre has developed, its unity and consistency have become clearer. Each play tends to throw light on the others, so that beyond the shock of their bizarre theatricality we can see how they are related. In this respect, two plays seem to me especially useful as coordinates in placing *Victims of Duty: Amédée,* produced the same year, and the later *Rhinoceros.* In *Amédée* the protagonist escapes from his intolerable situation simply by flying away with his burden of guilt while protesting to his wife and the neighbors he leaves behind: "I didn't want to run away from my responsibilities. It's the wind, *I* didn't do anything! . . . It's not on purpose! . . . Not of my own free will! . . . Forgive me, Ladies and Gentlemen, I'm terribly sorry! Forgive me!" This is escape drama in both senses of the term: a vivid fantasy, and an evasion on the playwright's part, as if he could not think how else to end his play. In taking the easy way out, he negates the essence of human nature as he showed it in *Victims of Duty,* and as it will appear in *Rhinoceros.* Amédée's resort to flight repudiates his humanity. This transcendence may free him from earth, but it also leaves him alone, cut off from his fellows. Honor Matthews has examined *Amédée* in connection with the theme of Cain and Abel in the theatre: "The weight of responsibility which will inevitably involve men with the weight of failure and of guilt, appears to be essential for the life which we recognize as human, and, if this pattern were ever to be broken, life as we know it would end." [21]

---

[21] Honor Matthews, *The Primal Curse: The Myth of Cain and Abel in the Theatre* (London: Chatto & Windus, 1967), p. 214. She calls *Amédée* "a fantasy of the integrated self" in which Amédée accepts the fact of his deed (the murder of love) and, by taking its consequences upon himself, transcends the limitations of his human condition, but at the cost of his nature.

Her further comment brings us to *Rhinoceros,* which in its situation is the obverse of *Victims of Duty,* and to a different solution: "So long as man desires his brother's keeping he must be his brother's keeper." [22] Like so many of his plays, *Rhinoceros* has its source in Ionesco's own life. As an adolescent in Rumania during the rise of fascism there, he saw people all around him joining the Iron Guard: "Everyone except me. Somehow, I didn't espouse the reigning ideology. To this day I still don't know how it happened. All I know is that I was quite alone." [23] Bérenger, the frightened "hero in spite of himself," as Ionesco calls him, feels that something must be done to save the world where everyone is going mad and turning into a rhinoceros; he even feels that he alone can do it (though he knows that is not true), but also that others ought not to leave him to do it by himself. So there he sits, half of him wishing he had joined the others in their trumpeting, the other half of him resisting. At the close, he is not even sure that he *can* hold out. But something inside him—a sense of duty—tells him he must try. Ionesco's dialectic of the absurd reduces itself to two propositions: His duty to humanity is the same as his duty to his own nature; for to betray himself is somehow to betray the others, and to betray the others is somehow to betray himself. Keeping faith (and it is a faith, for he does not know *why* it is so, only that it *is* so), he will not be able to say, "I am free." He will probably not be able to say, "I no longer fear death." But by his constancy he will have affirmed something without which neither statement would have any meaning or worth.

Ionesco presents an action that is an ironic inversion of ancient symbols and a picture of life that is at once funny and demonic. What we see in *Victims of Duty* is a mocking parody of the individual's initiation into society, into a new state of being, but without the supernatural meaning that initiation symbolized in older societies: " 'Initiation' means, as we know, the symbolic death and resurrection of the neophyte, or in other contexts, the descent into Hell followed by ascension into Heaven. Death—whether initiatory or not —is the supreme case of the rupture of the planes [of reality]," says Mircea Eliade.[24] The initiate, having undergone death and rebirth,

[22] *Ibid.*
[23] Quoted in Walter Wager, ed., *The Playwrights Speak* (New York: Delacorte Press, 1967), p. 158.
[24] Eliade, *Images and Symbols,* p. 49. See also p. 132 [The Existential Oedipus].

is by definition *one who knows*. As Ionesco presents him in Choubert, he is one who, through suffering that is communally inflicted, experiences the most intense life as he approaches absolute reality, both at the center of himself and at the center of the world, but who, afterward as well as before, *cannot remember*. This ritual of initiation is a ritual of alienation. He returns from his intense inner life to what is, by contrast, a zombie existence, a living death. Choubert's "death" cannot, like Oedipus' exile, lift the plague from society. Society *is* the plague. All its members are, like Choubert, mutilated. This is not the tragedy of an exceptional man who suffered a peculiarly horrible fate; it is the laughable tragedy of the ordinary man whose fate is irrational, gratuitous, and without meaning, all the more so for being unavoidable.

In the nonreligious world depicted in Ionesco's play, Choubert's quest for the ineffable in himself or in the transcendent world must end in failure, for it is not to be found in the profane life of the modern, desacralized *petit bourgeois* interior. "All that we dream is capable of realization," Ionesco has said. Artistically, perhaps; existentially, by no means. That is his burden in play after play. He dreams of the absolute, but cannot achieve it; he speaks of God, but cannot believe in him.

There is further irony in the means whereby Choubert is driven to search for Mallot with a t. What appears to be a brutal police interrogation also resembles psychoanalysis, a technique of remembering that is, however incidentally painful, ultimately intended to heal by bringing the patient to a new state of knowledge. But psychoanalysis itself reflects, on the plane of philosophic naturalism, the initiatory pattern of the ancient religious ordeals; and, as with them, there hangs over the crises in Choubert's unconscious a religious or mystical aura to which Ionesco can give no name.[25]

Once you have grasped the extent of evil, of cruelty and meaninglessness, in this waking world to which the initiate returns, you find it amazing that the playwright can hold to his conviction that man's plight is ridiculous, and that he can exemplify it in plays that are both horrible and funny. Ionesco does not mince words: "If you have been everywhere a foreigner and a stranger, as I have, you find that cruelty and hatred are the dominant factors in human affairs.

[25] Mircea Eliade, *The Sacred and the Profane: The Nature of Religion*, trans. Willard R. Trask (New York: Harper & Row, 1961), pp. 208, 210.

That's a discovery I've never got over—that people are out to kill one another; if not directly, then indirectly." [26] The guilt in *Victims of Duty* is only partly irrational—that is, arbitrarily imposed from without. It also springs from a desire to kill one's brother (whatever the actual relationship may be); and that desire, even without the deed, constitutes a grave crime and produces real guilt. What to Ionesco is absurd is that he does not know why this should be so; it simply is so. And if he does not resign himself to it, neither does he deny it.

We cannot, therefore, regard the individual man (Choubert or another) as good, and the group as evil. Ionesco does not subscribe to the old maxim: "The senate is a beast, the senators are good men." Nor will he subscribe to Rousseau's sentimental variant of it: "Men are good by nature and made bad by society." Yet he cannot subscribe to the older view: "Man is a fallen creature with a natural bias to do evil." [27] He cannot, although the play is suffused with a nostalgia for something precious that has been lost. His is a darker view: "As soon as an idea, a conscious intent, wish to be realized in historical terms, they are disfigured, become the opposite of what they were, turn monstrous. Social conditions may be based on the opposition which exists between conscious thought and the obscure tendencies which work against a concrete realization of the idea. . . . Does man always claim to do the opposite of what he deeply wishes?" [28] It is as if there were a demonic reversal operating at the heart of things. A conscious wish to do good at once releases an unconscious wish to do evil. The process is apparently not reversible: there is no indication that a conscious wish to do evil creates an unconscious wish to do good. That is why it is truly demonic. Choubert's father had cried out in his grief: "The good I did turned into evil, but the evil done to me never turned into good. . . ."

And where does art stand in this equation—art that is for Ionesco a sovereign good, a "secular prayer," solace in an absurd world, but that has its source in that same unconscious?

[26] Quoted by Vera and John Russell, "Ionesco on Death," *Chicago Sun-Times,* September 15, 1963.

[27] The latter two quotes are by W. H. Auden, "Criticism in a Mass Society," in Geoffrey Grigson, ed., *The Mint,* No. 2 (London: Routledge & Kegan Paul, 1948), p. 7.

[28] Ionesco, "Selections from the Journal," p. 6. Here he is very close to Sartre, who ascribes our insincerity and bad faith to that part of ourselves which we refuse to acknowledge.

For man's struggle to find his own center, of which Schlegel had spoken so urgently, Ionesco substitutes a vision of "racial introversion" reduced to a single motive: murderous hate. We see it as much in the persecution of Choubert as in the slaying of the Detective. It is through hate, not love, says Ionesco, that we are members one of another. We are bound by its invisible web, and there is no escaping it, except at the cost of our humanity or our life—and these turn out to be one and the same.

In view of this, one might think that Ionesco would end by echoing the sentiment of that Greek tragedian who concluded his masterpiece of "distinguished naturalism" with: "Never to have been born is best." But the modern playwright remains paradoxical. "I'm surprised to be," says Choubert; and the astonishment of consciousness, despite all its anguish, seems to Ionesco well worth it. That Ionesco should emerge as a playwright of affirmation is the most astonishing thing of all, but it is a fact which *Victims of Duty* demonstrates, and which his subsequent plays make even more apparent. It is why Ionesco can write in his journal: "A dream I will no longer remember will be that of universal existence, the dream of my actual self. 'What did I dream?' I ask myself often as I wake up with a hazy remembrance of captivating things which have disappeared in the night of eternal forgetfulness. The only thing I am left with is the regret of being unable to remember. I will die, torn abruptly from the dream of reality. . . . I will not remember, nor will there be an 'I' to do the remembering. *Yet this will have existed. No one can prevent this from having existed.*" [29]

Not even God.

[29] *Ibid.,* p. 4.

Ionesco's *L'Impromptu de l'Alma:*
A Satire of Parisian Theater Criticism

by Peter Ronge

Introduction

According to the author's allegation, the play *L'Impromptu de l'Alma,* written in 1955, is the only one of his dramatic works whose genesis cannot be traced to what he calls an "état affectif." Here, the creative impulse lies in the desire to dramatize a consciously selected subject which can be summed up in the following manner: "Theater critics attempt to influence an author to abandon his own concepts of the theater and to accept others, perverted ones."

The dramatization of this subject turns into a satirical comedy. As such, it is bound to two complexes of conditions which are of equal importance for the genesis and structure of the play. The first consists of an existent circle of people whose speech patterns and thought processes are incriminated. It is from this material that the author draws—sometimes in the form of source texts—the linguistic and intellectual matter, as well as the psycho-sociological models required to shape part of his *personae.* His satiric *volunctas auctoris* is directed towards ridiculing these existent models together with their ideas and ideologies and towards preventing them from gaining public ascendancy. The second results from the need to make the satire eminently clear and understandable, so that the intended individuals, or types they represent can be readily identified by the audience or reader. To further this end, certain formal and technical means must construct and maintain the recognizability of the satiric intent. The former are to be found, for example, in the works of the great satirists of French literature, Rabelais and Molière. Since the title of Ionesco's play echoes Molière's famous *Improptu de Versailles,* one can safely assume that the *calque* of the title is a form of opening or introduction to a more encompassing parallelism.

In the following sections, the structure of the play will be examined. We hope to prove that Ionesco's *Impromptu* is a traditional contribution to the reflective type of dramatic literature called "theater about theater," one which he obviously holds in high esteem.

Structure and Structural Characteristics of the Impromptu

The genesis of the over-all structure of *L'Impromptu de l'Alma* can be traced to two complexes of conditions: preserved traditional schemata of satire (source: Molière) and relationships in need of criticism (subject and source for the satirical presentations: R. Barthes, the semioclastic critic, B. Dort, the ideologue of "Theatre Populaire," and J. J. Gautier, the dramatic critic of *Le Figaro,* a representative of bourgeois theater criticism.) We will now examine closely the interweaving of the individual elements which form the structure of the play.

One can discern a tripartite division in a play, otherwise free of exterior structural separations into act or scene: a somewhat lengthy exposition (11, 1 to 18, 9), followed by a middle section (18, 10 to 55, 8) divided into seven major phases, and finally an epilogue (55, 8 to 58, 6).[1] The criteria for the divisions arise in the exposition phase from the introduction of the Bartholomeus group into the specific stage *locus,* Ionesco's "stage" workroom, and, when it comes to dialogue, from the initial, at first seemingly harmless contact established between the parties. The major phases of the middle part are separated from one another by the shifts in the dialogue situations. It is there that an "attempt at re-educating" Ionesco is made. Undertaken by the three B.s it founders at the very moment of apparent success. The final section clearly contrasts with the rest of the play to which it refers critically, letting itself be recognized as a play within a play.

[1] The divisions in the parentheses refer to pages in Eugene Ionesco, *Théâtre II* (Paris: Gallimard, 1958) which contains *L'Impromptu de l'Alma,* and to the particular tirade on each page.

We will now proceed to a description of the principal elements of the levels of objectivity and their concepts, the presentation of which is the major goal of the text. These reveal themselves in structure and disposition as functions—esthetic not effective—of the satirical intentions of the author.

The five characters in the play: Ionesco, Bartholomeus I, II, III, and Marie, are drawn schematically as types. Some rough character traits are provided. There is no serious attempt at characterization for even the *dramatis persona,* Ionesco, is stereotyped.

Ionesco, a dramatist upholding one point of view of the *Impromptu,* plays the role of a modest, patient, timid and submissive pupil. This attitude contrasts with that of the opposing parties which become dominant by virtue of number (there are three B.s) as well as by the nature of the relationships they establish.

The three B.s are immodest, impatient, aggressive, and, above all, terrified by all those who express views or opinions different from the ones they state. They are clearly slaves to hair-splitting pedantry. Their steering of the dialogue, and the content of their discourse reveal the following differentiation within the trio: B.I and B.II are representatives of a politically and culturally "leftist" psychosocial type. Their vocabulary and their faith in the dialectic method betray their adhesion to the ideology of progress; they seek the protection of established reputations, authorities in the field. B.II tends a bit more towards conciliation than B.III who is noteworthy for his anti-intellectual hedonism and pronounced xenophobia—traits which represent the mentality of the conservative or "reactionary" variant of the psycho-social type. B.III is also ignorant, the perfect common denominator of the audience he addresses: dull, silly gigglers.

Ionesco's cleaning woman, Marie, is a typical *femme du peuple.* Her prejudices and preferences are those most commonly associated with the concept of common sense (*le bon sens*). She can be compared to similar figures in Ionesco's plays such as the two *concierges* in *The Killer* and *The New Tenant,* as well as the devoted *bonne* in *The Lesson,* and is a recognizable literary descendant of Molière's Dorine (*Tartuffe*) and his Nicole (*Le Bourgeois Gentilhomme*).

All five characters are functions of the stage treatment of the subject stated above: "Ionesco and theater criticism."

Freely adapted from the Molière *servante,* Marie provides a direct reference to traditional satire, not unlike the above-mentioned elements of the scholar or pedant comedy. The *bon sens* of this naturally reasonable if uneducated person provides a sharp contrast with the ideological obstinacy (for Ionesco this trait can be equated with a lack of true culture) of the three B.s. A member of the *petite bourgeoisie,* the maid is refreshingly ignorant of the attitudes of "left-wing intellectuals." B.I and B.II detest the class represented by Marie, and consider themselves an anti-bourgeois elite. Thus, if a functional comparison can be made between Marie and Dorine, one can say that the *dramatis persona* Ionesco corresponds in the typology of comedy to Orgon in *Tartuffe,* in that he belongs, temporarily, to the type which is open to ideological persuasion, as Orgon was when he became the victim of Tartuffe. Marie's function, however, is not limited to providing static contrast. On the contrary, she has a dynamic role to play; she brings about the catastrophe of the play. After the completion of the education *d'un auteur* by the three B.s whose victim is awakened by a slap in the face from a quasi-hypnotic trance, it is Marie who disrespectfully drives the "doctors" from the stage with her broom, thus ending the play within the play.

Ionesco, the *dramatis persona,* must not be viewed as an attempt at psychological interpretation. No self-portrait this. The modestly submissive author has nothing in common with the "real" writer of *L'Impromptu de l'Alma.* The character provides the necessary counterpart to the exaggeratedly pedantic traits of the three B.s whose authoritarian intolerance, in turn, mirrors the inadequately reflective self-assurance of their "real" counterparts when they judge and condemn plays and theatrical performances. Thus, B.III (Gautier) always protests in the name of "good taste" and other equally vague, and subjective aesthetic categories. B.I and B.II raise their opposition in the name of social and scientific progress, that is of supposedly objective norms. The modesty of the character Ionesco is a contrasting correlative to the aggressiveness of the B.s; it is necessitated by the dramatic development of the satirical subject matter, the process of "re-education." The combined workings of *Ionesco*'s pupil-like subordination and the demanding, teacher-like conduct of the professors of theatrology, fosters the comic explosion of *Ionesco*'s about face. It is in this way that the basic premises for the drastic catastrophe are set up: the intellectual pretensions of the three B.s collapse, swept by the cleaning-woman's broom, a direct symbol of the cathartic action of healthy common sense.

The Action

Under "action" one can include here the totality of the characters'
altercations, in dialogue or physical action, as well as their motives
and affairs. The action can be summarized as follows:

A theater critic and *docteur en théâtralogie* by the name of B.I,
supporter of an "ultra-popular" and "ultra-scientific" theater visits,
in official dress, the playwright *Ionesco,* in order to question him
about his latest work and to hear a sample text from it, which, indeed, is offered him. The complete identity of the work in progress
with the stage reality (the visit of *B.I* to *Ionesco*) is thus demonstrated. In the course of the reading, a second theater critic and
docteur en théâtralogie, also in official dress, B.II, enters, followed
at once by a third, B.III. The latter two also insist on a test reading
which is synchronized with the reality of the stage action. Consequently, a convergence occurs between the "play" and the "play
within the play." B.I defines what has been called "cercle vicieux"
(18, 3) and his colleague B.II recommends locking out any people
who may knock at Ionesco's door. Thus ends the protasis or exposition of the play (11, 1–18, 9).

The definition of the first part as a *cercle vicieux,* and the ensuing
suggestion not to allow anyone else to enter, lead to a "party" dialogue as a *1st discussion phase,* in which *Ionesco* criticizes the paradoxical "philosophical" dialectic of his visitors *B.I and B.II* and
takes exception to the suspicions that he might be a pithecanthropus
endowed with a prehistoric mentality (21, 2) or a platonist (ibid).
This first diagnosis is followed by a *2nd discussion phase,* in which
Ionesco's scholarly knowledge—particularly of literature—is tested.
The examiners determine that *Ionesco* has read only such antiquated
French (22, 4) authors as Aeschylus, Sophocles and Euripides (22, 1–2),
foreign and therefore objectionable writers such as the Russian or
Pole Shakespeare (22, 3–6), and petty bourgeois reactionaries such
as Molière (22, 11–23, 11) who did not know how to express the
"social spirit of his epoch" (23, 11). The appeal to Shakespeare's
poetry is thrown out as unscientific, and the doctors come to the
conclusion from their examination that *Ionesco* is intellectually de-
formed (24, 10–13) and in need of "remedial education" (24, 14). To
this end the examinee is to answer a few more questions, and so be-

gins a *3rd discussion phase,* whose central theme appears clothed in the question, "What is theater?" (25, 9). The answers to this question of definition spread over the entire phase of discussion are commented on in dialogue. The first two *B.s* favor a complete system of correspondence, "theater as teaching and learning institution" (27, 16–28, 5; 29, 13–30, 25) and examine the conduct of the audience (28, 9–29, 12) after they have once more applied their paradoxical dialectic to the definition of theater and have therefore quarreled with *B.III.* Also in the *4th discussion phase,* this dialectic is used, even by *Ionesco* himself, to whom it proves useful in his defence against his aggressive visitors. Here the confession is wrung from him that he is an ignorant person in need of instruction (31, 19–32, 11). A dialectical attempt at the definition of this virtue leads to a new quarrel within the group of doctors (32, 12–34, 14), and allows *Ionesco,* unnoticed at first, to attempt flight. After the playwright's failure to carry out his escape, he justifies his action dialectically: he wished to flee "the better to stay" (34, 15–35, 11). Following a technical preparation of the "pupil" *Ionesco,* the *5th discussion phase* begins. It is devoted to the scholars' lecture on different "theatrological" sciences. Competing in generosity with one another (mock-politeness), each of the three *B.s* wants to allow the other two precedence. Finally, all three begin to speak simultaneously on *théâtralogie, costumologie, spectatologie* (37, 12–38, 1). These topics are then treated one by one, and developed separately. In the *6th discussion phase* the *B.s,* having stopped to admire the result of their work on *Ionesco,* see their plans for the new start for the play fulfilled in accordance with their principles. They allow *Ionesco* to let in his cleaning woman who has alredy been waiting for a long time (probably since the end of the exposition). This woman is declared useful as a representative of the popular audience, were the playwright prepared to apply to her the principles of "Verfremdung," *distanciation.* Obeying the demand of his visitors for distanciation, *Ionesco* carries out the principle literally by moving farther and farther away from the door he seeks to open. This sets the B.s dancing for joy, as they celebrate the successful re-education of their pupil. Crowned with a donkey mask by the similarly attired three B.s, *Ionesco* is drawn into a donkey dance punctuated by braying. It is at this point that Marie pushes her way into the room to free her master from his sorry situation. In the *7th discussion phase,* she criticizes the conclusions drawn from *Ionesco's* re-education. The three B.s are driven from the room, and Marie slaps the playwright's face twice in order to bring him back to his senses. *Ionesco* is now as we found him at the beginning of the play. The three B.s exit arguing, and the playwright declares the didactic play within the play completed. Thus ends the epitasis, or main body of the play.

The author *Ionesco* now gives a long lecture on the text just performed and its genesis, about theater criticism and its duties, the rights and duties of the playwright, the theater in general, and other comparable artistic disciplines. The tone and argumentation become increasingly indisputable; the doctors, called back on stage to hear the lecture, rightly reproach *Ionesco* for the fact that he detests being instructed and yet now is giving an instructional lecture on the theater. Confused, *Ionesco* recognizes this weakness, confesses to it, and promises that it should be the exception and not the rule.

The action of the *Impromptu* thus consists of the attempt of the three "theatrologists" to re-educate the author *Ionesco* turning him into a model author according to their (contrasting) principles. The conclusion is that the cleaning woman as representative of the average audience (if hardly as representative of the typical Ionesco audience) rejects the principles as nonsense and puts an end to their application on the guinea-pig *Ionesco*. Also, it subsequently appears that the main body of the play (framed by the exposition and epilogue) is a piece of "theater within the theater," staged by the author *Ionesco* with the participation of the three *B.s* for the latter's instruction. Both exposition and epilogue give commentary on the epitasis; in addition, in the epilogue the key to understanding the personal satire is given, as the list of excerpts from writings of the satirically represented models of the three *B.s* is offered as satirical compositional techniques used in the *Impromptu.*

The Ideological Background and Its Organizational Model

The characters selected by Ionesco and their goals mirror the basic ideas of this author about the theater.

Ionesco is here the representative of "autonomous theater," the only valid category of the genre. To that extent, it can be said that despite any lack of attempt at realistic characterization, the *dramatis persona, Ionesco,* and the playwright become one. Indeed, not only does the Ionesco of the *Impromptu* echo the theoretical views of his creator, the real Ionesco, but he also lectures with the indisputable precision which distinguishes the texts of *Notes and Counter-Notes.*

The party of the opposition, the three B.s, represents the two variants of existing bad theatre: B.I and B.II speak mostly in the name of theater of involvement, in particular of that patterned on the theories of Bertolt Brecht; B.III continually publicizes insipid entertainment, or "boulevard" theater.

While the representation of "autonomous" and "non-autonomous" theater by the two parties, *Ionesco* on one hand, Bartholomeus I, II and III on the other, can proceed organically, the theoretician *Ionesco*'s equally *dual* conception of "non-autonomous" theater is perhaps not fully rendered in connection with the trio of the B.s. The reason for this lies in the acceptance of an approved Molierian "model" for the comic representation of a professional group which appears outwardly as a unity, but which proves susceptible to crisis within that deceptive unity. The satirical schema of *L'Amour Médecin,* for example, Molière's caricature of the medical profession, presents pairs of representatives of this profession supporting bleeding and purging, and so involved in controversy that they forget their common interest, namely the protection of the *autorité doctorale,* until they are reunited by Filerin. Ionesco must have been prompted to utilize this schema by his intention of inserting grossly comic phases of the "methods quarrel" between the representatives of the dogmatically stubborn main party within a relaxed and amplified altercation confirming the equation, or *image initiale,* Barthes, Dort, etc. = docteurs.

On the Amplification of Dialogue in the Impromptu

Aside from the two main parties [*Ionesco*] and [*B.I, B.II* and *B.III*], a new party joins in toward the end of the epitasis. This new party fits into Souriau's category of *arbitre de la situation,*[2] insofar as she causes the catastrophe of the play, by apparently removing *Ionesco* from the definitive submission to the will of the *B.s: Marie.* These three parties and five dialogue partners receive a sum total of approximately 800 lines, of which *Ionesco* is engaged in only 170 and

[2] Etienne Souriau, *Les deux cent mills situations dramatiques* (Paris: Flammarion, 1950).

Marie in a little over 40. The rest, close to three-fourths of all spoken lines, fall to the share of the scholar party: *B.I.* about 225, *B.II* about 205, and *B.III* about 165 lines. These numerical relationships reflect the speech-activity of the characters and parties: *B.I* and *Ionesco* are both on stage from the beginning to end of the play; but *B.I* alone as one of three representatives of his party speaks over 50 lines more than his counterpart; even *B.III,* who enters last, speaks almost as often as *Ionesco.*

The function of this quantitative predominance—not only of characters, but also of lines—of the dogmatic advocates of bad or false theater is evident: their loquaciousness and the uniformity of thought of their allegations are means to their satirical characterization. The technical function is to lengthen the exposition of the B. party's total contribution to the dialogue—an effect which could have been achieved by using one third of the lines.—This technique is derived from the Molierian model, even when it is not followed directly.

Two main categories of the amplification schema can be isolated: the first type presupposes a unanimity of opinion on the part of the three B.s, the second belongs to the internal party quarrel type. These two polar categories lend the B. party's contribution to the dialogue its dialectic tone.

The first category is marked by a tendency toward repetition. It is the counterpart of the figure of speech called *repetitio* in the rhetoric of monologue. It consists of the full or partial repetition of the preceding sentence by one or two speakers of the last speaker's party; content and wording remain the same. Here are some examples of partial repetition of wording:

> *B.III.* Lisez-nous au moins le début.
> *B.II.* Au moins le début . . .
> *B.I.* . . . moins le début (17, 11–13)

There are also full repetitions:

> *B.II to B.I.* Tiens, Bartholoméus, comment allez-vous?
> *B.I to B.II.* Tiens, Bartholoméus, comment allez-vous (16, 5–6)

The second variation on the main type can be called the *synonym* or *affirmation-schema*. It consists of the unlimited acknowledgement or repetition of the content of the preceding line, where the wording is paralleled by the synonyms:

B.I. Je m'en doutais . . .
B.II. Moi aussi.
B.III. Moi aussi. (25, 16–18)

The amplification is then further elucidated by the line: "Je me doutais bien que sa pensée était viciée." (25, 19).

There are pairings of etymological figures of speech:

B.I. (. . .) Voilà.
B.II. Voici.
B.III. Voyons. (18, 15–17)

Since none of the speakers intends to operate a change or variation on the content of the preceding lines, the effect is simply one of quantitative amplification. The doctors appear as a loquacious group of pedants who believe in repeating thrice the most banal statements.

The quantitative dialogue amplification is abetted by the schemata in which the content of the first line in the schema is either negated or replaced with its opposite in the second line, and then, alternately negated or negotiated in the following lines. Here are examples which will demonstarte that B.III alters the content of his sentence, and that the lines grow progressively meaningless:

B.II. to Ionesco: Taisez-vous!
B.III. Dites quelque chose!
B.I. and *B.II,* to Ionesco: *Parlez* . . .
B.III, to Ionesco: Taisez-vous! (31, 3–6)

B.I. C'est pourtant clair.
B.III. Cela me parait obscur.
B.II. C'est du clair-obscur.
B.I. Je m'excuse, c'est de l'obscur clair . . .
B.III. Pardon, l'obscur clair n'est pas le clair-obscur. (32, 25–33, 4)

Conversations are also reduced, dialogue abstracted:

B.III. Non . . .
B.I. Si.
B.III. Non . . .
B.I. Si . . .
B.II. Si et non.
B.III. Non.
B.I. Si.
B.II. Non et si.
B.III. Non. (33, 13–21)

Clearly B.III negates, B.I affirms while B.II negates and affirms simultaneously, varying however the order of the particles.—As in *Scène à quatre* which starts with a "non/si dialogue" the schema offers the possibility of the briefest form of wording for the realization of "meaningless dramatic conflict."—Variations on the "abstract dialogue" schema use alliterative material developed from the schema's first line:

> *B.I.* (. . .) Le théâtral est dans l'antithéâtral et vice versa . . .//vice versa . . . vice versa . . .
> *B.II.* Vice-verso . . . Vice-verso . . . Vice-verso!
> *B.III.* Vice-verso? Ah non pas vice-verso, mais bien versa-vircé.
> *B.I.* Je dis vircé-versa.
> *B.III.* Je maintiens versa-vircé!
> *B.I.* Vircé-verso!
> *B.III.* Vous ne me ferez pas peur: versa-vircé. (26, 8–14)

It is interesting to note that the excerpt from // to the end of the quotation did not appear in the *Impromptu*'s first printing. It was inserted in the book version for the sake of quantitative amplification. On the other hand, the line closing the insertion:

> *B.II* to the other *B.s.* Ne vous disputez pas devant lui . . . Cela affaiblit notre doctorale autorité . . . (26, 15)

clearly demonstrates an ethopoetical function related to Molière's *L'Amour Médecin*.

These dialogue schemata based on contradiction,—the category mentioned above as "the internal party quarrel,"—represent for Ionesco dramatic dialogue *in nuce*. Contradiction precludes compatibility of judgment, or unification of characters. On the deepest level, it reflects the "antagonismes qui font qu'il y a théâtre." (*Notes et Contre-Notes*, p. 126) It must be added, however, that even in *L'Impromptu* not all contradictory pairs of lines are developed into individual polemic dialogue phases and dealt with in accordance with their function. (See 27, 16–18, 29, 1–2, 45, 5–6)

The Schemata dealt with so far demonstrate the main function of ethopoeia so far as the speaking B. party is concerned. The content of their discourse is unimportant as compared to the unity or disunity of the speakers belonging to this party, revealed by the tone of their remarks. In other schemata, however, the content or wording, carefully selected, find themselves in the foreground. *The catalogue schemata* can be said to belong to this group:

B.II. On doit venir au théâtre pour apprendre!
B.I. Non pas pour rire!
B.III. Ni pour pleurer!
B.I. Ni pour oublier!
B.II. Ni pour s'oublier!
B.I. Ni pour s'exalter!
B.II. Ni pour s'engluer!
B.I. Ni pour s'identifier! (27, 19–26)

B.I. (. . .) populairement, c'est-à-dire . . .
B.II. Scientifiquement . . .
B.III. Tout bonnement.
B.I. . . . et dialectiquement, c'est (. . .)
B.I. Elle (l'oeuvre) est dans ce qu'on en pense.
B.II. Dans ce qu'on en dit . . .
B.I. Dans l'interprétation qu'on veut bien lui donner . . .
B.II. Qu'on lui impose . . .
B.I. Que l'on impose au public. (32, 6–10)

This type unfolds thoughts and words synonymically and enumeratively relevant to the satirical situation of the play. The first of the catalogues has as its content prescriptions and proscriptions for the behavior of the audience. Ionesco suggests that these are the goals of the Brechtians, Barthes and Dort, and of their dramatic representatives. In the second example, we are faced with the "marxist-scientific" vocabulary indulged in by the editors of *Théâtre Populaire.* "Tout bonnement" is a pet expression of J. J. Gautier, the model for B.III.

In what we call *interruption-schema,* a lengthy span is divided among several lines and speakers, rather than using duplication or accumulation of analogous grammatical and syntactic unities. Even here, however, strict separation is not possible.

B.I. (. . .) Car, plus on est distant . . .
B.II. . . . plus on est proche . . .
B.I. . . . et plus on est proche . . .
B.II. . . . plus on est distant . . . C'est l'électrochoc de la distanciation, ou effet Y. (19, 2–4)

This type of schema is parallel to the catalogue schema.

Another type of dialogue which can be analyzed schematically as well can be found on the periphery of the forms analyzed above. We have a syntactically and semantically independent discourse followed by one or several lines related to the content of a preceding speech, carrying that speech further, or detailing it. This is the author's solution to his own difficulty with a discursive point of discussion not actually suited to dialogue. In the final analysis the same is true of both the catalogue and the interruption schemata.

Basically, in all these examples of what can be called a *free amplification style,* we can isolate two specific functions: the quantitative widening of the total text, and the calculatedly cliché characterization of all three B.s as dogmatists in the tradition of Molière doctors. It is also obvious that raw material of satire better suited to discursive treatment has been artfully turned into dramatic dialogue. In fact, *Ionesco,* the second major "party" of the play, is never once involved as a speaker in the actualization of the schemata examined above. Information on the attitudes in regard to dramatic aesthetics of the playwright *Ionesco* (with few exceptions) is given only in the author's long monologue. Thus, the discursive form is used but only in an epilogue to the "play within a play." True dialogue by the major parties on questions of dramatic theory is left to the presentation of the perverted (according to Ionesco) aesthetic of the B.s, or their models, Barthes, Dort, Gautier. We can safely conclude therefore that in composing *L'Impromptu de l'Alma,* the author was primarily concerned with condemning the views and practices of his ideological and aesthetic adversaries, rather than with developing his own point of view.

On the Structural Characterization of the Course of the Text

The text of *L'Impromptu* is outwardly undivided: there is no division of acts or scenes. Yet, clearly marked segments can be discerned. There are signals, which in form are parallel except for the slightest variations. The different partners of *Ionesco* use the following signals:

1. Ringing at *Ionesco's* door (= acoustic signal)
2. Knocking at *Ionesco's* door (= acoustic signal)
3. Call: *Ionesco! Ionesco!* (or similar) (= linguistic signal)
4. Call: *Ionesco! Vous êtes là?* (or similar) (= linguistic signal)

Ionesco himself uses the following signals:

5. Sitting at writing-desk (= optical signal)

6. Stereotyped answer to the acoustic signals of each partner: *Oui
    . . . une seconde . . . Q'est-ce qu'il y a encore?* (= linguistic
    signal)

In a total of five places in the text at least three of these signals—
in the order 5, 2, and 6—are combined. In the schema of the plot:

1–3. Entrance of *B.I., B.II* and *B.III*
4.   Demand for admittance by an otherwise unspecified person at
      the end of the exposition.
5.   The preparation of the final admission of *Marie.*

Each time, when *Ionesco* is in position 5 and reacts to signals 1
to 4 (but least to 2) of the opposite party by giving signal 6, it indicates the beginning of a new part in the over-all structure of *L'Impromptu.* The arrival of the three *B.s* introduces in each case a part
of the exposition. The stereotyped progress of these three major
phases of the exposition ensures its schematic unity, by showing them
as a series of formally equal moments and preparing the typological
uniformity of the *B.*-party. The desire for admission of the one who
only knocks (signal 2; and who thus for lack of linguistic expression
or optical appearance is only a 4th unidentifiable visitor) at the end
of the exposition is at this point misinterpreted by the audience or
reader as that of a 4th *B.* This error is only cleared up when *Marie*
has first spoken (directions after 35, 11: *Ionesco! Monsieur Ionesco!*)
and the subdued author begs his visitors

Messieurs, Messieurs, permettez, je dois ouvrir, elle est là depuis long-
temps. (35, 12)

Here the audience notes that the silence of the person knocking
was intended to give rise one after the other to the interpretations
"a 4th *B.*" and "the cleaning woman *Marie.*" By *Ionesco's* reaction
—signal 6—the main part of the play, i.e. the performance of the
"play within a play," is introduced. From the point of view of the
over-all structure, it entails the postponement of *Marie's* entrance.
Marie's call, a later addition to her merely acoustic signal, falls in
the episode of *Ionesco's* oppression by the *B.s.* Only his sly change
of interpretation, making the cleaning woman into a representative
of the public (whereby she is integrated into the body of the "play
within the play"), and the fulfillment of the *B.s* requirement for
admission of the "public" make it possible for *Ionesco* to appear
as the stage direction after 48, 3 specifically states, *dans sa position*

du début. Thus signal 5 is fulfilled, so that *Marie,* can precipitate with signals 2, 3 and 4, *Ionesco's* decisive reaction, signal 6, which leads to the "catastrophe" of the "play within a play."

The overall structure of the text can thus be understood as a series of phases of unequal length, delineated by signals approximately equal in form. These signals are introduced by the author whenever a character enters or is supposed to come in. Thus, each major phase of the text can be compared to the conventionally structured scenes of French drama wherein divisions are marked by the entrances and exits of the *dramatis personae.*

Even the epilogue of the *Impromptu* is framed by the exit and re-entrance of characters, though without the use of the signals punctuating the exposition and the "play within the play." When the character *Ionesco* calls the three B.s to return: "La pièce est finie . . . Revenez en scène!" (55, 10) we see that the "play within the play is indicated after the fact, *extra artem.* We are provided with a stage direction by the "stage manager" of the completed play. At this point B.I, B.II and B.III re-appear on the stage, no longer as characters, but as doubles of the audience in the theatre. After all, we must recall Bartholomeus II's declaration: "On ne répétera jamais assez qu'il n'y a pas de théâtre sans public!" (39, 10)

Utopia and After

by Richard N. Coe

In France, it is enough—almost—that a writer should be profoundly and influentially revolutionary in *form* for the critics to
consider him "committed," and committed, without question, to the
Left. To belong to the *avant-garde* is *ipso facto* to be against the
Establishment; exceptions are so rare—Claudel alone, perhaps, since
the beginning of the present century—that even open hostility towards other Left-committed writers counts scarcely in the balance.
"Saint Ionesco, the Anti-Brecht," whatever his past history, is still
assumed by the majority of French critics to be *un homme de gauche*.

In England, the position is vastly different, for the Great Divide
of mutual contempt between politicians and writers has for so long
prevailed, while genuinely "committed" men of letters are so much
the exception rather than the rule, that English critics are perhaps
not wrong to apply the dictum of Paul Guth and to proclaim that
"to opt out of politics is to side with the Establishment." [1] It follows,
therefore, that Ionesco's doctrine of "belligerent non-commitment"
has been subject to widely varying interpretations on different sides
of the Channel. In particular, Kenneth Tynan, strongly backed by
Orson Welles, has accused Ionesco of trying to "opt out" of politics,
and thus has seriously misinterpreted, or at least oversimplified, this
important aspect of his work.

For Ionesco's position with regard to politics, like most of his
thought, is decidedly complex. Death and the fear of death—the
subconscious and the metaphysical—comprise the central themes of
his drama, whereas problems of political and social organisation,
concerning as they do almost exclusively the conscious and material
aspects of existence, can rarely be of more than marginal significance,

[1] Paul Guth, *Le Naïf aux quarante enfants* (Paris, 1954), p. 62.

and in fact may dangerously obscure the real issues at stake. On the other hand, the "horror" of existence and the universal imminence of death, above all the universal awareness of the *fear* of death, are specifically linked with certain definite political combinations in the modern world, and, consequently, these combinations are never negligible. To put the same conclusion in another form: if it is true that Ionesco has roundly condemned both Sartre and Brecht and all "committed" literature, it is no less true that he could never have written the plays by which he is known, if indeed he had written at all, were it not for Hitler and Hiroshima. English criticism, not a little puzzled by the appearance of a major French writer who flatly refuses to harness his theatre to this party or to that, has tended to overlook (because it is concealed) the violence of his onslaught against certain all-too-current political attitudes of our time. But, over and beyond this, there is in addition the fact that to reject the traditional attitudes towards the human condition is *ipso facto* to criticise the current ideologies which these attitudes have bred. A new view of man is in itself an argument for the Left. The heavy-handed sociological tirades of a Wesker may be missing; yet for all that, Ionesco's drama is none the less a drama of dissent. By no argument in the world can a writer who publishes, for preference, in the quasi-anarchist *Cahiers de 'Pataphysique,* or in the off-beat, anticlerical *Bizarre,* be counted among the pillars of the Establishment.

One fact is incontrovertible: Ionesco is inextricably involved in his own plays, "committed" willy-nilly to the struggles and destiny (if not to the actual language) of his characters. And these characters, despite the dream-surroundings in which they exist, are involved in reality. There is all the difference in the world between imagination and "illusion"; imagination is a means, not of avoiding, but of coming to grips with reality, whereas the philosophy which "deems this world of ours naught but illusion" is not so much wrong, according to Ionesco, as irrelevant. "Right or wrong, no matter; it *seems* real to us, and obviously this reality (however precarious it may prove) is the one we have to deal with." [2] Again and again, Ionesco insists upon the extent of his own intimate participation in the theatre which he has created. "Each play of mine has its roots in a kind of self-analysis," he declares;[3] and elsewhere: "More often than not, the

[2] "Entretien," from "Entretien avec Eugène Ionesco," in *Cahiers Libres de la Jeunesse,* no. 2 (March 15, 1960), 12–13.

[3] "Finalement, je suis pour le Classicisme," in *Bref,* no. 11 (February 15, 1956), 1–2.

theatre—my theatre—is a confession; all I do is to make personal avowals (incomprehensible, of course, when the listener is deaf—how should it be otherwise?); for what else could I do?" [4] The very intensity of this subjectivism, moreover, carries it above the level of the merely personal, the idiosyncratic. Between the "I" and the "not-I" there is no inherent conflict. The inner world (the "subjective" element) is simply a reflexion of the outer world of "objective" reality; the microcosm, all "tattered and disjointed" as it is, is nothing but the perfect miniature of the macrocosm, "the very mirror and symbol of contradictions on a universal scale." [5] Between "subjective" and "objective" there is no clear line of demarcation; the poet's awareness "bears witness" to the character of reality—bears witness to it subjectively, yet at the same time creates an image of it, and, by doing so, "objectivises" its own awareness. To perceive reality in a certain way is in itself an act which alters the character of reality. "What is objectivity, if not a consensus of different subjectivities?":[6]

> I believe that, by dint of being subjective, I am creating an objective type of drama. Perhaps, without even being aware of it, I am really socially conscious.[7]

In these statements, the phenomenological undercurrent which determines much of Ionesco's theoretical argument is clearly apparent. To the phenomenologist, the act of perception is in itself a dual act of creation: the subjective image in the mind is created or modified by an awareness of the outside object; but, at the same time, the object itself is created, or modified, or *given meaning,* by the nature of the awareness which it has itself provoked. For Ionesco, therefore, the very process of perception—let alone that of artistic creation—is literally an *act:* an act which, no less than any other, is the starting-point of an infinite series of repercussions and responsibilities in every sphere. It is not a question of whether one wants or does not want to be "committed"; one *is* committed by the simple fact of being alive, of being conscious. The first of all commitments is existence; the rest are incidental. The solitary is as deeply involved in the ultimate destiny of man as is the Party Member; to join a

---

[4] "L'Invraisemblable l'insolite, mon univers," in *Arts,* no. 424 (14/20 August, 1953), 1–2.
[5] *Ibid.*
[6] "Entretien," pp. 12–13.
[7] "Finalement," p. 2.

group, to adhere to a programme is merely a clumsy, noisy, and possibly dangerous way of doing what is inevitable in any case. It is also, perhaps, an easier way—a delegation of responsibility, a form of escapism, a "detachment system," as Madeleine and Choubert realise all too well.[8] In *Le Tueur*, it is the Soldier, the member of the "group," who refuses to participate ("I don't know . . . *I've* got my flowers"),[9] while Bérenger, the very symbol of loneliness and isolation, bears on his shoulders the total responsibility of man:

> You'd think I was frightened, but I'm not. I'm used to being alone . . .
> I've always been alone. . . . And yet I love the human race, but at a
> distance. What does that matter, when I'm interested in the fate of
> mankind? Fact is, I *am* doing something. . . . Doing . . . acting . . .
> acting, not play-acting, doing! [10]

That history is made, not by political movements, nor by the application of carefully-evolved, rationalistic doctrines, but by the imperceptible creative action of the individual consciousness, is fundamental to Ionesco's attitude of dissent. It is, admittedly, a romantic attitude; yet Ionesco's very mistrust of "history," his stress on the themes of solitude, anguish, and death, is an apt historical comment upon this particular age—an age in which, in Professor Schérer's words, "the appearance of new social structures has confronted the individual with problems which he cannot solve with his own unaided strength." [11] For Ionesco, the "historical" (or, for "historical," read "political") solution of such problems is not merely foredoomed to failure, but, by the operation of a universal "law of contradiction," is predestined to achieve precisely the opposite of what it sets out to perform. So intense and deep-rooted is Ionesco's mistrust of the self-advertised "political man" that he resorts to a positively 'pataphysical argument—reminiscent of Rousseau—to present his case. The individual, in relation to society, has not one "will," but two: a conscious will to improve the lot of his fellow-men, and a subconscious *anti*-will which desires exclusively their destruction:

> No sooner does an idea, a conscious intention, seek to realise itself
> *historically*, than it finds an incarnation in its own opposite; it becomes

[8] N.R.F., I, 178–9 (II. 267–9).
[9] N.R.F., II. 152 (III. 88–9).
[10] N.R.F., II. 159 (III. 95–6).
[11] Jacques Schérer, "L'Evolution de Ionesco," in *Lettres Nouvelles*, n.s. no. 1 (March–April, 1960), 91–6.

a monstrosity. [. . .] We wish the contrary of what we wish. There is a will and an anti-will; a wish-for-this, a corresponding anti-wish-for-that. And this anti-will is revealed (for we are not aware of it, it remains hidden) in the experience of *facts:* in the immediate contradiction that it brings about. . . .[12]

For Rousseau, it was the *conscious* desire of the individual to realise his own personal interest (*la volonté particulière*) which constituted the obstacle; yet every citizen had deep within him a *subconscious* wish for the general prosperity of the community, and it was this hidden reflexion of the *volonté générale* which the wise legislator was concerned to exploit. For Ionesco, the position is reversed. The conscious will may desire the salvation of mankind; but there is always the all-powerful subconscious to wreak vengeance on the illusion of good intentions. In Ionesco's "Man," there is more than a suspicion of original sin; more than a hint of Manichæism in his philosophy of contradiction. For as long as he remains alone, remains himself, his "will" may dominate his acts; but as soon as he renounces his solitude, as soon as he conforms to the pattern of a class or party, then the secret "anti-will" takes over, and universal devastation is the outcome.

This, then, is the background to Ionesco's unremitting hostility to the notion of "commitment," when commitment involves the conscious acceptance by the individual of a party programme, whose aim is to "reform" the existing state of things. "My Plays make no Claim to Reform the World"[13] is the characteristic title which, echoing the 'Pataphysicians, he once chose for an article published in *Express*. Between "reform" and "revolution" lies all the difference in the world—all the difference between Lenin and Makhnò. The mutual mistrust between Ionesco and his "committed" critics is precisely that between the genuine anarchist and the Left-wing committee-men, who, precisely because they constitute a revolutionary *party*, can no longer pursue the dream of revolution to its logical conclusion.

Far from being a "formalist," a silent supporter of the Right, Ionesco glories in the "subversive" character of his own drama. "The

---

[12] "Le Bloc-notes d'Eugène Ionesco," in *Arts*, no. 763 (24 February 1960), 2.

[13] "Mes pièces ne prétendent pas sauver le monde," in *Express*, 15/16 October, 1955, p. 8.

avant-garde writer is, as it were, an enemy in the very heart of the
city—a city which he is fighting to destroy, against which he is in
active revolt. . . ." [14] In fact, there is no such thing as "formalism"
in such a context, for to destroy a "formula" is to destroy an ideology, to reveal the absurdity of a jargon is to reveal the absurdity
of a whole social structure, of which the logic of language is more
than the expression, is indeed the very core and essence. The *political* revolutionary is at best a reformer, altering the appearance of
society while leaving intact its inner structure; the artist alone can
destroy and refashion the mentality upon which that society is
based:

> Science and art have done far more to change thinking than politics
> have. The real revolution is taking place in the scientists' laboratories
> and in the artists' studios. Einstein, Oppenheimer, Breton, Kandinsky,
> Picasso, Pavlov, they're the ones who are really responsible [. . .].
> Penicillin and the fight against dipsomania are worth more than poli-
> tics and a change of government.[15]

In other words, given the true revolution, the "revolution which is
a change in mentality," [16] the corresponding upheaval in social structure will necessarily follow after; by contrast, to impose a social re-
construction without first revolutionising the minds of those who
are due to be reconstructed is to coerce the fabric of society against
the nature of its own material—a process which can only be achieved
by brute force. Ultimately, Ionesco is not so much hostile to "committed" literature as such—after all, "every writer has wanted to
make propaganda; the great ones are those who have failed" [17]—as
afraid of its results. The assertion that "all ideologies are aggressive,
even the most revolutionary," [18] is one which is not easily contra-
dicted from the evidence of European history over the past fifty
years; and over Ionesco's argument there hangs constantly the

[14] "Eugène Ionesco ouvre le feu" (textual report of Ionesco's opening address
to the Eighth Congress of the International Theatre Institute, Helsinki, June
1959), in *Théâtre dans le Monde,* VIII (Autumn, 1959), 171–202.
[15] N.R.F. II. 144 (III. 82).
[16] "Le Cœur n'est pas sur la main," in *Cahiers des Saisons,* no. 15 (Winter,
1959), 262–7. This article, Ionesco's final reply to his English critics, was written
for the *Observer,* but not published therein.
[17] "Finalement," p. 2.
[18] Quoted by P. Sarisson in *Aux Ecoutes,* 16 January, 1959.

shadow of Belsen. "A committed theatre is dangerous—exceedingly dangerous. It leads directly to the concentration camp." [19]

But this is not all; for not merely are revolutionary politics, like all politics, "fatal to man," but they are not even, in the deeper sense of the term, revolutionary. Before it can be fashioned into a "programme," an idea must already have been disseminated, popularised, diluted—in other words, bandied about from platform to platform, from committee to committee, until its novelty is tarnished, its subversive violence tamed, its unfamiliarity made acceptable. But by this time, it is no longer revolutionary; it is no longer even alive. "Once an idea has been formulated, it is already dead, and reality has hurried on ahead." [20] Politics, more than any other aspect of the "conformist" society in which we live, feeds on platitudes, for no idea, unless it be already dead as mutton (from the artist's point of view) can figure on a "programme" without scorching a hole in the paper. Political fingers are easily burnt by the fire of live ideas. Consequently, for a writer to harness his art to the politics of a party is to surrender his right to be revolutionary and to chain his living language to the senseless cadavers of words which have already lost half, if not all, their meaning. And to accept a form of language, a way of thought which is already out-of-date and platitudinous is to betray the truth, to distort reality—in short, to propagate a *lie.*

In the summer of 1958, Ionesco was soundly taken to task for these and other related ideas by Kenneth Tynan, Orson Welles, Philip Toynbee and others, in a series of articles which appeared in the *Observer.*[21] The essence of Tynan's criticism was that Ionesco's unappeasable mistrust of *a priori* political value-judgments had led him to divorce his art *entirely* from its social context, and to produce a subjective, "formalistic" type of drama (cp. Arnold Wesker, Shelagh Delaney, etc.), in which his own, purely private obsessions and inner preoccupations were puffed up, all sheathed in a cascade of glittering linguistic fireworks, into a sort of cheap and spurious "universality." Yet a drama which rejected ideology, Tynan suggested, was at once narrow, dangerous, and hollow: narrow because it could have only a limited, *"élite"* appeal; dangerous because, by

[19] Georges Lerminier, "Clés pour Ionesco," in *Théâtre d'Aujour d'Hui,* January–February, 1959, 42–5.
[20] "Eugène Ionesco ouvre le feu," pp. 176–7.
[21] *Observer* (London), 22 and 29 Jun., 6 and 13 Jul. 1958.

its "formalism," it suggested that all was well in the world of "You-
never-had-it-so-good"; hollow because, by professing to despise "man
as a social animal," it could offer no more than a partial and incomplete portrait of reality:

> Art and ideology often interact on each other; but the main fact is that
> both spring from a common source. Both draw on human experience
> to explain mankind to itself; both attempt, in very different ways, to
> assemble a coherence from seemingly unrelated phenomena; both
> stand guard for us against Chaos.[22]

—to which Ionesco retorted: "Social man is hell; other people are
hell; if only one could do without them!" [23] . . . and the controversy became slightly embittered.

To dismiss this controversy as a simple misunderstanding of Ionesco's purpose, or even as a (mistaken) attempt to judge Ionesco
in terms of Brecht, is perhaps to oversimplify the problem. The argument reflects a conflict of tradition, as well as a clash of historical
experience; and the whole attitude towards Ionesco in England and
America is coloured by the implications of the debate. Ionesco has
been recognised in the English theatre almost as widely as in France
—but for rather different reasons. It takes an audience brought up
against a background of Cartesian logic to accept Ionesco's anti-logic
at its face value; the English empirical tradition looks rather for the
practical implications—and sometimes finds them. For English audi-
ences, it is necessary that the unexplainable should be explained,
should even help in explaining something else (compare the productions of *Rhinocéros* by Orson Welles in London and by Jean-Louis
Barrault in Paris);[24] and when it fails to do so, they feel that they
have been deceived. Not that Ionesco deceives them *in his plays,* for
his drama is so complex, contains so many threads, that (to take an
instance), *Les Chaises* has been interpreted either as a study in the
breakdown of "classical psychology," or, alternatively, as a straightforward and realistic psychiatric case-history (*"folie à deux"*) in
dramatic form. Similarly, *La Leçon* has been taken as a "myth"—
a full-scale political allegory of a "people" oppressed by a "Dictator," of its desperate and futile attempt at revolt (the Girl-Student's

[22] *Observer,* 13 Jul. 1958.
[23] "Le Cœur n'est pas sur la main," p. 266.
[24] Dorothy Knowles, "Ionesco's Rhinoceroses," in *Drama,* Autumn, 1960, pp.
35–9.

toothache), and of its eventual repression.[25] "Apparently," Ionesco
himself remarks somewhere, "one can get a lesson out of anything
—even out of *La Leçon*." But the shock comes when, having allowed
his audience their rationalistic interpretation as they sat in the
theatre, he then denies them the slightest right to such Anglo-Saxon
self-indulgence in his theoretical commentaries. *La Leçon* is an
allegory of nothing; it is just . . . a lesson. Even *Jacques*—apparently a political and social satire on the bourgeoisie—is "totally un-
committed." In a way—given the contrasting national attitudes—
both the antagonists are right: Tynan to insist that the play should
mean what it does, or might, or conceivably could be made to mean;
Ionesco to retort that all meaning is subordinate to absurdity:

> The theatre, like all art, must serve no utilitarian purpose; the theatre
> is not *engagement* but *dégagement;* none the less, this "disengage-
> ment," this alienation, this forgetfulness of self, this violent separation
> from the utilitarian world, is a usefulness *without which we cannot
> live.* . . .[26]

The question, however, as put by the English side of the controversy, is wrongly presented: the argument is not whether Ionesco
should or should not be committed, for Ionesco—as I have tried to
show—*is* committed, and the argument is fruitless. The problem is
to see precisely *to what* he is committed, and in what way. He is
committed to "Man," to "the Left," to revolution, to anarchy even:
but he is *not* committed to Marx or to Marxism, to the Trotskyists,
the Socialists, the F.L.N., or the New Left. Whereas, in the English
view—or in the Sartrian view—he should be; for revolutionary
dreams divorced from political action are nothing, are worse than
nothing, a snare, a delusion, a gift handed on a silver platter to the
ogres of the Establishment.

But here, between these irreconcilable views, the actual experience of history intervenes. English political history has on the whole
been kind to the principle of opposition; the English intellectual
who dissents from the accepted platitudes of the Establishment risks
seldom more than a certain notoriety, a certain amount of defama-
tion and vituperation, a couple of stormy scenes in Parliament or

[25] Pierre-Aimé Touchard, "Eugène Ionesco a réinventé les myths du Théâtre,"
in *Arts*, no. 608 (27 February/5 March, 1957), 2.

[26] "Théâtre et anti-Théâtre," in *Cahiers des Saisons*, no. 2 (October, 1955)
149–51. Reprinted as "Essays: (ii.) Theatre and Anti-Theatre" (trans. Leonard C.
Pronko), in *Theatre Arts* (New York), June, 1958, pp. 18, 77.

in the police-court, a few mass-meetings, protest-marches—and ultimately he stands to gain a measure of adjustment in the law. In
such a context, a greater or lesser degree of opposition is scarcely
less than a duty consequent upon the possession of intelligence. In
France, the background, although different, is still comparable. In
the absence of a deeply-rooted parliamentary tradition, the intellectual's responsibility is from the first more sharply focused on *activity*
—on party warfare (still largely verbal), on propaganda, speech-
making and organisation. But Ionesco's experience is neither French
nor English, but fundamentally *Nazi:* Nazi Roumania, Nazi-occu-
pied France, with the politics of the post-war "People's Republic"
in Bucharest thrown in for good measure. And the quintessential
lesson of this experience is that parties which begin as ideological
minorities will necessarily develop—under contemporary European
conditions—into dictatorial police states, so that the final condition
of the unhappy citizen is infinitely worse than the first. Admittedly,
the poet's first duty is to "impose his universe" [27]—but to do so from
within, never from without. To codify this "inner universe," to formulate it in the neat phrases of an ideology, to cease to be a "witness" and to become an "orator," is directly to hasten the advent of
the concentration camp, the mass-execution, and the pogrom.

And, indeed, the hidden theme of much of Ionesco's drama is precisely this: the denunciation of the police state as the final, most
nefarious incarnation of the "bourgeois" mind. Concerning the various Communist régimes in Europe, he has little to say—an isolated
outburst of indignation at the time of the Pasternak "affair," [28] a
few generalised criticisms of Marxism (of no great weight) in *Pages
de journal,*[29] an occasional *boutade* in the vein: "Nothing is more
conducive to pessimism than the obligation to eschew pessimism . . .
or go to gaol!";[30] and, indeed, in certain Communist countries, notably in Poland and in Jugoslavia, Ionesco's drama has enjoyed a
quite phenomenal success. But where Fascism is concerned (not forgetting the crypto-Fascism of the petty, would-be Nazis, the bullies,
the *agents de police,* the *concierges*), his pen can never be bitter
enough nor "committed" enough to express the fullness of his fear,

[27] "Eugène Ionesco ouvre le feu," pp. 190–91.
[28] "Celui qui ose ne pas haïr devient un Traître," in *Arts,* no. 711 (3 March,
1959), 1–2.
[29] "Pages de Journal," in *Nouvelle N.R.F.,* no. 86 (1 February, 1960) 220–33.
[30] Frédéric Towarnicki, "Ionesco des *Chaises* vides . . . à Broadway," in *Spectacles,* no. 2 (July, 1958), 6–12.

contempt, and hatred. From *Le Maître* and *Victimes du devoir,* by
way of *Tueur sans gages,* to *Rhinocéros,* Ionesco's drama is an implacable diatribe against the oppression and poison of the Nazi
state; the nightmare which absorbs all other nightmares is that of
Adolf Hitler.

The grotesque and horrifying episode of La Mère Pipe and her
goose-stepping regiment of thugs in *Le Tueur* needs no comment;
but some critics (especially in England) have been less aware of the
implications of *Rhinocéros.* The fell disease of "rhinoceritis" is the
condemnation, not of *any* ideology to which man may feel the urge
to conform, but specifically of the *Nazi* ideology. Not that the allusion is in any way historical; Fascism is far from belonging exclusively to the past, and indeed, the urgency of the play, the menacing
tempo of its dramatic rhythm, makes it very much a warning to be
heeded here and now. The average audience is all too eager to find
any excuse not to apply a dramatic moral to itself, and it was probably in an attempt to avoid the pitfall of "history" that Ionesco deliberately omitted all references which might associate the drama
with a specific place and epoch. Having avoided the particular,
however, he found himself caught out on the general; for all too
many of the critics, their safe refuge in history being denied to them,
have retaliated by turning the play into an *abstraction*—a "universal
parable" on the subject of "conformism." Universal it may be; but
when "universality" is used as an excuse for making oneself deaf to
a call to action, then it is time to restate the particular.

The theory that *Rhinocéros,* in its initial conception, is a deliberate onslaught against Fascism is borne out, not only by Ionesco's
own occasional assertions, but by the evidence of the origins of the
play as such. One of the recurrent themes of *Rhinocéros* is the conflict between the "ideal of civilisation" and the "ideal of nature":

> *Jean.* After all, rhinoceroses are living creatures the same as us; they've
> got as much right to life as we have!
> *Bérenger.* As long as they don't destroy ours in the process. You must
> admit the difference in mentality.
> *Jean.* Are you under the impression that our way of life is superior?
> *Bérenger.* Well at any rate, we have our own moral standards which I
> consider incompatible with the standards of these animals.
> *Jean.* Moral standards! I'm sick of moral standards! We need to go be-
> yond moral standards!
> *Bérenger.* What would you put in their place?

Jean. Nature!
Bérenger. Nature?
Jean. Nature has its own laws. Morality's against Nature.
Bérenger. Are you suggesting we replace our moral laws by the law of the jungle?
Jean. It would suit me, suit me fine.
Bérenger. You say that. But deep down, no one . . .
Jean. We've got to build our life on new foundations. We must get back to primeval integrity. . . .[31]

In this passage (as in the later arguments between Bérenger and Dudard) the rhinoceros incarnates the dream of simplifying the complexities of an over-civilised society, of a return to "natural innocence" and to a "state of nature" in which the degeneracy of modern man will be finally purged and redeemed. But, to Ionesco, it is precisely this glorification of nature which constitutes by far and away the most dangerous aspect of the Nazi ideology—dangerous because it may have a quite genuine appeal to the over-civilised mentality. In an essay written some ten years earlier, we find the same theme worked out in detail; this time, however, with the allusions made plain and the missing references filled in. This article (unfortunately unpublished) is entitled: "Un Témoignage faux: La Vingt-cinquième Heure," and is a highly critical review of C. Virgil Gheorghiu's popular novel, *The Twenty-fifth Hour.*[32] In many ways, it may be considered the germ of the later play. Among other fashionable intellectual pursuits, declares Ionesco, is that of denouncing the "oppressive automatism of a robot machine-age." But this is an error; the machine, on the whole, is beneficial to man, is at least a product of *civilisation;* even the automatism and impersonality of bureaucracy has its advantages, precisely *because* it is impersonal. The real danger lies not in the robot, but

in the automatism of passions and of evil instincts, the biological and physiological automatism of the Fascist beast [. . .]. The automatism of the machine is *not* dangerous; it is the sub-human automatisms which are [. . .] Nazism likewise was opposed to the "machine age" and to "abstractions"; Nazism was this and nothing else—the revolt

[31] *Rhinocéros,* pp. 126–7 (*Plays,* IV. 66–7) (London: Calder, 1960, trans. Derek Prouse).

[32] Virgil Gheorghiu, *La Vingt-cinquième Heure,* Fr. tr. by Monique Saint-Côme (who originally introduced Ionesco to Nicolas Bataille, and thus was indirectly responsible for the first production of *La Cantatrice*), Paris 1949, Engl. tr. by Rita Eldon, London 1950.

of nature and of the instincts of the brute against civilisation, to the point where the "man of the future," as Hitler wished to see him and was prepared to fashion him, was the *wild beast*. What, in point of fact, was the S.S.? A machine? No, rather a stupid bird of prey, with the brain, it goes without saying, of a bird. . . .[33]

—while, in a later passage from the same work, one comes across a sentence which, in one neat phrase, summarises the whole of the plot on which *Rhinocéros* is built:

Nature against mind—there you have the whole of Nazism.[34]

This, obviously, is not the total content of *Rhinocéros*, which, like all Ionesco's plays, is extremely complex in its thematic structure; but it is certainly the *leitmotiv*, the initial inspiration, without which the play would not have been written at all. The picture of the progressive transformation of man into rhinoceros (with all that this implies) is as explicit and as "committed" a statement as one could wish: a warning of the most peremptory order against the ever-present menace of the Fascist "appeal to instinct."

On the other hand, the superficial impression that Ionesco's theatre by and large is a-political is strengthened, not only by the dramatist's own deliberately provocative assertions, but also by the fact that his satire rarely touches upon identifiable details; most of it is concerned with issues so broad (the ultimate bankruptcy of the bourgeois ideology, etc.), that its immediate social or political implications are lost sight of in the general chaotic dissolution of accepted standards which ensues. Not that even Ionesco can resist letting off an occasional squib—the Swastika arm-band in *La Leçon*, as the Professor proceeds to dispose of his forty corpses; the drunken American soldier in *Amédée*, who, threatened with the Military Police, retorts simply (in English!): "Military Police? I belong to it!";[35] the bloated patron of the arts in *Le Tableau* exploiting and humiliating his toadying little painter—even allusions of a more personal kind, such as the readily-identifiable trio of critics in *L'Impromptu*,[36] or the oblique reference to M. Morvan-Lebesque in *Le Tueur*.[37] But, of all the plays, perhaps *L'Avenir* alone relies on this sort of irony to any considerable degree. On the other hand, there

[33] *Un Témoignage faux*, MS (in the possession of Eugène Ionesco), pp. 12–13.
[34] *Op. cit.*, p. 13.
[35] N.R.F., I. 298 (II. 217).
[36] Bernard Dort, J.-J. Gautier, Roland Barthes; see "Finalement," p. 1.
[37] N.R.F., II. 109 (III. 52, footnote).

are two broad and constantly-reiterated themes which carry strong political implications, and which, when they occur finally in combination, contrive to make *Rhinocéros* one of the most significant political plays of the twentieth century.

The first of these is the idea that the forces of social order which hold the state together—the police, the civil service, the army—are the highest incarnation of the principle of "logical necessity," as conceived by the bourgeois mind. But once the illusion of logic has disintegrated, as in Ionesco's view of the world it has, then nothing remains of these forces but an empty shell. Just as meaning has departed from language, leaving only a hollow crust of platitudes, just as the concept of a rational justice has evaporated, leaving only the echoing reverberations of legalistic formulæ, so likewise the controlling forces of society have lost their *raison d'être*. A police-force is just as gratuitous in a society without justice as an army is in a world of hydrogen bombs. When all clues are meaningless (and this is one of the problems of *Victimes du devoir*), how should a detective set about detecting? But, even when deprived of meaning, the shells of authority still remain; indeed, like all inanimate objects, not merely remain, but proliferate at the expense of man; and *power without sense* is the most evil, the most dangerous phenomenon with which poor "modern man" can be confronted.

The theme of senseless brutality substituted for order and justice is found everywhere in Ionesco, but above all in *Victimes du devoir* and in *Le Tueur*. The beating-up of the Old Man and of the Soldier-with-the-Bunch-of-Flowers, followed by the total moral disintegration of Bérenger when ordered to "show his papers," [38] are merely the logical development of the "brain-washing" sequence which forms the central episode of *Victimes du devoir*. It is significant that whereas Ionesco's soldiers tend to be harmless, even despicable, individuals, the civilian authorities (who incarnate the very concept of social logic) are menacing and evil. "Everything will have to be changed," declares Bérenger; "first we must start by reforming the police force." [39] Even the Fireman of *La Cantatrice* is vaguely threatening; more so the Concierge of *Le Nouveau Locataire*; more so still (although apparently benevolent) is the City Architect of *Le Tueur*. For the Architect (who is also the *Commissaire de Police*) symbolises, not merely power without sense in a disintegrating social order, but

[38] N.R.F., II. 153–5 (III. 89–91).
[39] N.R.F., II. 159 (III. 95).

also "the Administration"—that insubstantial father-figure whose authority alone can satisfy the subconscious of the Common Man. The "Administration" is not so much menacing in itself (although it appears so to both Choubert and Amédée), as dangerous on account of what might happen should it prove illusory. Relying upon the all-wisdom of Authority, the common man can shrug off his responsibilities, confident that this intangible *something* will accept the burden in his stead, and, in return for surrendered liberty, give justice, order, and a comfortable quietude. For such is the principle of Social Contract—that scintillatingly logical pillar of the bourgeois state. "We ought," says Jean, upon the appearance of the first Rhinoceros, "to protest to the Town Council! What's the Council there for?" [40] But, in Ionesco's world, as poor Dany had already discovered, "the Civil Service [*l'Administration*] is *not* responsible";[41] there is no all-wise, all-provident "Town Council" to guarantee the order of society, because there *is* no order in society. The Social Contract is repudiated, and willy-nilly man must take back his liberty, and manage it as best he can. The menace, therefore, which emanates both from the Police and from the Architect is of a similar order: in the general disintegration of the bourgeois system, rational discipline, now void of meaning, is replaced by *force* emanating absurdly from the "automatism of instinct," while, for the victim, the last redress, the ultimate court of appeal, has vanished into smoke. In such a context, even to *try* to apply the criteria and conventions of social morality is totally absurd. Bourgeois society has lost its reason for existence, and henceforward (until the time of that *inner revolution* which is destined to "transform his mentality") the life of bourgeois man is destined to be "solitary, poor, nasty, brutish, and short."

But man is not merely betrayed by the forces which incarnate the bourgeois-rational ideal of society; he is more directly and more fatally betrayed by reason itself. This is the second general theme of *Rhinocéros*. *Rhinocéros* is more than a simple study of the herd-instinct; the point that Ionesco has striven to make is that the "herd" (the mad rush of Dostoevskian "possessed") is no longer composed of the old "unthinking mass." Ours is, all in all, a *thinking* civilisation; the modern mob is not a rabble of *sans-culottes,* but a mutinied regiment of reasoners and logicians, of all those who exploit the

[40] *Rhinocéros*, p. 30 (*Plays*, IV. 14).
[41] N.R.F., II. 83 (III. 29).

illusion of logic to justify the unjustifiable. The danger of the illusion is that the same type of logical argument which, in the field of abstract speculation, exploits logic and reason to disguise the non-logical essence of reality, can be used, and is used, on the political level, to justify any form of oppression, atrocious cruelty or exploitation—in brief, any variety of Fascism—that may happen to come into existence. This, ultimately, is the theme to which Ionesco is committed: the betrayal of man by his own intellect.

Rhinocéros is fundamentally an analysis of this betrayal. The problem is not "What is Fascism?" but "How does a rational and civilised nation come to accept the Fascist ideal?" And Ionesco's answer is that, accustomed to veil all reality behind the illusion of logic, the bourgeois mind has come to rely on reason to supply an *a posteriori* justification for whatever phenomenon may happen to arise. How a phenomenon achieves existence (how the first rhinoceros appeared) is not Ionesco's problem; it is the reactions of the thinking mind *after* the appearance which fascinate and horrify him. Faced with the sudden crisis, the first reaction is to disguise the fact of reality with meaningless words and platitudes; then to side-track the significant issue altogether (". . . for it is possible that since its first appearance, the rhinoceros may have lost one of its horns, and that the first and second transit were still made by a single beast . . .");[42] next, to shift the responsibility on to the "Town Council"; and finally to deny that the phenomenon had ever occurred at all.

Confronted ultimately, however, with incontrovertible evidence of the fact, the second series of reactions is more sinister. The real evil begins with M. Botard, the "Brechtian," the "committed propagandist," obsessed with his resolve to discover "the whys and the wherefores of the whole business":

> I know my own mind. I'm not content to simply state that a phenomenon exists. I make it my business to understand it and explain it.[43]

But, as Sukhanov remarks somewhere, *à propos* of the Menshevik theorist, Martov, "in politics, to understand too much is inadmissible, *parce que comprendre, c'est pardonner.*" In the same way, in Ionesco's context, to "understand" and to "explain" a phenomenon is merely a disguised way of justifying its existence, a trick, once

⁴² *Rhinocéros*, p. 67 (*Plays*, IV. 36).
⁴³ *Rhinocéros*, p. 104 (*Plays*, IV. 54).

again, to divert the awareness of the mind from the terror of the fact to some nice, comforting and totally irrelevant consideration. Once the fatal assumption has been made that, in a world supposedly logical, each and every existing phenomenon must partake of this necessary logicality, the harm is done. If it exists, therefore it *must* be the necessary result of a given and ascertainable cause; and since the law of cause-and-effect is inescapable, the phenomenon is inescapable likewise. Rationalism, in other words, is merely fatalism disguised. The necessity of the phenomenon *justifies* its existence, and what is logically justified cannot logically be opposed. Worse: for the logical mind soon grows so exclusively preoccupied with demonstrating the necessity, that it contrives secretly to do what it has been aspiring to do all along: namely, to lose sight of the phenomenon altogether, to disregard its implications, and to hide reality behind a smoke-screen of argument. M. Botard himself having (inevitably) become a rhinoceros, the thread is taken up by M. Dudard:

> My dear Bérenger, one must always make an effort to understand. And in order to understand a phenomenon and its effects you need to work back to the initial causes, by honest intellectual effort. We must try to do this because, after all, we are thinking beings. I haven't yet succeeded, as I told you, and I don't know if I shall succeed. But in any case, one has to start out favourably disposed—or at least, impartial; one has to keep an open mind—that's essential to a scientific mentality. Everything is logical. To understand is to justify.[44]

This, then, is the final betrayal of intellect. Because it has accepted, lock, stock, and barrel, the illusion of logic, reason has allowed itself to degenerate into the slave and sycophant of facts; as the facts proliferate, so reason is progressively "victimised" by the material world, while at the same time it contrives to hide its impotence and degradation under the flamboyant banners of "understanding," "tolerance for others," and "scientific detachment." Bérenger alone resists the general infatuation: his salvation, his "originality" (like that of Amédée) lies in his positive acceptance of the irrational; he alone, in his *naïveté*, receives the facts for what they are, instead of striving to demonstrate their "logical necessity," thus obliterating the significance of the facts themselves. In such a context, reason is no longer "wisdom," but "oriental fatalism"; if reason—*any* reason—can serve to justify the Nazi creed, then reason by that alone stands finally condemned. The principles of rational-

[44] *Rhinocéros*, p. 158 (*Plays*, IV. 83).

ism are inadequate to deal with the world of Hitler and Hiroshima, and Bérenger's despairing cry is hauntingly significant:

> Well, in that case, I . . . I *refuse to think!* [45]

Ultimately, politics are rational; and therefore the political solution *cannot* be the final solution in an irrational world. Like Bérenger, who feels himself "responsible for everything that happens . . . involved . . . unable to be indifferent," [46] Ionesco is deeply committed to the cause of man. But man, as he sees him, is not fundamentally a political animal, because the political solution, *even when achieved,* will still leave the eternal, the essential problems unanswered. Utopia *may* lie ahead—but what happens after? Ionesco is committed—urgently—to averting the cataclysms towards which present politics seem unerringly to be heading; he is committed—less urgently—to bringing about "a world where economic worries are a thing of the past, a universe without mystery where everything runs smoothly";[47] but his ultimate commitment is to the solution of the problems of man in the world *beyond* Utopia. It is not true that he is "neutral" (as Orson Welles suggests) in the conflict of ideologies; but both as a dramatist and as a philosopher, he is possessed of that "thirst for the absolute" which must, for all time, fail to be satisfied with the temporary shifts and compromises of practical politics. As a dramatist, because the problems of politics, like those of Molière, are "in the last analysis relatively secondary, sometimes sad, certainly even dramatic, but never tragic: for they can all be resolved";[48] as a philosopher, because the political solution can never go beyond Utopia, whereas it is precisely with the coming of Utopia that "we shall see that this solves nothing, indeed that our problems are only just beginning." [49] Even in Utopia, man will still be faced with death, with boredom, with absurdity; and the confrontation will be all the more intolerable for taking place in a universe devoid of wars and crises and distractions, amid the boundless silence and "emptiness of a world without metaphysics." [50]

[45] *Rhinocéros,* p. 161 (*Plays,* IV. 85).

[46] *Rhinocéros,* p. 149 (*Plays,* IV. 78).

[47] "The World of Eugène Ionesco," in International Theatre Annual, no. 2, ed. Harold Holson, London (Calder), 1957. Reprinted in *Tulane Drama Review,* III. 1 (October, 1958), 46–8.

[48] "Discovering the Theatre," trans. Leonard C. Pronko, in *Tulane Drama Review,* IV., 1 (September, 1959), 3–18.

[49] "The World of Eugène Ionesco," p. 46.

[50] *Op. cit.,* p. 47.

To Ionesco, man's isolation is fundamental. No mass-meeting, no communal parade with banners, be it a million strong, will alleviate for one instant the obsessive loneliness which springs from the simple awareness of death. If there *is* an escape from such loneliness, it can only lie in another *kind* of community—a community whose bonds are deeper, more intimate than the superficial links of Welfare economics:

> The truly social, the authentic community, is *extra-social*. To reach the heart of the matter, we must discover a broader, profounder type of society—that of our common anguish, revealed to us through our desires, our unfathomable longings. The entire history of the world is governed by longings, by anguishes such as these, and political activity has never succeeded in realising it otherwise than imperfectly, partially. No society has ever succeeded in abolishing such sadness; no political programme can ever deliver us from the *malaise* of existence, from our fear of death, from our thirst for the absolute. It is the nature of man which dictates the nature of society, and not *vice versa*.[51]

[51] "Ionesco à l'heure anglaise," in *Théâtre Populaire*, no. 34 (1959), 132–4.

This essay was written in 1960, shortly after the première of *Rhinocéros*, and its assessment of Ionesco's political attitudes was based on the evidence available at the time. Since then, however, Ionesco has written scenes for the stage (notably, the last act of *La Soif et la faim* and the "orator" episodes in *Jeux de massacre*), together with numerous polemical and autobiographical articles (in particular, the two extracts from the *Journal* in *Preuves*, September and October, 1965, and the essay "L'Auteur et ses problèmes" in the *Revue de Métaphysique et de Morale*, 1963) which situate him far more clearly on the political Right, and in the light of which the earlier plays should perhaps be reinterpreted. It is plain that his development has been in two directions, both tending to reinforce his hostility towards left-wing radicalism of the Sartrian type: firstly, towards a fairly traditional type of religious mysticism; secondly, towards what he himself describes as "right-wing anarchism." Yet probably what matters more, at this date, than to re-assess Ionesco's own political position is to query, in the light of events since the middle 1960s, the political implications of the "Absurdist" drama as a whole. It could be argued that all irrational literature is subversive, and that therefore all such literature is important in creating a climate appropriate to revolutionary social change. But it could also be argued that all true human progress has been based on the critical use of reason; that no doctrines were more irrational than those of Hitlerism; and that therefore any literature which exalts the irrational at the expense of the rational is fundamentally hostile to progress and thus, in the long run, reactionary. Ionesco uses the first of these arguments to justify himself, and it was also the argument I adopted in this essay; but his critics who use the second argument have a strong case in their favour.

—Richard N. Coe, November 1970

Eugene Ionesco and
the Metaphysical Farce

by Rosette C. Lamont

For me, the theatre is the projection onto the stage of the world within: it is in my dreams, my anguish, my dark desires, my inner contradictions that I reserve the right to find the stuff of my plays. As I am not alone in the world, as each one of us, in the depths of his being, is at the same time everyone else, my dreams and desires, my anguish and my obsessions do not belong to myself alone; they are part of the heritage of my ancestors, a very ancient deposit to which all mankind may lay claim. It is this which, surpassing the superficial diversity of men, brings them together and constitutes our deepest fellowship, a universal language.

In this manner does Ionesco, the principal character of his own *Improvisations or The Shepherd's Chameleon (L'Impromptu de l'Alma)*, answer the questions of Bartholomeus I, II and III, the Molieresque doctors in theatrology who have come less to interview the dramatist than to impose on him their own theories of dramaturgy. Ionesco's retort reveals how far removed his theatre is from the traditional well-made play. In his drama there is to be no explanation, or exposition, no logical development of character and events. A dislocation of reality is effected before reintegration can be achieved. Thus a pure reality, a deeper truth—*vérité* as against *réalité*—is opposed to realism and naturalism. It is by means of this a-logical, a-psychological inner truth that the dramatist hopes to establish a contact of profound poetic significance between his audience and himself, a kind of communion.

The parallels between this philosophy of drama and the one developed by Nietzsche in his seminal *The Birth of Tragedy* are striking. There is no evidence that Ionesco himself is aware of any such influence since he had not even read Nietzsche's heir, the passionate pamphleteer Antonin Artaud, when he first began to write his plays and to elaborate a consistent philosophy of stagecraft, now unified in his *Notes and Counter Notes*. It is important, however, to recall that it was Nietzsche who was responsible for one of the first and most significant statements about the instinctual, subconscious forces basic to the genesis and shaping of dramatic form. In his "Preface to Richard Wagner," Nietzsche declares that art, not ethics, is the properly metaphysical activity of man. In his early Romantic phase the German philosopher sought to discredit Judeo-Christian standards of morality, and to substitute for them his own myth of paganism based on a personal interpretation of pre-Socratic Greece. He baptized his counter-dogma with the name of an ancient deity, Dionysos.

The son of the nymph Semele, who, having wished to see her lover Zeus in his glory, was consumed by the fires which surrounded deity, Dionysos was reared by nymphs, muses, and the aged, drunken spirit of the forests, Silenus. The last, according to an ancient legend, was questioned once by King Midas, who had gone hunting in the woods, as to his beliefs about what constitutes man's supreme good. The daemon answered: "First, to be *nothing*. Second, if you have not had the good fortune of not being born, to die as soon as possible." Silenus' disciple, his divinity confined to a mortal shape, is the suffering god of ecstasy, dispensing at once the joyous inebriation of wine and revelry, and the dark fermentation of cruelty. As he treads the earth, making his way from the golden lands of Lydia and Phrygia, moving towards Thebes through the sun-beaten Persian plains where "Greeks and Orientals swarm together," as Euripides says in the *Bacchae*, Bromius-Dionysos, god of thunder and of flaming destruction, orchestrates transformations. Those who refuse to celebrate his cult are punished by loss of sight or sanity. Those who, like Pentheus, deny by word and action, natural law, ready to haunt their own mother and her sisters to bring them from their bacchic revelry, will die at the hands of these very women, who, blinded by the opiate, mistake the young ruler of Thebes for a lion cub. Such is the power of the "effeminate stranger," the "girl-faced thing who introduces/This new disease to women" (*Bacchae*). Before he destroys his enemies, the deity teaches them to submit to life. He is to be worshipped through dramatic enactments, expressions of man's freedom from morality and social constraints, and followed by ever rising multitudes walking in the wake of his chariot bedecked with flowers and garlands. As Nietzsche writes: "All the rigid, hostile walls which either necessity or despotism has erected between men are shattered" (*The Birth of Tragedy,* Ch. I). Luxuriant existence rises from the ground of being. The *Sparagmos* in which the royal victim is torn asunder, the cannibalistic feast of men and gods, is transformed into the celebration of rebirth through the dramatic imitation of the deeper life of nature and the psyche. According to Nietzsche, tragedy, comedy, ballet and opera have this common origin and must combine into total theatre. This last form, which springs from the Dionysian desire to represent man in a state of trance, will also allow access to that transcendence in the course of which bonds are broken and nature explored.

Two forms of apprehension are present simultaneously in the act of creation: the Apollonian, art of the shaper, and the non-plastic, ecstatic condition of revelation, the Dionysian. Euripides' *Bacchae* dramatizes the opposition of these two aspects of the human psyche, but, in so doing, the play reconciles or synthesizes them at the end. Gilbert Murray regards Pentheus as another form of Dionysos, so that the death of the Prince is followed by the re-birth of the god. At the end of the play, the chorus sings: "The gods have many faces./ They manifest themselves/ in manifold ways." Before the Cambridge School of Cultural Anthropology, Nietzsche saw that myth and tragedy embody the conflicts and contradictions which are generated by the cycles of our universe. He formulated a modern view of myth, revealing its kinship to rituals, such as the celebration of spring and the new harvest. The chorus and the audience are united by this feasting, and the members of the public identify with the satyrs and the chorus, beholding at the same time as these do the transcendental Apollonian images arising at the center of the amphitheater. The phenomenon is "epidemic," since "a whole crowd becomes rapt in this manner" (*The Birth of Tragedy,* Ch. VIII). Thus, drama is born, according to Nietzsche, when the Apollonian *principium individuationis* is shattered, the normative myth of *sophrosyne* dispelled, so that the knowledge of suffering may shine through. Wagner's admirer adds that this miracle is achieved by the lyric poet's language entering a "musical mood" (*The Birth of Tragedy,* Ch. V). At this point, the poet "becomes his images, . . .

objectified versions of himself" (*ibid.*). In the act of creation, the artist, an amoral divinity, frees himself from the anguish of fulness and from the contradictions inherent in his nature as in the world. He enters a realm beyond good and evil. Nietzsche affirms that art alone can save since "the spirit of the sublime . . . subjugates terror," and "the comic spirit . . . releases us . . . from the tedium of absurdity" (*The Birth of Tragedy,* Ch. VII).

Nietzsche's interpretation of the theatrical experience as spiritual exercise is both Romantic and strikingly modern. When, in the Postface to *The Birth of Tragedy,* the mature philosopher casts "a critical backward glance" at the young man's work, yet admits with some pleasure that in this book "a sort of maenadic soul . . . stammering out laborious phrases in an alien tongue—as though the speaker were not quite sure himself whether he preferred speech to silence—" And what could be closer to Beckett and Ionesco than the question: "Or is there such a thing as a strong pessimism?" Contemporary dramatists and directors are indebted to Nietzsche's early formulation of what constitutes total theatre. Nietzsche affirmed with Schiller that the chorus, which represents the spectators seated around and above it, constitutes a "living wall which tragedy draws about itself in order to achieve insulation from the actual world, to preserve its ideal ground and its poetic freedom" (*The Birth of Tragedy,* Ch. VII). As the dithyrambic chorus unburdens itself of ancestral images, or myths, it can no longer be considered as composed of individual citizens of Athens, each bringing to the solemn occasion of the Dionysia the prestige of his civic rank. Selected for religious office, trained by the dramatists themselves, the members of the original satyr choruses found their names and personalities submerged in the enchantment of the revel. As to the audience, "given the terraced structure of the Greek theater," it viewed through the eyes of the dancing singers the Apollonian dream sphere, "each spectator quite literally surveying the entire cultural world about him and (imagining) himself, in the fulness of seeing, as a chorist" (*The Birth of Tragedy,* Ch. VIII). In this way, the individual emerges from the lethargy in which personal experiences are morassed, and recaptures the instinctual powers of the visionary. Freed from the bonds of everyday existence, the spectator consents both to the delight of life and its dissolution. This process cleanses archetypal man of the "illusion of culture" (*ibid.*).

Echoing these sentiments, the French poet Baudelaire, who like the German philosopher was an intense admirer of Nietzsche, writes in his essay, "Richard Wagner et Tannhaüser": "Nothing is more cosmopolitan than the Eternal."

Among contemporary critics, pamphleteers and practitioners of the drama, none came closer to Nietzsche's analysis of the transcendental nature of the theatrical experience than Antonin Artaud. In *The Theatre and Its Double,* Artaud states that the spectacle is a mirage, the double of an archetypal and dangerous reality. Psychology, which attempts to reduce the unknown to the knowable, is a method of inquiry that aims to allay fears, extinguish anxiety. These, however, are essential ingredients of a primitive, archetypal, alchemical theatre. The spectator, according to Artaud, must suffer the sacred malady, the plague of cruelty which alone can bring him in contact with the metaphysical verities contained in total theatre.

Artaud praises the Oriental theatre, Japanese and Balinese, for its metaphysical tendencies, as opposed to the psychological emphasis of the Occidental theatre. All great art invites the mind to share a delirium, and thus, violent forces—present in the universe and potentially manifest in all human beings—must be unleashed upon the stage. As this "cruelty" discharges itself into the audience, it allows, in turn, the audience's sensibility to discharge itself. In this manner does the twentieth century Dionysos re-define *catharsis.* Nor is theatre the only way in which purgation is achieved. A police raid, Artaud suggests, is like a dangerous, cruel ballet staged through the streets of a town. It is closer to the ritual solemnity of theatre than any naturalistic melodrama could ever be. Since all of us share in the anguish, the victory, the fulfillment of the participants, be they victims or victors, a catharsis is reached at the sight of this spontaneous spectacle. Drama must then seek to reproduce a sense of danger, a state of alert. When the spectator enters the space where a spectacle is about to be performed, he ought to sense that he is about to be involved in a violent, potentially threatening happening, a sentiment not unlike that experienced upon entering the office of a dentist, or being wheeled into an operating room. What is essential is the knowledge that something will take place which cannot leave one whole, unaltered. The spectator and the performer are united in their decision to take risks with their psyches and even their lives.

Clearly Antonin Artaud reacts against a deeply ingrained French tradition, that of the seventeenth-century respect for *les bienséances* based on the idea that one must not shock the sensibilities of reasonable men, and of the eighteenth-century espousal of Diderot's theories as to "le paradoxe du comédien." No longer does Artaud think that the actor remains uninvolved, cool, nor does he believe that the spectator sits back, observing, passing judgment, convinced of his own superiority, or at least reassured as to the stability of his status and his mental balance. According to Artaud, the classical idea of verisimilitude which also forms the basis for all slice-of-life plays is a lethal illusion. Theatre must seek within the autonomous universe to make a work of art that will be as lice of eternity. Truth rather than reality will erupt upon the stage, or in the theatre space (Artaud's plays must not be confined to a traditional stage) and bring to the fore a universe tangential to our own. When the world is captured at the moment of disintegration, the spectator is able to assume his place "between dream and events" (*First Manifesto of the Theatre of Cruelty*).

Artaud's extremely revolutionary theories of dramaturgy have been systematically misunderstood and misinterpreted. Semantic differences over his use of the terms "cruelty" and "plague" have served to obscure his profoundly spiritual view of the dramatic experience. The great question for Artaud is whether the theatre will be able to restore to all of us "the natural and magic equivalent of the dogmas in which we no longer believe" (*The Theatre and the Plague*). Our world is "committing suicide without knowing it" (*ibid.*) and we must shake it out of its indifference. Only a greater sickness can, through crisis, cure us of this paralysis of the will, diagnosed in the preceding century by Nietzsche. "The theatre like the plague is a crisis which is resolved by death or cure" (*ibid.*) writes Artaud. He seeks therefore the purification which can emerge only out of the extreme suffering, the mortal danger, of a disease which wipes out multitudes. There is little doubt that this seer envisioned the chaos of our troubled, demonically ruthless century. Poised on the edge of madness, aware of the erosion of his mind, Artaud felt that lucidity coupled with pain conferred special powers, or at least "the right to speak" as he states in a post-scriptum to his letter of January 29, 1924 to the poet Jacques Rivière. Wracked by migraine headaches, the result of meningitis contracted in childhood, Artaud contemplated suicide and sought relief in drugs. Yet, he also possessed a strong will to live. In his essay "Is Suicide a Solution?" he speaks of his longing to reach "the other side of existence, but not that side which is death." He might have preferred, like Silenus, *not to have been.*" When in the last ten years of his life Artaud sank into madness—his state was being disputed even while the poet-pamphleteer was being shuttled between various hospitals —one cannot help but feel that the lines written by Nietzsche about Oedipus apply both to the French theoretician's and to the German philosopher's ends:

> It is as though the myth whispered to us that wisdom, and especially Dionysiac wisdom, is an unnatural crime, and that whoever, in pride of knowledge, hurls nature into the abyss of destruction, must himself experience nature's disintegration.

The sight of Balinese dancers performing for the first time in Paris at the Colonial Exhibition of 1931 brought Artaud to a passionate consciousness of the sacred roots of drama. This new vocabulary of gestures and expressions, this language beyond language, made him feel as though he had been able to witness the birth of tragedy. If one is to speak of a Renaissance of religious (in the deepest sense) theatre in Europe, one could date its beginning from this appearance of the Balinese group, or rather with the impressions these "umbilical, larval" movements made on a poet weary of his environment. Suddenly, words, or rather the understanding of words, did not seem to matter. The strange howls emitted by the Balinese dancers together with their music suggested to Artaud (who had never heard gamelan nor these percussion instruments) the cutting of wood, the rustling of branches moved by the wind, and made him feel connected to the great Void. The author of *The Umbilicus of Limbo* wondered at that evocation of the Oneness of nature by what he came to regard as animated sorcery. The dancers appeared to him as "hieroglyphs" clothed in "geometric robes," their motions suggesting a quest for perspective in ideal space. Was this not what Artaud himself had pursued in those hermetic symbolist prose poems, his early works? One is reminded of a Mallarmean statement in Artaud's confessional "Paolo Uccello" (Paul of the Birds) in which the writer identifies himself with the artist trying to capture "the vanishing form, not the line that encloses all others, but the one that begins not to be." In the same way, when Artaud began to reflect on the art of the Balinese dancers he realized that "when this abstraction, which springs from a marvelous scenic edifice to return to thought, encounters in its flight certain impressions from the world of nature, it always seizes them at the point at which their molecular combinations are beginning to break up" ("On the Balinese Theatre"). The Dionysian aspect of this exploration of the cosmos in the process of disintegration is further revealed in the same essay when Artaud states that the gestures of the Balinese performers narrowly divide us from chaos. But it is perhaps in his letter of September 18, 1932 to *Comoedia* that the planner of a *Nouvelle Revue Française* theatre exposes with greatest clarity the purpose of his suggested enterprise. In that letter, Artaud begins by agreeing with Jean Cassou's use of the term "ceremonial" as applied by that writer in a piece published by *Nouvelles Littéraires* (September 17, 1932) about Jean Cocteau's theatre. Cassou had detected Cocteau's fascination with the circus, and stressed the parallelisms between prestidigitation and a desire for a secular imitation of the miraculous. Cocteau's endorsement in his Preface to *Les Mariés de la Tour Eiffel* (*Wedding at the Eiffel Tower*) of what the poet-dramatist calls "poetry of theater" as opposed to "poetry in theater"—that is, the poetry of spectacle rather than that of language alone—finds an echo in Artaud's idea that "gestures equal words."

Both Cocteau and Artaud learned from the Symbolist poets—Baudelaire, Mallarmé, Rimbaud, Lautréamont—that poetry is the instrument of exploration and discovery. One rides the newly invented poetic form like a magic capsule projected into space, or a ship gone wild upon an ocean, in order to get a glimpse of the unknown. For the Symbolists—and here we must include the Surrealists, and the avant-garde dramatists—the poem, the spectacle, reveals to the mind, which welcomes the death of rationality in order to be reborn as spirit in the vertigo of revelation, the profound anarchy of hitherto familiar connections and relationships. This upheaval of analogies is a form of cruelty. To understand the much maligned notion of "theatre of cruelty" we must turn to a letter written by Artaud to Rolland de Renéville, a member of the *Nouvelle Revue Française* whose support the dramaturgist tried to secure:

> We need an active theatre, capable of taking drastic measures. I do not mean by this that we must come out on the stage perpetually armed with a butcher knife, but that we must find once more the principle at the basis of all reality. One cannot deny that life in its

devouring and implacable aspects must be identified with cruelty. And this does not take place on the visible, physical plane alone, . . . but above all on the invisible, cosmic plane where the very fact of being, combined with the immense sum of suffering it presupposes, appears as a cruelty.

The "theater of cruelty" must also be an "archeological" and "alchemical" dramatic art form in which the poet, searching for perfect alloys, and for the "apparition of gold" will operate "the organic expulsion of all inert values" (Letter of July 13, 1932 to Rolland de Renéville). The absolutism of Artaud's quest leads to the statement in "The Theater and the Plague": "Theater can be theater only from the moment the impossible really begins."

It was Mallarmé, the high priest of the Symbolist movement, who expressed the thought that a real artist must always be a "sublime failure." He is a failure in his own eyes since he is looking for the impossible, since he explores the outer limits of being. Mallarmé's longing to create The Poem or The Book, and to evolve the "orphic explanation" of our universe, acquires the proportions of a myth in which the Oneness of Being in the work of art comes dangerously close to destruction, Non-Being.

Samuel Beckett, who creates on the edge of silence, took his cue from Mallarmé, particularly in his "Three Dialogues," (interviews with Georges Duthuit on three painters, Tal Coat, André Masson and Bram Van Velde). The abstract canvases of Van Velde inspired Beckett to make a statement which defines not only the art of the painter, but his own as well:

> My case, since I am in the dock, is that Van Velde is the first to desist from this estheticized automatism, the first to submit wholly to the incoercible absence of relation, in the absence of terms or, if you like, in the presence of unavailable terms, the first to admit that to be an artist is to fail, as no other dare fail, that failure is his world and the shrink from it desertion, art and craft, good housekeeping, living.

Yet, despite this knowledge both Mallarmé and Beckett went on writing. The reason for it was perhaps also given by Beckett in the same conversations with Duthuit when he states in the Tal Coat piece that he prefers to any standard definition of the creative activity "the expression that there is nothing to express, nothing with which to express, nothing from which to express, no power to express, no desire to express, together with the obligation to express."

It is no accident that there should be such a meeting of minds between one of the purest practitioners of avant-garde drama, and the "poet of absence" as Mallarmé is sometimes called. Had Mallarmé been more successful in creating for the stage the works he wrote with production in mind they would doubtlessly have been thought of as forerunners of *Waiting for Godot, Endgame, Krapp's Last Tape, Happy Days, Act Without Words,* and, the most recent, *Not I.* Under the influence of Baudelaire and of that poet's boundless admiration for the character of Hamlet, Mallarmé elaborated a doctrine of a poetic drama of the soul. In his numerous essays on the art of staging, Mallarmé envisioned a return to the most ancient Greek theatre. A single actor on a bare stage would enact explorations of inner conflicts. Such could have been the stage versions of "L'Après-Midi d'un Faune," and "Hérodiade." Both poems, written over a period of years with some production in mind, are actually short plays. Mallarmé went so far as to go to Paris to discuss details of the recitation of the first with the famous actor, Coquelin. The performance never took place, but Mallarmé went on to write his own *Hamlet, Igitur* published posthumously.

Hamlet was for Mallarmé "la pièce que je crois celle par excellence" ("Hamlet"). It seemed to the poet that Shakespeare's protagonist was that adolescent "vanished from us all at the beginning of our life." In his highly private interpretation of the play, Mallarmé sees Hamlet as the emblematic fusion of all the other characters of the tragedy. Book in hand, "le seigneur latent qui ne peut devenir" negates those around him and destroys them with utter unconcern. It is the poison of his solitude and the black bile of his philosophic doubt, rather than the point of the young prince's sword, which kill them. When he uses the latter, it is to push aside "the pile of loquacious vacuity" he might become were he to grow as old as Polonius. In this essay on Hamlet, Mallarmé warned his readers that no subjects exist beyond the ineluctably mythic one of the antagonism between man's dreams and the fatalities imparted to his existence. It was, on the poet's own avowal, the figure of the great Romantic actor, Mounet-Sully, which imprinted on Mallarmé's mind its "disquieting and funereal" presence; it appeared to exorcise with a wave of the hand "the pernicious influence of the House."

We know from George Moore that Mallarmé intended to write a monologue for the stage entitled "Hamlet et les vents" of which *Igitur* must be a first draft. Time and timelessness are the basic preoccupations of Igitur, filled with the horror of disintegration as he watches the work of time in the mirror. At the precise hour of midnight, when the hands of the clock are fused, time exists beyond their oneness as future and past, but potentially the same, so that Igitur can feel that his future death can bring him to the pre-natal phase, that he can recede through the embryonic stage into nothingness, be unborn, leaving in the room only a world of inanimate objects: a mirror, curtains, armchairs. (One is again reminded of a Beckett work, his cinematic essay, *Film*.) By uncreating himself, Igitur, the hero of a culture, would annihilate humanity of which he is the last representative. Another Phèdre, he will restore purity to the world.

"Theatre is of a superior essence," affirms Mallarmé in his essay "Le Genre ou des modernes." The seer of Symbolism associated in his mind the functions of priest, poet, dancer and conductor. For him, theatre, in its most perfect form, would be a dramatized ode, a reenactment and majoration of self. Long before Craig's *On the Art of the Theatre* and even Appia's *Die Musik und die Inszenierung,* Mallarmé toyed with the concept of a new mental milieu, a fusion of stage and theatre space. For the poet as for Nietzsche it was Wagner who proved to be a major source of inspiration. Mallarmé, however, evolved his own theory of total theatre as secular ritual. Theatre, as he saw it, could in a sense become a kind of mass, spiritual nourishment and renewal not being derived from the blood and flesh of the Saviour but from a communion with the spectacle and the hero-protagonist. Thus, actors and priests have for the poet one thing in common: they are intruders in the myth. Both must achieve transparency as they mediate between the communicants, or spectators, and the idea of a Divine Presence (deity or universal myth). As for Artaud, half a century later, drama for the symbolist poet is metaphysical in aim and character.

Although Mallarmé's dramaturgy was too abstract for realization on the stage in his own lifetime, it served to help sever the theatre from its realistic, naturalistic traditions, and to pave the way for the poetic drama of the twentieth century. A belief in the dream image and in the freedom of the imagination is the common denominator between the Symbolist poets, the Dadaist pranksters, and the Surrealists. André Breton called man "an inveterate dreamer" (*First Manifesto of Surrealism*) who should live out his existence as though everyday life were poetry—with all the risks and commitments this entails—and who, in turn, ought to experience poetry as an authentic act. Breton is the true heir of Alfred Jarry who would exclaim when awed by an event: "C'est beau comme la littérature!" ("As gorgeous as literature!")

"I belong to the cabaret school of literature," Ionesco likes to joke in all seriousness. This quip may reflect his rejection of the academic attitude, but it reveals that the dramatist is an excellent literary historian and theoretician. The newest avant-garde art has indeed come out to a great extent from the *Cabaret Voltaire,* the birthplace of Dada. In 1916, the German conscientious objector Hugo Ball and his friend Hennings, later joined by Jean Arp, Tristan Tzara and Marcel Janco, rallied to the cry: "Dilettantes arise!" The name of their movement was chosen—so the legend goes—by opening a dictionary at random. This game of chance yielded a truly international word—hobby in French, horse in French baby talk, yes-yes in Russian (a thoughtful, hesitant affirmation bordering on negation) and, in Krou, according to Tzara, the tail of a sacred cow. Thus, a subversive movement was born on neutral ground, in an old section of Zurich. It was a group, or association of people in opposition to all groupings. If they had any program it was to will their platform out of existence, to annihilate all theorizing and all recognized, enthroned masterpieces.

The first dada manifesto appeared in 1918. It stated that art was not a serious pursuit, and proceeded to equate self with non-self, order with disorder, affirmation with negation. It proclaimed the age of *j'menfoutisme* (not giving a damn), which must end with a bang, the explosion of the time bomb of anarchic humor. The Dadaists were the creators of the Happening, or the first anti-plays. One hears of noisy poetry recitals conducted at the *Cabaret Voltaire* with the voice of the reader drowned out on purpose by the loud tam tam of drums and African music, while, at the same time, Tzara and Richard Huelsenbeck performed pastiches of primitive dances, "le noir cacadou." One must not take this for a form of entertainment. Michel Sanouillet, the historian of the movement, explains in his comprehensive book, *Dada à Paris,* that these manifestations, or protests, were attempts to suggest a "demonic microcosm, a reflected image of the apocalyptic events of the rest of the world, the echo of shouts rising from one battlefield, then another . . . and which drowned out intelligence" (p. 18). Above all else, the Dadaists were weary of the so-called enlightened Western man. In their eyes this

Renaissance ideal had become the contemporary equivalent of the nineteenth-century *homme sensuel moyen,* Flaubert's *bête noire.* So, it becomes increasingly obvious that Ionesco, more than any of his contemporaries, is in that sense the heir of Tzara when the dramatist derides literary critics by telling them in conversation: "You are all so much more intelligent than I am. You *know* what I'm saying." It is an echo of Tzara's declaration in his manifestoes that Dada seeks the "triumphant instauration of the idiot, a rare, precious, free, anti-human being." Tzara also enjoyed describing himself as a "short, insignificant idiot."

The destruction of the edifice of literature and the arts had to be followed by a movement of spiritual regeneration. Although the Surrealists rejected the concept of the Apollonian image sifted through the conscious mind in favor of an objectification of the subconscious Dionysian revelation, they believed that regeneration would follow the dissolution of the ego. For them, verse, sentence, image or act arose from the subterranean forces of man and did not belong to the individual. Breton recounted the strange circumstances in which a sentence began to haunt him, "knocking at (his) window pane" (*First Surrealist Manifesto,* 1924). The initial phrase: "There is a man cut in two by my window" was followed by others, utterly gratuitous. Having communicated this experience to his friend Soupault, Breton asked him to join him in an experiment with automatic writing. Though they wrote separately, the two young men found a surprising unity of tone in the pages when they compared the result of their "dictated" texts. Breton began to see the anonymous clusters of meaning as vestiges of a universal consciousness. Since the Surrealists developed a mystique of the value of hallucination, as Coleridge, De Quincey, Nerval, Rimbaud and Lautréamont had done before them, they saw their work as a communal simulation of delirium. This was the principle behind the *assemblages* of writing by Eluard and Breton, collected under the mock-religious title *L'Immaculée Conception.* These were contemporary with the collages of Picasso and Braque whose similarity in design and color scheme made it impossible for either artist to acknowledge a particular work as his own. Although one must admit that a good deal of mystification entered into these cubistic games, Surrealism was in earnest when it prophesied in *The First Manifesto* (1924), "the future resolution of two seemingly contradictory states of being, that of dream and that of reality, into an absolute reality, or surreality."

The adjective "absolute" reveals the extent of Breton's indebtedness to Mallarmé who used to say that he had not special gifts for anything "outside perhaps the absolute." As to the surreality or suprareality of the dream world, it sends us back to Ionesco's statement in *Improvisations*. For Nietzsche, the Symbolist poets, the Surrealists and the avant-garde dramatists, there is clearly a spiritual, metaphysical universe as palpable to the psyche as our paltry realities are to our clumsy fingers. Breton's manifestoes constitute a lore of the art of understanding and perceiving psychic reality. "Man proposes and disposes" declares the self-appointed Pope of Surrealism, a statement worthy of the nineteenth century exclamation: "God is dead!" By freeing man from God, Breton destroys bourgeois conventions and forces one to view the abyss of infinite possibilities. At the same time, Freud's exploration of dream opened new avenues for poetry. Turning away from the realism of the world of adults— those makers of world wars—poets and playwrights traveled through the lost continent of childhood memories, probed the ocean floor of mental derangement. Both the child's astonished gaze and the psychopath's richly distorted vision seemed to offer an approach to suprareality. This is still, to a great extent, the direction explored by the avant-garde dramatists. In his book *Découvertes,* a kind of essay-journal illustrated by the author himself for Skira's new series *Les Sentiers de la Création,* Ionesco writes: "Explanation separates us from astonishment which is the only gateway to the incomprehensible" (p. 72). Ionesco can be said never to have recovered from the state of childhood. To step away from that moment of timeless illumination is to enter history, the universe of planners, scientists and tyrants. To become an adult is to look for answers when there are only questions.

For the child, the grown-up is an evil giant, a monstrous Gargantua. The tiny, clown-like genius Alfred Jarry, who lived in what he called a reduction of a house—his apartment house in Paris had been cut horizontally by a greedy landlord—slept on a pallet, the reduction of a bed, had a library composed of Rabelais and a couple of volumes from a series of children's books for little girls, *La Bibliothèque Rose,* kept owls for pets, and put a drop of ink in his absinthe glass for a proper writer's cocktail—he christened it *herbe sainte* (holy grass)—was that glorious anomaly necessary to the crea-tion of an entirely new artistic universe.

In 1889, the *potache* of the Lycée de Rennes and his classmates the Morin brothers presented in the latter's attic a series of puppet plays, *Les Polonais,* so entitled because "Poland is No Place." The central guignol character designed by Jarry himself was a monstrous creature with a pear-shaped head so that whether in assent or denial he could always be said to "shake-his-pear" (a pun on the name of a famous predecessor). He was also endowed with a tremendously developed belly, the visible sign of his appetites, and an embryonic heart. Of the three states of man differentiated by Plato, only the one dealing with the lower portions of the body had become in Ubu's case sufficiently mature. Among the attributes of this strange creature one could list the strength of the pig, a nose in the shape of a crocodile's jaw and the general properties of the horseshoe crab. Three subjects filled the tiny mind of this mythical being based on the boys' physics teacher, Hebert, better known as Le Père Heb: *Physics,* which had come to represent for Jarry not only his enemy's field of interest but nature against art, scepticism against faith, medi-cine against alchemy—to counterbalance science, Jarry created Pata-physics, "the science of imaginary solutions"—; *Phynances,* spelled in an ancient, mock-erudite manner to remind the reader of Rabe-lais' own spoofs on scholasticism, and stress perhaps the gigantic avarice of Ubu—the materialistic preoccupations destroy, according to Jarry, self-respect as surely as physics destroys the sense of the world's mystery—; when Ubu is not concerned with taking the mechanism of the world apart, or sticking the whole thing into his pockets, he is left with the residue of knowledge and wealth, *Merdre.*

When on December 10, 1896, Firmin Gémier bellowed the open-ing word of *Ubu Roi* from the stage of *Le Théâtre de l'Oeuvre,* the public rose in its seats. The *mot de Cambronne,* also known as *les cinq lettres,* had suddenly acquired, through the addition of a rum-bling extra "r," a second syllable. Blown up to equal the expres-sionistically distended belly of Ubu, the familiar, coarse but recog-nizable exclamation, hurled from the stage in the teeth of the audi-ence, fell like the toilet brush tossed by the grotesque king upon the banquet table. William Butler Yeats, who was present at the first performance, wrote in his *Autobiography* that the play heralded "the coming of the Savage God." Indeed, the prophetic, archetypal figure of a leader compounded of cruelty, cowardice, stupidity, cunning, avarice, ambition and obscene vulgarity seems the apocalyptic incarnation of the dictators and tycoons of our twentieth century. In his chapter "Suicide by Hallucination," Roger Shattuck, the author of *The Banquet Years,* speaks of "the inverted dignity of Père Ubu." Shattuck makes a very important point when he reminds us that we "cannot laugh (Ubu) off." Troubled epochs have always tended to be dominated by great humorists. We recognize in Jarry the heir of Rabelais, Cervantes, Swift and Gogol. His Ubu is an abstract cartoon, a caricature of the grossness of our appetites, the futility of ambition and the disintegration of human discourse. But if Ubu is Stalin, Hitler, Nasser, General Amin and Aristotle Onassis rolled into one, he is also Sancho Panza, Gargantua, Panurge, Falstaff, Brutus, Macbeth, Hamlet and even the demonic Maldoror. Composed of quotations and familiar situations, he is a literary creation with no life beyond that conferred on him by the dramatist; he lives on the printed page and on the stage. Yet, this mask is so compelling, so powerful that it began to take over its creator. More and more, Jarry became Ubu, talked in a strange, flat, nasal voice, moved with the stiff dignity of a doll. When Gémier wondered how he should interpret the role, he was advised to watch Jarry and imitate him as much as possible. In his correspondence with his friend Madame Rachilde, the famous *salonnière* married to Vallette, the editor of the powerful *Mercure de France,* Jarry speaks of himself in the third person, and calls himself Père Ubu. Shattuck writes: "Ubu obsessed and possessed him totally, swallowed him whole. Thereafter it was as if, like Jonah, he could communicate only from inside the whale. He had found his Other, the flesh of his hallucination."

Jarry knew that a dramatic character has greater reality than a living human being because he is viewed in his totality, and because a play is a wider and deeper form of life. He tried therefore to create a walking abstraction, a comic character who would not be a type. It is difficult to laugh at Ubu for he is as terrifying as the ancestor figures of the Africans, a grotesque, occult presence, expressing in its bearing the absurd quality of existence, the precariousness of all standards. Behind the double figures of Père and Mère Ubu, we glimpse the smiling Hermaphrodite, Shiva, the Great Destroyer, the inverted aspect of creation. As Ubu and his wife, a concierge version of Lady Macbeth, move through a hybrid, heraldic set, a decor of the mind which suggests a polytonal, cubistic time capsule, we realize that the proceedings are vested with a quality of eternity.

Perhaps Jarry's most significant innovation, and the one that
brings his farce close to the spirit of Greek tragedy which he knew
well and had read in the original language, is the use he makes of
masks. He aimed for a crystallization of emotion, a mineral gesture
of petrified horror or ecstasy. The atonal voice issuing from below
a covering which he wanted to extend to the entire body is that of
a medium, an oracle, speaking in riddles through lips of stone. Perhaps Jarry recalled what the poet Baudelaire had written in his
strange journal, *Fusées*: "I would like to see actors wear high bus-
kins, and masks since these are more expressive than the human
face." Jarry felt that the marionette is universal, that it transcends
reality. He wanted his actors, men of flesh and blood, to imitate the
doll.

When Ionesco states that he thinks theatre ought to be a-psychological, and when he expresses his malaise at the sight of actors
"making a public exhibition of themselves" (*Notes and Counter
Notes*, p. 16), he echoes the feelings that Jarry voiced to Lugné-Poe,
the director of *Le Théâtre de l'Oeuvre*. In *Notes and Counter Notes*,
Ionesco writes:

> Why could I not accept the truth of theatrical reality? Why did it seem
> false to me? And why did the false seem to want to pass as true and
> take the place of truth? Was it the fault of the actors? Or the text?
> Or my own fault? I think I realize now that what worried me in the
> theatre was the presence of characters in flesh and blood on the stage.
> Their physical presence destroyed the imaginative illusion. It was as
> though there were two planes of reality, the concrete, physical, impov-
> erished, empty and limited reality of these ordinary human beings
> living, moving and speaking on the stage, and the reality of imagina-
> tion, face to face, overlapping, irreconcilable: two antagonistic worlds
> failing to come together and unite. (pp. 16–17)

Ionesco did not like to visit the theatre in what he calls "a spirit . . .
unsanctified" (p. 17), and thus, he realized, that to restore to the
stage its quality of ritual magic one ought to magnify effects, "push
drama out of that intermediate zone where it is neither theatre nor
literature . . ." (p. 26). In this desire to raise everything "to paroxysm" Ionesco reveals his Dionysian leanings, and shows that he is
the heir of a line of thinkers which begins with Nietzsche, and continues through Jarry and Artaud to the present. All of these theore-
ticians or practitioners of the theatre, or both, have in common
this discovery that "drama lies in extreme exaggeration of the feel-

ings, an exaggeration that dislocates flat everyday reality" (*Notes and Counter Notes*, p. 26).

Since a play is an invention, a fiction, not an imitation of nature, the dramatist must be both poet and builder to concretize upon the stage the universe of his imagination. Guillaume Apollinaire, the inventor of the term "Surrealism," states in the Prologue to his play, *Les Mamelles de Tirésias*:

> It is right for the dramatist to make use of
> All mirages at his disposal
> It is right that he allow crowds, inanimate objects to speak
> If such is his pleasure
> And that he disregard time
> And space
> The play is his universe
> Wherein he is God the Creator
> Commanding at will
> Sounds gestures movements masses colors
> Not merely in order
> To photograph what is called a slice of life
> But to summon forth life in all its truth.

Written in 1903, performed on June 24, 1917, at the time when the problem of repopulation had been made acute by the war, *Les Mamelles de Tirésias*, a mock *pièce à thèse* which encourages the French to "make love" and its by-product, children, is Apollinaire's answer to what he calls "le théâtre en trompe l'oeil." A friend of Jarry whom he visited at his "Grande Chasublerie,"—a manufacturer of ecclesiastical vestments occupied the second floor of 7 rue Cassette, while Jarry lived on the third floor and a half—Apollinaire did not fail to learn something from the strange young man whom he describes as looking "like the personification of a river, a young, beardless river, wearing the dripping clothes of a drowned man." He must have been fascinated with Jarry's redefinition of theatre as "a civic celebration, a festival in which all must participate," since he himself explains in the Preface to *Les Mamelles de Tirésias* that "one must return to nature but without imitating it as photographers do." In a statement which seems to foreshadow Ionesco's *Notes and Counter Notes* Apollinaire says:

> Theatre is no more like the life it interprets than a wheel is like a leg. Thus, it is legitimate . . . to bring to the stage new, striking aesthetic principles which stress the theatrical aspect of the characters, and widen

the pomp of mise en scène, without modifying the pathetic or comic tone of the situations which must speak for themselves.

Despite many divergences, Dadaists and Surrealists clearly recognized that Jarry was their common source. In his *Anthologie de l'humour noir* Breton calls *Ubu Roi* "the incarnation of the Nietzschean-Freudian synthesis of subconscious, frustrated, unknown forces." Thus, when in September 1926, Antonin Artaud, Robert Aron and Roger Vitrac decided to form a new theatrical group, they christened it *Le Théâtre Alfred-Jarry*. The latter offered four programs between 1927 and 1930, but, despite the paucity of performances and the lack of funds, these productions made theatre history. The first of these four, presented on June 1st and 2nd at the *Théâtre de Grenelle,* included *Ventre Brûlé* by Artaud, a "pochade" or humorous attack against the cinema, Vitrac's *Les Mystères de l'Amour,* "a real drama" as Artaud calls it, and *Gigogne,* a sketch by Robert Aron who wrote under the pseudonym of Max Robur. On January 14, 1928, the group presented Claudel's *Le Partage de Midi* without the author's permission since "any published work must be considered to be in the public domain" and, together with this play, a controversial film based on Gorky's *The Mother,* chosen expressly because it had been censored by the government.—Thus, the second program was not merely an artistic event, but an act of political terrorism. Artaud declares in his essay, *"Théâtre Alfred-Jarry,* Saison 1928": "The Alfred-Jarry Theatre has been created to make use of theatre, not to be used by it. The writers who have formed this group feel no special respect for authorship, or for texts. . . . If they come upon plays which seem in their most absolute and original substance significant of the state of mind they seek, they will welcome them over others. But, if none such appears, some Shakespeare, or Victor Hugo, or Cyric Tourneur they may stumble on will do" (*Oeuvres Complètes,* tome II, p. 31). This explains why Artaud chose Claudel's play, put it on despite the author's interdiction while the latter was beginning his term as ambassador to Washington D.C., and introduced the show by declaring that the play was written by "a traitor." This program to take any text, and act *against it* rather than act it is profoundly Dadaist, and reveals that the whole enterprise is a second wave of the Dada movement.—On June the 2nd and the 9th of the same year, Strindberg's *The Dream Play* was given its premiere performance in France by the Théâtre Alfred-Jarry. Assisted by Yvonne Allendy, Artaud collected 3,000 francs for a subsidy, and invited an elite audience to opening night. The Surrealists led by Breton came *en masse* also. They, however, were gathered to stage a protest against the defection of their erstwhile friends who now clearly sought success and material gain. The fact that Artaud had the support of the Swedish embassy made matters particularly acute for these modern saints who had taken a kind of vow of poverty. After a preliminary exchange of letters between Breton and Artaud, the latter decided to call on the police for protection. On the 9th, when Breton arrived with his cohorts, he saw Artaud, standing at the entrance of the theatre between two policemen. The Surrealists never forgave Artaud his independence, nor the fact that he refused to adhere to the Communist movement. The fourth and final spectacle of the *Théâtre Alfred-Jarry* was given on the 24th and 29th of December 1928, and on the 5th of January of 1929. It was Vitrac's brilliant take-off on bourgeois salon melodrama, *Victor ou les enfants au pouvoir*. It is perhaps with the performance of this play that we can date the birth of a new genre, the Metaphysical Farce.

Victor presents what appears to be at the start a perfectly conventional, bourgeois situation. The Paumelle family is celebrating the ninth birthday of their son Victor. They have invited for the occasion their friends the Magneaus with the latter's daughter Esther, Victor's friend. Since every self-respecting French family has at least one general in its circle of acquaintances, one of the guests is Le Général Lonségur. There is of course the family maid, Lili. It is, however, with the appearance of the mysterious, uninvited Lady in black, Ida Mortemart, that the play veers, revealing the rotten underside of the situation and introducing the threat of dissolution. Death—the name of the Lady suggests her secret essence— turns the bourgeois comedy of manners into a vulgar farce tinged with tragic undertones. The play ends, in mock-Greek tragedy manner, with the demise of the protagonist, Victor, and that of his parents "shown fallen on each side of their son's bed, a smoking revolver between them." The bourgeois world ends with a bang, the apocalyptic explosion foreshadowed by the discreet rumblings emitted by Ida Mortemart, the "pétomane."

A disquieting weirdness is present, however, from the moment the curtain rises. Empty frames, suspended in front of the audience, suggest a fourth wall grown transparent, and let the public know they are "voyeurs," as is every audience at a so-called "realist" drama. By this striking device of mise en scène, Artaud, who directed

Vitrac's play, reveals that we are dealing with a pastiche. As to Victor, supposedly a child of nine, he is played by a six foot tall adult. We know his measurements, or rather those of the original actor, from Antoine Magneau's declaration as he enters in scene 7, Act I: "Here you are. You keep on growing, don't you! How old are you? Nine, and you're six foot tall!"—In the first scene, between Victor and the maid, Victor picks up and breaks a huge Sèvres vase, the prize possession of his family. He also threatens Lili with telling his parents that she has broken it, and, since he has been "a model child" these nine years, they will believe him. The sacrilegious destruction of an objet d'art valued at "ten thousand francs" sets the mood for the anarchic destruction of the bourgeois universe which is the aim of the play, and that of the whole *Théâtre Alfred-Jarry* group.

The underpinnings of this bourgeois world are far from clean. Esther reveals to Victor that she has seen her mother and his father making love. She paints the scene in semi-surrealist terms which nevertheless allow us to recognize despite the surface absurdities, and the mock-poetic language, a typical adulterous encounter.

> Esther.—They were sitting on the sofa. Daddy was asleep in the next room. This is what I heard. Mother was saying: "Frizzy, frizzy, frizzy." Your father: "Rizzy, rizzy, rizzy." Mine: "Carlo, I idolize myself in you" or something to that effect. Yours: "Thirteen, oh silent swimmer." Mine: "But, if all of a sudden, Antoine were to . . ." Yours: "Your neck would save me." Mine: "Ravished horizon." Yours: "Let go this pink octopus." I'm absolutely certain of octopus, the rest is an approximation.

This revelation seems to throw the erotically inclined Victor into a fit of delirium. Whether momentarily insane, or feigning madness, this latter day Hamlet is clearly planning to catch the conscience of his father in the mousetrap of a play. After a quotation from Racine's *Britannicus*, Victor recites a list of typical *dramatis personae* straight out of boulevard melodrama. When, a little later, the children are ordered to conform to one of the bourgeois rituals, the recitation of a poem for the entertainment and ego satisfaction of their parents, they comply by putting on a play within the play. As they repeat line for line the dialogue overheard by Esther, miming in child-like fashion an adulterous rendezvous, a pall falls on the festivities. The cuckolded husband who is insane, or perhaps also pretends madness the better to endure his misfortune, leaves the

room. Act I ends with the General asking the birthday child to state
what he would enjoy most. Victor makes the General take a solemn
oath that he will accede to any wish or even whim. This done,
Lonségur is told to go down on all fours. "Je voudrais jouer à dada
avec vous," explains Victor ("I'd like to play horsy with you"). The
childish word recalls the well-known movement, and indeed, as Victor whips and spurs his mount, he appears as the embodiment of
Dadaist irreverence. Having sapped the prestige of bourgeois family
life, the *Théâtre Alfred-Jarry*, destroys that of the military.

It is in Act II, however, that *Victor ou les enfants au pouvoir*
acquires a metaphysical dimension. At this point the grown-ups are
clearly befuddled. Esther, wearing the General's képi, is singing the
revolutionary song, *la carmagnole*. It looks as though power has
really gone to the children. Victor's father is saying that a miracle
is needed. It is at this moment that a beautiful woman, dressed in
a black ball-gown enters the room. "Here's the miracle!" shouts
Victor, running toward her. Ida Mortemart, dignified, aloof, seems
to know the family.

> *Ida.*—I'm Ida, aren't you Emily any longer?
> *Emily.*—I've known three Idas in my life. The first. . . .
> *Ida.*—I'm the last, that's certain. I'm Ida Mortemart.

As Ida is introduced to the guests doubt is cast as to whether she
meant to visit this household. She was supposed to see a Madame
Paumelle, of rue Lagarde. "But this is rue Lagarde," says Charles.
Perhaps there are two Paumelle families on the same street, each
unaware of the other's existence.—The scene is strangely reminiscent of the conversation between the Martins in Ionesco's *The Bald
Soprano*.—As the guests are trying to puzzle this out, the General
says something about a canon, and the word brings about a strange
reaction on the part of the lovely lady: "She farts." The General
thinks he is being insulted:

> *The General.*—It's a joke, isn't it?
> *Ida*, who does not understand, who cannot understand.—No, sir, an
> infirmity.

Ida's "fartomania" is not only a grotesque characteristic for a woman
who describes herself as "beautiful, rich and loved," it suggests the
putrification of the society in which she lives, and, beyond that, the
sulphurous depths of hell. In a letter written to Domenica Blazy,
the actress who played Ida Mortemart, Artaud explains: "The au-

thor is not wallowing in disgusting, ignoble ugliness. Everything that is stinkingly dirty has meaning, and must be understood directly. Here, we find ourselves in a magical element, at the very core of human alchemy." He goes on to say that the actress ought to suggest a peculiar mixture of ghost and woman. Each of Ida Mortemart's words has a double or triple meaning, says Artaud, and the tone of her voice conveys the fact that she has come from a world beyond, and retained a superiority, a special intelligence, due to her passage from that universe to ours. The director also tells the actress not to be frightened, or repelled by this role; she must interpret it with complete sincerity, utter freedom. He reminds Domenica Blazy, who replaced Alexandra Pecker, a young woman who felt that this role would injure her future career, that Ida Mortemart "represents moral pain, and the poisoning of matter." For Artaud, it is the character of Ida which lends dimension to the play. "I am as sure of this play," he writes, "as of a mechanism loaded with an explosive charge which must be triggered off at a given moment."

Unlike the grown-ups, and even his friend Esther, who is already too much of a woman not to fear Ida, Victor is attracted to the lady in black. At a certain moment, taking advantage of the fact that they are left alone, he asks her to initiate him to the secret of love-making. "I wouldn't like to die . . . and one can die at any age, isn't that so? . . . without knowing," he says. After a bit of hesitation the mysterious visitor whispers the secret in the boy's ear. One has the impression of witnessing a *rite de passage*. Victor is no longer a child. We know, now, that he will die soon.

After Ida's departure the household is profoundly shaken. *Angst* has entered the spirit of handsome Charles. He confesses his adulterous love for Thérèse to his wife, and also his fears, though he is not sure what it is he fears. Victor is sick with a strange stomach ache. Soon, we are informed by a frantic Thérèse who appears in the middle of the night in the Paumelles' bedroom, that her cuckolded husband has taken his life by hanging himself from the balcony of their room. In his suicide note, the unfortunate man claims that he is the French flag since under his white nightshirt he is wearing the blue coat and the red trousers of the dragoons of Napoleon. He asks Charles to take care of Esther who might after all be Victor's sister. The threat of incest hangs now over the Paumelle home.

A sacrificial victim is needed to avert the catastrophe; it will be

Victor. He is sick, feverish. In this state he asks his father not to smoke, and to give his pipe to Emily. It turns out that the pipe is a revolver. Victor, who has not seen this bit of stage business, whispers: "Don't press too hard on the spring of the Unique One." These are mysterious words, prophecies from the world beyond. Victor promises his mother to reveal to her "what the springs of the Unique One are," but he will die "of Death" before having a chance to do so. It is his mother who tells him that he was born at eleven thirty P.M. "What time is it now?" asks Victor. "Eleven twenty-five," answers his father. We realize that Victor has five minutes of life left. The last spring of the Unique One is Death.

"I expect *everything* from this daring, scandalous play," wrote Artaud to Domenica Blazy. In his manifesto, "Le Théâtre Alfred-Jarry en 1930" he states:

> The *Théâtre Alfred-Jarry* will not make use of anything which touches on superstitions such as religious, patriotic, occult, or poetic feelings, except to denounce and combat them.

He goes on to say that the group plans to exploit and bring to light "the poetry of fact," and that of "humor" since the only attitude worthy of man's dignity is one which takes into account the oscillation between the tragic and the comic. "We pursue *absolute laughter*," he writes, "the one that goes from drooling immobility to the paroxysm of tears." The great master of this kind of humor is the Jarry of *Ubu Roi*.

With its fourth and last program, the *Théâtre Alfred-Jarry* had an artistic success. The Vitrac-Artaud collaboration yielded one of the first anti-plays in the sense that *Victor* is a parody of the well-made play, and even of classical French tragedy with its unity of time, place and action. The humor is subversive, sapping all the institutions of French society. Above all a new mode is created, the tragicomic mode, as Death is presented as a haunting, beautiful, elusive, but grotesquely afflicted figure of fear and fun. With the apocalyptic end, we realize that *Victor ou les enfants au pouvoir* is not merely an absurdist play, or a play of the absurd, but something more profoundly philosophical, and more shatteringly humorous, a Metaphysical Farce.

It has often been said that in the twentieth century tragedy is as dead as our gods. This may be so, yet the tragic apprehension of life in art must survive. Faith lives on beyond the death of religion.

On the other hand comedy, once considered a low, popular form of entertainment, is assuming in our times some of the Dionysian character of the drama. The terms *catharsis through laughter, catharsis through comedy* are being used by critics such as Charles Lalo in his book *Esthétique du rire,* or Serge Doubrovsky in his seminal essay "Ionesco and the Comic of Absurdity." The two genres, comedy and tragedy, tend to flower in the same epoch, since fear, tension, sympathy, pity can bring about a comic explosion, a liberation through laughter, as well as a purgation through pity and terror. Laughter liberates us, yet it dissolves at the same time any pre-established harmony, any pact between man and nature, between the justice of God and that of society. According to Lalo, comedy suggests an unsteady, fluid element of shifting values tumbling downwards. It is comedy, however, which saves us from sinking in the shipwreck of our standards. This is achieved through the device of devaluation. Some examples of the latter are Charlie Chaplin's caricature of Hitler in *The Great Dictator,* and Molière's mockery of intelligence, or what we take for culture, in his portraits of doctors, lawyers and *femmes savantes.* The devaluation of the living process occurs when life is viewed as something rigid, mechanical, when, according to Bergson, the mechanical forces overlap the living ones. Death itself, and the universal fear of death, are devalued by gallows humor. (Victor says: "I am dying of Death." In Act II, scene 5 he tells his mother: "Mother, you are pregnant with a dead child." These bitterly humorous statements seem to announce Beckett's "They give birth astride of a grave.") According to Schopenhauer, the function of art, and in theatre of tragedy, is to bring about this salvation. In our time, transcendental humor has assumed this responsibility.

In a world turned upside down, a world deprived of heroes, tragedy is no longer possible. It presupposes, according to Friedrich Duerrenmatt, "guilt, despair, lucidity, vision, a sense of responsibility" ("Problems of Theatre," *Tulane Drama Review,* October 1958, p. 20). It necessitates, above all, the existence of a hierarchical order. In a society ruled by mass production, a civilization which equates people and things as products to be consumed, the state loses its physical reality. The mighty, who were formerly our standard for measuring virtue, have turned into replaceable expressions of blind cruelty; they are puppets of Evil. According to Duerrenmatt, "The comical exists in forming what is formless, in creating order out of chaos" (*ibid.*). Thus "the tragic is still possible if tragedy is not" and "we can achieve tragedy out of comedy" (*ibid.*). Laughter through tears, a mouth hesitating between the upward grin of the comic mask and the downward tilt of lips grimacing with suffering as in the mask of tragedy, this is the emblem of our ironic age.

It is no accident that a couple of years after the end of the Second World War, the arts witnessed a resurgence of the nihilist spirit of Dadaism, and of the terrorist humor, and philosophic interests of the Dada-Surrealist baby, *Le Théâtre Alfred-Jarry*. It is no easy task to determine among the newest of the avant-garde artists what came first, the chicken or the egg. For instance, Romain Weingarten, a poet and playwright in his middle forties who had a *succès d'estime* in 1961 with his play, *Les Nourrices*, and has come into his own with a dramatic fable, *L'Eté*, is assumed to be Ionesco's disciple. Yet, *Akara*, the play he wrote in his student days at the Sorbonne in 1948, is the first anti-play of the new wave. It was presented by *Le Groupe de Théâtre Moderne de la Maison des Lettres*, with the author in the main role of Le Chat. The stir created by this amazing play was such that the dramatist Audiberti nicknamed it *Hernani 48*. Had Ionesco seen the young man's work, a neat case could have been made for the influence of Weingarten on Ionesco. We find out, however, from a generous article written by the older dramatist in defense of the struggling young vanguardists that the former had no acquaintance with *Akara* till 1953. Literary historians know how deceitful dates can be. All one can point out is that a *famille d'esprits* was in the making in the 1950's, and that it had emerged from Surrealism. But, as Ionesco says:

Surrealism is not new either. All it did was discover and bring to light, in the process of reinventing, a certain way of knowing, or certain tendencies in human nature that centuries of rationalism frowned upon and suppressed. What, in short, does surrealism try to release? Love and dreams. How can we have forgotten that man is quickened by love? How not to have noticed that we dream? Like all revolutions, the surrealist revolution was a reversion, a restitution, an expression of vital and indispensable spiritual needs. If finally it became too rigid, if one can now talk of academic surrealism, it is because every idiom wears out in the end . . . surrealism is itself a rejuvenation of romanticism; its origin, or one of its sources, is in the German romantics' power to dream. An extension of the frontiers of known reality depends upon a rediscovery of method and a rejuvenation of idiom. A genuine avant-garde movement can only be of value if it is more than a fashion. . . . I believe that in recent times we have forgotten what theatre is. And I am not excepting myself; I believe that, step by step, I have discovered it once more for myself, and what I have just described is simply my own experience of the theatre.

(Notes and Counter Notes, p. 35)

He was not alone in this rediscovery. Boris Vian, Jean Vauthier, Jean Tardieu, Audiberti, Georges Schehadé, Arthur Adamov, Samuel Beckett, Jean Genet, and more recently Romain Weingarten, Roland Dubillard, Marguerite Duras, François Billetdoux, Francisco Arrabal, René de Obaldia, assisted by such fine directors as Jean-Louis Barrault, Jean Vilar, Roger Blin, Nicolas Bataille, Jacques Mauclair, Victor Garcia, Jorge Lavelli, have sought and are seeking to do what Artaud tried to perform in creating his *Théâtre Alfred-Jarry,* and to some extent what the directors of *Le Cartel des Quatre* had striven for in that transitional period known as *l'entre-deux-guerres,* to renew the language of the stage by creating a poetic, comitragic and tragicomic drama.

It is not the purpose of this final essay to analyze in detail Ionesco's plays. This has been done, for at least a great many of the more difficult ones, by the essays in this volume. It is important, however, at this stage in our epoch, to situate Ionesco in literary history, both in relation to the recent past, and to his contemporaries. It is Ionesco's greatest achievement—and it may also be the test of what makes a great writer—to have remained over the years in tune with himself. Bartholomeus I, II, and III (Barthes, Dort, and Gautier) attempted to refashion him in the image they had of what a dramatist ought to be or do. Kenneth Tynan deplored Ionesco's a-political, anti-Brechtian attitudes. Ionesco listened, read, entered politely but firmly into public debate with all of them, but he went on being Ionesco.

To go on being himself, he had of course to become many Ionescos since, as we pointed out in the Introduction, to be true to oneself one must grow, develop. Thus, we have the prankster who claims to belong "to the cabaret school of literature," the creator of the term anti-play, we have the philosophical dramatist who presents man's situation on this fragile planet, and his fear of the beyond, there is also the social satirist, and the metaphysico-political commentator. In this essay we have attempted to show in what way

Ionesco re-discovered the theatre and created in the process a form we call the Metaphysical Farce.

Born of a French mother and a Rumanian father, brought up first in France, then from the age of thirteen till early manhood in Bucharest where he also began to teach French literature at the lycée, Ionesco cannot be said to belong totally to one culture, or to be of one mind. This divided self, the essence of the intellectual according to Albert Camus, was perhaps a problem, but proved also a great advantage. Nor is Ionesco the only dramatist of his generation to become a great French writer despite foreign or mixed origins. It is curious to notice that the dramatic literature of today in Paris is dominated by the following names: Beckett (Irish), Adamov (Russian), Ionesco (French and Rumanian), Arrabal (Spanish). In this sense also the avant-garde is not unlike the Dada movement, created by Tristan Tzara, Hugo Ball, Huelsenbeck, Marcel Janco, and continued by the poet of Polish-Italian ancestry, Guillaume Apollinaire. Both the Dadaists and the vanguardists have in common the fact that they were not brought up exclusively in the tradition of Cartesianism. There is a quality of wildness, of abandon which does not come naturally to the French. To this, the new dramatists —and some of them, like Beckett, are also novelists—added a subconscious knowledge that one proceeds by affirmations and negations, or by aporia. Suspended judgment replaces the necessity of choice, the either/or proposition. Thus, more often than not, their laugh is the mirthless, dianoetic laugh ("the laugh laughing at laugh," as Beckett writes in *Watt*).

As we explained in the Introduction, Ionesco seems to have become a dramatist by accident. A religious man would call such an accident a revelation. What is clear is that the reading of the *Assimil* method textbook set off a metaphysical reaction in this man who, as he tells us himself, had not planned in 1948 to become a playwright, but merely wished to acquire a third language, English. Up to that time, this man had lived in two languages, two cultures. He had recently escaped from a fascist regime, and lived in semi-hiding in occupied France. Now, as he sat copying out phrases from the English-French conversation book, he felt like a child who sees the world for the first time. The commonness—the absurdity of a universe he had begun to take for granted, a prisoner of habit as all of us are—stood in his sight, flat, yet flowing with colors, like a stained glass window. It was through language (trying to assimilate a new tongue, and thus a new manner of seeing reality, this leading to the knowledge that in order to express a new reality one needs to create another language) that Ionesco learned that the Word is indeed the true act of creation. He, the inventor, the poet, could only re-create through words. The deceptively simple exercise of copying sentences from the textbook proved to have been a spiritual exercise, not unlike those practiced by the followers of Loyola, or the students of Zen Buddhism. The result of this exercise was a mystical vision, a state of exaltation similar to that experienced by the holy man, or by the opium eater. Here is the description Ionesco gives us of this state:

> While writing this play (for it had become a kind of play or anti-play, that is to say a real parody of a play, a comedy of comedies), I had felt genuinely uneasy, sick and dizzy. Every now and then I had to stop working and, wondering what devil could be forcing me on to write, I would go and lie down on the sofa, afraid I might see it sinking into the abyss; and myself with it.
>
> *(Notes and Counter Notes,* p. 179)

Was it a devil or a daemon urging Ionesco to become Ionesco? At any rate, the language student was becoming more ambitious. He tells us that he wanted "to communicate to his contemporaries the essential truths of which the manual of English-French conversation had made (him) aware" *(ibid.,* p. 177).

The "comedy of comedies" having turned into "the tragedy of language," Ionesco became a playwright, and a metaphysician. But it was with *The Chairs* that he embarked on the exploration of the abyss he had feared sinking into. No longer amazed by what was happening to him, he set out on the exploration of the "ontological void" *(Notes and Counter Notes,* p. 190). This does not mean that he had not come into his own with the writing of *The Bald Soprano,* but simply, as he says over and over again, that he knew now that he was a dramatist, and that, as such, it was incumbent upon him to re-invent theatre.

The theatre he wanted to create was mythical, abstract, universal. It would be primitive because it would spring from the soul of the people. It would explore the Jungian archetypes, the world of dreams, common to all people whatever their social condition, their place of origin, their sex. The new drama would unmask the murderous will, the destructive instinct, the longing to kill and perhaps be obliterated as well, basic to all creatures. Above all, ideologies would be demystified since a work of art has nothing to do with doctrine. It is the work of art which is the source of ideologies to come not the other way around. By going deep into himself, and extracting from these depths a universe of images, of sensations, the poet is at one with the whole world, by not fearing his solitary state, he experiences the true fraternity. True society transcends social machinery, Ionesco likes to affirm. It also transcends history, the lethal illusion of cruel ideologues. Ionesco says that his ancestors are Job and King Solomon. Thus, by conquering time and space, the Ionesco play, the Ionesco universe, allows us to realize that we are free. We may fear death like Bérenger Ier, or tremble at the sight of The Killer, but because another human being reaches out to us and shows us that he too is afraid, that he too is horrified, disgusted, we are filled with the knowledge of our humanity, and thus of our freedom. To be a man is to be free; such is the message of Ionesco, and those who have for so many years emphasized his pessimism have misread him. Few writers have greater love for the human being, greater respect for the other, greater pity and tenderness. Literary man, being the sum of his dreams, is the one creature capable of winning the existential race against time, and if we trust him, he will take us with him. We would do well to listen to his message, for, unlike the Orator of The Chairs, Ionesco is not afflicted with aphasia:

> It is pedants of every kind, educators, re-educators, propagandists for all kinds of beliefs, theologians and politicians who finally constitute the oppressive forces against which an artist must struggle. . . . Freedom of imagination is not flight into the unreal, it is not escape, it is daring and invention. And invention is not evasive, nor is it an abdication. The paths of imagination are without number and the inventive powers are boundless.
>
> (*Notes and Counter Notes*, pp. 81–82)

Finally, the miracle of art is that the artist is able to impart something he does not always fully possess, yet together, artist and reader, artist and viewer, can begin to travel away from the stereotype in the direction of the archetype.

Chronology of Important Dates

1912   November 26: Eugene Ionesco born at Slatina, Rumania.

1913   Ionesco is brought to Paris by his parents.

1921   His mother takes Ionesco and his sister to La Chapelle-Anthenaise, a small village in Mayenne which will play an important part in the playwright's private mythology. It is described in his *Journals,* and appears in some of his plays.

1925   Ionesco returns to Rumania and begins to learn Rumanian.

1929   He is admitted to Bucharest University.

1930   His first article is published in the review *Zodiac.*

1931   Publication of a volume of poetry, *Elegy for Minuscule Beings.*

1932   Ionesco contributes to *Azi, Viata Literara.*

1934   Publication of *Nu* (No), a collection of essays in which one chapter deals with the fusion of opposites.

1936   Ionesco marries Rodica Burileano.

1937   He teaches French at the Lycée in Bucharest.

1938   Ionesco receives a fellowship from the Rumanian government to write a thesis in Paris on the subject of Death in Modern French Poetry.

1939   Ionesco and his wife arrive in Paris. During the war they settle in Marseilles.

1944   Their daughter Marie-France is born.

1949   Ionesco writes *La Cantatrice Chauve* (*The Bald Soprano*).

1950   *La Cantatrice Chauve* is presented on May 11 at the Théâtre des Noctambules (directed by Nicolas Bataille).
Ionesco writes *La Leçon* and *Jacques ou la soumission.*

1951   *La Leçon* (*The Lesson*), directed by Sylvain Dhomme, is presented at the Théâtre de Poche on February 20.

Ionesco writes *Les Chaises (The Chairs).* He plays a part in a dramatization of Dostoyevsky's *The Possessed.*

1952   Ionesco writes *Victimes du Devoir (Victims of Duty).*

1953   Jacques Mauclair directs *Victimes du Devoir.* Publication of Volume I of his *Théâtre,* with a preface by J. Lemarchand.

1954   *Amédée ou comment s'en débarrasser,* directed by Jean-Marie Serreau, is presented at the Théâtre de Babylone on April 14. "Oriflamme," the novella on which the play is based, is published in *The Nouvelle Revue Française.*

1956   Performance of *L'Impromptu de l'Alma* at the Studio des Champs-Elysées on February 20. Ionesco's story *La Vase* ("Slime") is published by the *Cahiers des Saisons.*

1957   Ionesco writes *Tueur sans gages (The Killer)* in London. *Le Nouveau Locataire (The New Tenant)* is given on September 10 at the Théâtre de l'Alliance Française.

1958   Ionesco writes *Rhinocéros.* He gives a public reading of the last act at the Théâtre du Vieux Colombier. *Rhinocéros* is first presented at the Schauspielhaus in Düsseldorf.

1959   *Tueur sans gages (The Killer)* is given at the Théâtre Récamier.

1962   *Le Roi se Meurt (Exit the King),* directed by Jacques Mauclair, is presented at the Théâtre de l'Alliance Française. Gallimard publishes *La Photo du Colonel (The Colonel's Photo),* a collection of stories, and *Notes et Contre-notes.*

1963   Jean-Louis Barrault directs *Le Piéton de l'Air.*

1966   The Comédie Française gives *La Soif et la Faim* in February.

1967   The Mercure de France publishes *Le Journal en Miettes (Fragments of a Journal).*

1968   The Mercure de France publishes *Présent Passé Passé Présent,* the second volume of Ionesco's Journals.

1969   Skira publishes *Découvertes,* illustrated by the author.

1970   *Jeux de Massacre,* directed by Jorge Lavelli, is given at the Théâtre Montparnasse.

1971   Addresses the Académie Française as a new member on February 25.

1972   *Macbett,* directed by Jacques Mauclair, is given at the Théâtre Rive Gauche (ex-Alliance Française).

Selected Bibliography

Ionesco's Works Available in English

The Colonel's Photograph and Other Stories. 1969, tr. Jean Stewart and John Russell. Evergreen.

Exit the King. 1967, tr. Donald Watson, illus. Evergreen.

Four Plays. (*The Bald Soprano; The Lesson; The Chairs; Jack, or the Submission*) 1958, tr. Donald M. Allen. Evergreen.

See also Samuel Moon, ed., *One Act.* Evergreen.

Fragments of a Journal. 1968, tr. Jean Pace.

Hunger and Thirst and Other Plays. (*The Picture; Anger; Salutations*) 1969, tr. Donald Watson. Evergreen.

The Killer and Other Plays. (*Improvisation, or The Shepherd's Chameleon; Maid to Marry*) 1960, tr. Donald Watson. Evergreen.

Notes and Counter Notes: Writings on the Theater. 1964, tr. Donald Watson. Evergreen.

Present Past, Past Present. 1971, tr. Helen R. Lane. Evergreen.

Rhinoceros and Other Plays. (*The Leader; The Future is in Eggs*) 1960, tr. Derek Prouse. Evergreen.

A Stroll in the Air and Frenzy for Two or More. 1968, tr. Donald Watson. Evergreen.

Three Plays. (*Amédée; The New Tenant; Victims of Duty*) 1958, tr. Donald Watson. Evergreen.

Ionesco Criticism Available in Book Form

Coe, Richard N. *Ionesco.* New York: Barnes & Noble, 1965; London: Oliver and Boyd Ltd., 1961.

———— *Eugene Ionesco: A Study of His Work.* Rev. ed. New York: Grove Press, 1968.

Dickinson, Hugh. *Myth on the Modern Stage*. Urbana: University of Illinois Press, 1969.

Esslin, Martin. *The Theatre of the Absurd*. New York: Doubleday/Anchor Books, 1961; London: Eyre and Spottiswoode, Ltd., 1962.

Fowlie, Wallace. *Dionysus in Paris*. New York: Meridian Books, Inc., 1960.

Guicharnaud, Jacques (with June Beckelman). *Modern French Theatre from Giraudoux to Beckett*. New Haven: Yale University Press, 1961.

Pronko, Leonard Cabell. *Avant-Garde: The Experimental Theater in France*. Berkeley and Los Angeles: University of California Press, 1962.

Wulbern, Julian H. *Brecht and Ionesco*. Urbana: University of Illinois Press, 1971.

Notes on the Editor and Contributors:

ROSETTE C. LAMONT, editor of this volume in the Twentieth Century Views series, teaches at the Graduate Center of the City University of New York, in the French Ph.D. Program and in the Department of Comparative Literature. Her book *De Vive Voix* is an anthology of contemporary French plays with advanced conversation exercises. She has published essays on Modern French Drama, Symbolist European poetry, and the Russian novel.

RICHARD N. COE lives in England and is the author of books on Beckett and Ionesco.

HUGH DICKINSON is Professor of speech and theater at the University of Illinois, Chicago Circle Campus. He is the author of *Myth on the Modern Stage*.

JEAN-HERVÉ DONNARD is Cultural Attaché of France in New York City. He is the author of *Balzac, les réalités économiques et sociales dans La Comédie Humaine; Balzac, Les paysans;* and *Ionesco dramaturge ou l'artisan et le démon*.

SERGE DOUBROVSKY is Professor in the French Department of New York University. He is the author of *Corneille et la dialectique du héros, Pourquoi la nouvelle critique,* and a novel, *La Dispersion*.

JACQUES GUICHARNAUD is Professor in the French Department of Yale University. He is the author of *Modern French Theatre—Giraudoux to Beckett* and *Molière, une aventure théâtrale*.

DAVID MENDELSON lives in Israel and teaches at the Tel-Aviv University. He has acted in films and is the author of *Le verre et les objets de verre dans l'univers imaginaire de Marcel Proust*.

PETER RONGE lives in Germany and is the author of *Polemik, Parodie, und Satire*.

RICHARD SCHECHNER is Professor of Drama at the New York University School of the Arts and Co-Director of The Performance Group. He is the author of *Dionysus in 69* and *Public Domain*. Hawthorne Publications will shortly bring out his *Environmental Theatre*.